SOUTHAMPTON FINDS VOLUME TWO

THE GOLD, SILVER AND OTHER NON-FERROUS ALLOY OBJECTS FROM HAMWIC, AND THE NON-FERROUS METALWORKING EVIDENCE

David A Hinton

With contributions by
Justine Bayley, DR Hook, AD Morton, WA Oddy, Alison L Parsons, MS Tite and Paul Wilthew

To the memory of

JOHN BARR

Councillor, Alderman, Sheriff and Mayor of the City of Southampton

Chairman of the Southampton Archaeological Research Committee, 1971–1980

SOUTHAMPTON ARCHAEOLOGY MONOGRAPHS 6

Published by Alan Sutton Publishing, in association with Southampton City Council

This monograph is published with the aid of a grant from the Historic Buildings and Monuments Commission (England). Crown copyright is reserved in respect of material in it resulting from central government expenditure.

© 1996 David A Hinton

ISBN 0-7509-1167-0

The cover photograph is by John Lawrence, City Arts Services, Southampton City Council.

Alan Sutton Publishing, Stroud
Printed in Great Britain by WBC Ltd, Bridgend

CONTENTS

List of Figures	v
List of Tables	v
Preface and Acknowledgements	vi
Introduction	1

Catalogue of Non-Ferrous Objects

Catalogue Preface			2

Dress and Personal Items

Brooches:	A:	Equal-arm bow-	3
	B:	Disc-	3
	C:	Small-long	5
	D:	Roman bow-	6
Buckles and buckle-fittings			6
Chain			8
Finger-rings			8
Hooked tags			9
Loops and distributors			11
Pendants			13
Pins.	By David A Hinton and Alison L Parsons		
	Introduction		14
	Type A:	Spherical-headed	14
	Type B:	Polyhedral-headed	21
	Type C:	Bi-conical-headed	25
	Type D:	Spiral-headed	28
	Type E:	Disc-headed	30
	Type F:	Rhomboid-headed	32
	Type G:	Ring-headed	32
	Type H:	Oval-headed	33
	Type I:	Linked	33
	Type J:	Miscellaneous	34
	Type K:	Headless	34
	Discussion		35
Strap-ends:	Introduction		37
	A:	Single-riveted, with narrow shafts, small triangular split ends and spherical terminals	37
	B:	Single-riveted, with various terminals	39
	C:	Double-riveted, with flat convex-sided shafts, animal-mask terminals and plain reverses	40
	D:	Double-riveted, with various shafts	43
	E:	Folded and other sheet-metal strap-ends	44
Tweezers and other toilet implements			44

Fittings

Discs	46
Hooks and handles	47
Keys and locks	50
Mounts, studs and attachments	50
Rings and loops	54

Miscellaneous

'Forks' and 'spoons'	55
Scales and weights	56
Other identified objects	62
Unidentified objects	62

Metallurgical analyses of pins and other mid-Saxon copper-alloy objects from Saxon Southampton. By Paul Wilthew — 66

Non-ferrous Metalworking Evidence

The evidence of metalworking from Saxon Southampton, Site SOU 8. By AD Morton — 75

A mortar for grinding gold and mercury found in Saxon Southampton, Site SOU 169
- Description — 80
- Report on three samples taken from the grinding mortar. By DR Hook and MS Tite — 80
- Fire-gilding in early medieval Europe. By WA Oddy — 81

Clay piece-moulds. By Justine Bayley	83
Stone moulds. By AD Morton and Justine Bayley	84
Tile moulds. By AD Morton	85
Crucibles and cupels. By Justine Bayley	86

Discussion

The non-ferrous metal collection from Saxon Southampton	93
Dating	95
Production	97
Exchange systems and Hamwic's function	98
The range of objects	101
'Marginality', gender and ethnicity	102

Concordance	105
Summary	109
Sommaire	109
Zusammenfassung	110
Bibliography	111
Index	117

LIST OF FIGURES

Frontispiece	viii
Figure 1. Brooches	4
Figure 2. Buckles and buckle-fittings	7
Figure 3. Finger-rings	8
Figure 4. Hooked tags	10
Figure 5. Loops and distributors	12
Figure 6. Pendants	13
Figure 7. Pins, types Aa and Ab	16
Figure 8. Pins, types Ac and Ad	20
Figure 9. Pins, type B	22
Figure 10. Pins, type C	27
Figure 11. Pins, type D	29
Figure 12. Pins, types E and F	31
Figure 13. Pins, types G–K	33
Figure 14. Strap-ends, type A	39
Figure 15. Strap-ends, type B	40
Figure 16. Strap-ends, type C	42
Figure 17. Strap-ends, types D and E	43
Figure 18. Tweezers and toilet implements	45
Figure 19. Discs	47
Figure 20. Hooks and handles	49
Figure 21. Keys	51
Figure 22. Mounts, studs and attachments	52
Figure 23. Rings and loops	55
Figure 24. 'Forks' and 'spoons'	57
Figure 25. Scale-pan	59
Figure 26. Other identified objects	63
Figure 27. Unidentified objects	64
Figure 28. Ternary diagram	66
Figure 29. Site SOU 8, pits	76
Figure 30. Folded wire debris	79
Figure 31. Stone grinding mortar	80
Figure 32. Clay piece-moulds	83
Figure 33. Stone ingot moulds	85
Figure 34. Tile ingot moulds	86
Figure 35. Crucibles	87

LIST OF TABLES

Table 1. Pins without heads	36
Table 2. Weights of Roman coins	60
Table 3. Bar chart of Roman coins	61
Table 4. XRF analyses of pins	68
Table 5. XRF analyses of other objects	71
Table 6. Crucibles from Site SOU 8	89
Table 7. Crucibles from Site SOU 14	89
Table 8. Crucibles from Site SOU 15	90
Table 9. Crucibles from Site SOU 17	90
Table 10. Crucibles from Site SOU 24	90
Table 11. Crucibles from Site SOU 30	90
Table 12. Crucibles from Site SOU 31	91
Table 13. Crucibles from Site SOU 34	91
Table 14. Crucibles from Site SOU 99	91
Table 15. Crucibles from Site SOU 169	91
Table 16. Crucibles from Site SOU 254	92
Table 17. Objects of silver	94

PREFACE AND ACKNOWLEDGEMENTS

This volume has had a longer gestation period than was anticipated by Robert Thomson of Southampton City Museums, when he suggested it to me. Had it not been for his insistence that its production, and that of others about Southampton's archaeology, was a duty that should not be disavowed by those responsible for the city's heritage, despite problems caused by the departure from Southampton of those who carried out excavations in it, I suspect that this report would not have seen the light of day. It is, however, dedicated to the late John Barr, a councillor who had a wider vision of his city than merely its division into electoral districts. He chaired the Southampton Archaeological Research Committee, and it is fitting that his contribution to Southampton's archaeology should be commemorated.

Although the Southampton Archaeological Research Committee all but disappeared in 1983, it nevertheless played a part in the production of this volume, for it had some residual funds which were used in 1992–3 to make possible work towards publication of the Six Dials excavations by Philip Andrews. His expeditious completion of that report, which I have had the advantage of reading in typescript, helped to persuade English Heritage that Southampton was again worth supporting, after a long period in which funds had not been provided because so little progress could be seen. Consequently, money was made available for the preparation of the illustrations in this report, all of which are the admirable work of Simon Griffin of the Southampton Heritage Services Unit, directed by Andrew Russel.

Modern excavations conducted on a large scale lead to considerable problems of publication, and there is no consensus on how these are best dealt with. This report on Hamwic's non-ferrous metalwork has been driven largely by expediency; if specialists could be found who were willing to work on the material, they have been encouraged to do so. I am grateful to all of them for their contributions, and to many of them for their patience, as they have had to wait a long time for their reports to appear. It would, of course, have been preferable for volumes on all the Hamwic finds to have been published together, but this has not been possible. The most obvious gap as far as the present volume is concerned is the ironwork, and therefore two major points that need always to be borne in mind in the following discussions are, firstly, that when it is said that there are, for instance, few copper-alloy buckles, there may be many iron or bone buckles which could have served similar functions fitted on to similar objects, and, secondly, that there is no discussion of the use of silver, tin and other metals to plate iron, nor of such metals inlaid into iron. The full range of the uses of the non-ferrous metals in Hamwic cannot yet be considered.

Because production of this report has been delayed, some of those to whom thanks are due will by now have forgotten that they once answered my questions, or that they were even involved with the objects catalogued in it. Vanessa Fell, however, has spent even more time than me on most of them, while she was funded by English Heritage to work at the Conservation Laboratory maintained by Wiltshire County Council at the Salisbury and South Wiltshire Museum. I am very grateful for her work, and for that of her successors, notably Margaret Brooks; many of the details on these objects would not have been revealed but for their care and attention, and I should certainly have missed many of them had they not been pointed out to me in our discussions. Other contributions of various kinds have been made by Christopher Arnold, Mark Brisbane, William Brooks, Michael Corfield, Ann Fahy, Susan La Niece, Alison Parsons, David Peacock, Chris Scull, Paul Wilthew and Susan Woolgar.

During the 1980s I visited various archaeological units, and looked at metalwork finds that might be relevant to Southampton: I have occasionally referred to material seen on these visits, but in general I have thought it preferable to cite published examples only. I am grateful to those who showed me these collections: Pam Garrard and Tim Tatton-Brown (Canterbury); Keith Wade (Ipswich); Jenny Mann

(Lincoln); and John Clark (London). I saw many of the exciting new discoveries made at sites like Flixborough at a very useful meeting of the Finds Research Group organised by Kevin Leahy at Scunthorpe in 1991, but I have only referred directly to those that have been published in short reports or exhibition catalogues.

It is always a pleasure to be able to thank English Heritage for their money and for their *imprimatur*, in this case particularly Stephen Trow as the Inspector for Southampton, Chris Scull in his dual capacity of report processor and Saxon specialist, and Justine Bayley of the Ancient Monuments Laboratory, who is also a major contributor. Sue Margeson of the Norfolk Museums Service kindly read the typescript, and made many useful suggestions and comments. I am grateful to Richard Bryant of Alan Sutton Publishing for taking on its publication. I have been helped and supported by many of those who operate within various permutations of Southampton's labyrinthine cultural heritage resource management structure, notably by Kevin White (managerially), Karen Wardley (curatorially), Duncan Brown (locationally), Lindsay Ford (unravellingly), Vince Allen (practically) and especially by Alan Morton (inimitably). Finally, I should like to thank Geraldine Bailey, who uncomplainingly turned a difficult and often tedious manuscript into an immaculate typescript.

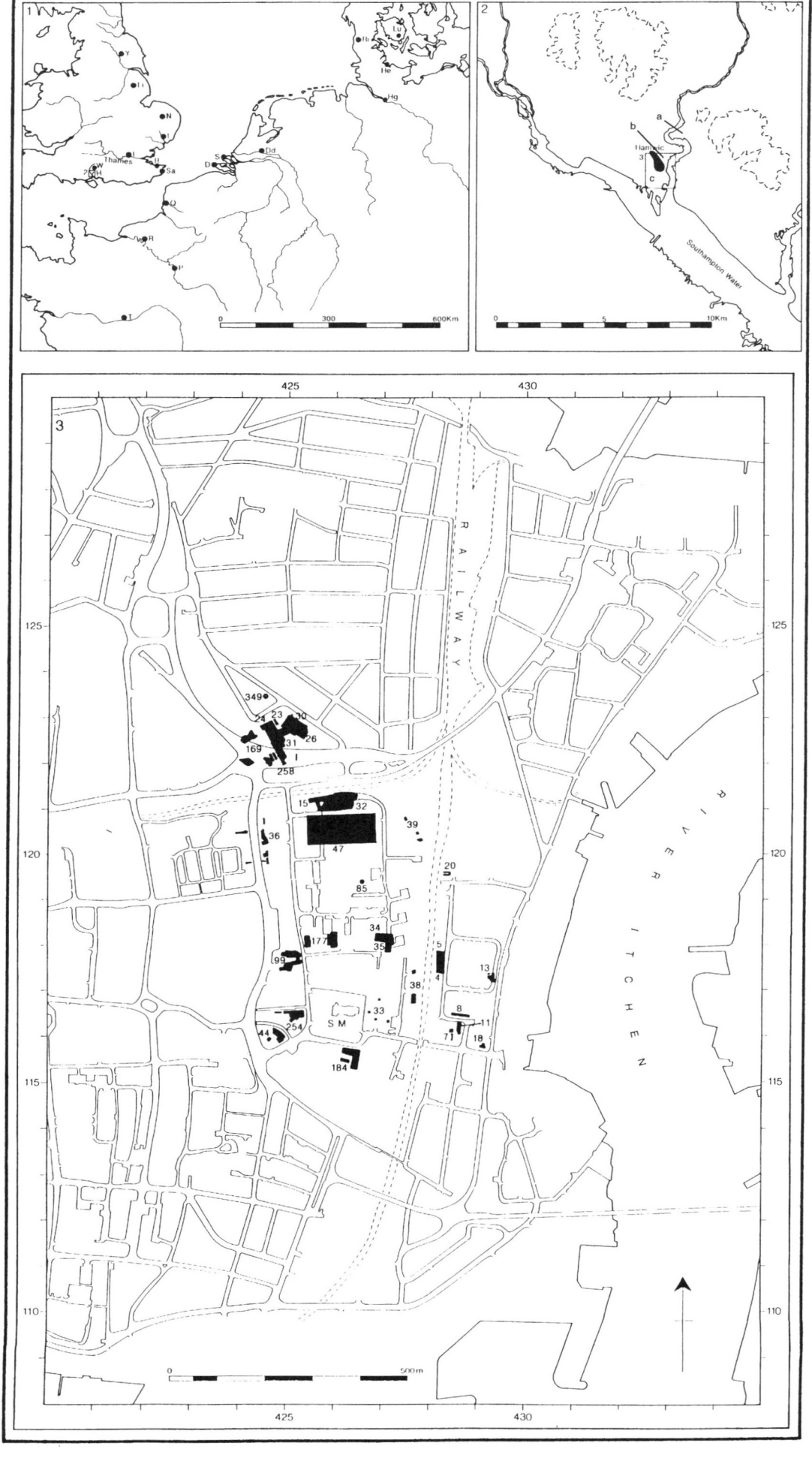

INTRODUCTION

Since the middle of the nineteenth century, it has been known that there was a major trading establishment of the Saxon period in Southampton near the mouth of the River Itchen, and material has been collected from the area ever since (Frontispiece). Archaeological excavation began in the late 1940s, and all this work up to 1983 has been scrutinised by Morton (1992). In the mid-1980s a large zone in the northern part of the occupied area was excavated (Andrews 1995), and subsequently there has been investigation in the southern part (Garner 1993). The non-ferrous objects and the evidence of non-ferrous metalworking from all these sites is considered in this volume. It has to be borne in mind, therefore, that very different information is available about the different contexts, and that very different methods and standards of recovery were applied. Consequently, fewer useful comments can be made about associations and intra-site sequences than are possible with many reports where excavations have been both more recent and more uniform.

Morton has shown that Saxon occupation at Hamwic began perhaps at the very end of the seventh century, but in his opinion probably in the very early eighth, despite the discovery of a few objects that would usually be taken to pre-date c 700 (1992, 26–8). The area was never totally abandoned, as limited occupation continued around St Mary's Church, which remained the mother-church of Southampton; but the centre of activity from at least c 1000 was on the Test side of the peninsula between the two rivers. The decline of the Itchen-side settlement took place during the ninth century, but the precise chronology is a matter of debate, and is discussed further in Part Three. Most of the Hamwic objects would therefore have been deposited between c 700 and c 850, but slightly earlier dates cannot be absolutely precluded, and the possibility of later ones cannot be discounted.

Hamwic's parameters have no precise English counterparts. Nearby Winchester, of course, was a Roman site, but whatever its usage subsequently, the small number of objects and the almost total absence of coins from it shows that its usage was very different from Hamwic's until the later part of the ninth century. The bulk of its Saxon objects date from the tenth and eleventh centuries (Biddle 1990A). Seventh- to ninth-century shoreside occupation has now been shown to have been quite dense in the Strand area of London (Vince 1990, 13–25), but the finds have not yet been published in detail, so there is as yet no comparison to the admirable volume on the later material from the City (Vince 1991). Ipswich was, like Hamwic, a 'green-field' site in the Saxon period, but has cemetery evidence that suggests earlier beginnings: unlike Hamwic, occupation remained on the same site (Wade 1988; Newman 1993). The objects from Ipswich have, for the most part, not yet been published, but there are useful East Anglian compendia from Norwich (Margeson 1993; Ayers 1994) and Thetford (Rogerson and Dallas 1984): these towns have some, limited, eighth-century data, rather more ninth-, and continue thereafter. A better parallel to Hamwic is therefore York's Anglian district, discovered in the mid-1980s in the Fishergate area south of the Roman town, and dated from c 700 to the mid-ninth century, with reoccupation from the late tenth (Kemp 1993, 1205–11). This means that four very relevant urban publications have already appeared in the 1990s, which has made possible comparanda that were not expected when the volume on Hamwic was first proposed. At the same time, recent work at Flixborough, Brandon and other sites has yielded an abundance of metalwork (Webster and Backhouse 1991, *passim*) which may ultimately put a rather different perspective upon sites such as Hamwic which now seem less exceptionally prolific than heretofore.

Frontispiece
Location of sites. Key: Map 1: *D* Domburg; *Dd* Dorestad; *H* Hamwic (inset, map 2); *Hg*, Hamburg; *He* Hedeby (Haithabu); *I* Ipswich; *L* London; *Li* Lincoln; *Lu* Lundeborg; *N* Norwich; *P* Paris; *Q* Quentovic; *R* Rouen; *Ri* Ribe; *S* Schouwen; *Sa* Sandwich; *T* Tours; *W* Winchester; *Y* York. Map 2: *a* Roman site at Bitterne (possibly Clausentum); *b* Hamwic, Saxon Southampton; *c* later medieval Southampton. Map 3: *SM* St Mary's Church. On Map 3 are shown only the excavation sites (SOU prefixes) which have yielded non-ferrous metalwork objects and other evidence discussed in this volume (see catalogue preface).

CATALOGUE OF NON-FERROUS OBJECTS

CATALOGUE PREFACE

The catalogue is divided into object categories, some of which are explained in the individual discussions. Within the categories, objects are ordered by site code number and site item number. In cases where more than one type of object occurs in a category, each number is followed by the object's putative name, with a question-mark to indicate any gross uncertainty.

Descriptions begin with the metal content. In cases where analyses have not been carried out, the metal is described merely on superficial examination as copper alloy, lead alloy or silver. Many objects have been analysed by X-ray fluorescence by Paul Wilthew, formerly of the Ancient Monuments Laboratory, Historic Buildings and Monuments Commission for England. His report (Wilthew 1984, AML Rep No 4334, August 1984; copy in City Heritage archive) is summarised below, and metal terminology used in the catalogue resulting from his work is identified by the reference 'XRF analysis, table 4 (or 5)'. In other cases, references are to '(AML)': these are derived from the archives prepared during conservation, and are largely the work of Vanessa Fell. A few objects were shown to Susan La Niece of the British Museum Laboratory, and her valuable comments on the niello are individually paraphrased or quoted: her reports are also in the archive.

In the individual descriptions, it should be noted that information in the general headings and sub-headings is common to all the objects in a category, and is not repeated. Some objects have already been published, and references are given to scholarly works but not to casual mentions in pamphlets and so on. The context number is given, and there is a concordance. If the context has particular significance, it is referred to in the discussion. Inevitably, many objects are from general clearance layers, the tops of pits, or other unsealed contexts; objects demonstrably later than the eleventh century have been excluded. A few of uncertain date are included despite reservations which are expressed in the discussions. Where two context numbers separated by an oblique line (eg 1234/5678) are given, the double reference is to both halves of a single layer, which were separately excavated and numbered.

The sites from which objects derive are mapped on the Frontispiece. There are two large groups, the Six Dials complex at the north end of the settlement, and another around Clifford Street a little to the south. There is a scatter of small central sites, and another around St Mary's Church at the south end of the settlement. There are also a few along the eastern side, the largest group being the Melbourne Street sites. The SOU numbers are:

    Six Dials group: 23, 24, 26, 30, 31, 169, 258, 349
    Clifford Street group: 15, 32, 36, 39
    Central group: 34, 35, 85, 99, 177
    St Mary's group: 33, 44, 184, 254
    Eastern group: 4, 5, 7, 8, 11, 13, 18, 20, 38

The concordance at the end of this volume lists the objects from each site which are described in it.

DRESS AND PERSONAL ITEMS

BROOCHES

A. Equal-arm bow-brooches (fig 1)

15 1 (fig 1)
Leaded bronze (XRF analysis, table 5), with iron from the pin. Circular, flat terminals each with a central ring-and-dot and irregularly spaced dots around the circumference. Plain bow, thickening to the centre. Hinge-lugs and catch-plate on back, with traces of the iron pin in the former.
L 23mm
Context F1, 14

32 134 (fig 1)
Leaded bronze (XRF analysis, table 5), with iron from the pin. Circular, flat terminals each with a lozenge inside a circle in relief. On the bow is a counter-sunk cross set saltire-wise. Hinge-lugs and catch-plate on the back, with traces of the iron pin in the former. Now slightly bent.
L 40mm
Context not known
Published Addyman and Hill 1969, 71 and fig 27, 9

254 811 (fig 1)
Copper alloy. Undecorated, with straight, unexpanded arms. Hinge-lugs and catch-plate on back.
L 32mm
Context 2580
Published Hinton 1993C, no 3

There is a fourth equal-arm bow-brooch (a form also called 'ansate' brooches) from Southampton, but from the Westgate site within the medieval walls, not from Hamwic (SOU 25). This is of the 'caterpillar' type, like 254/811, having unexpanded arms (Holdsworth 1984, 340).

The number of equal-arm bow-brooches recorded from England is now quite high – a contrast to the situation at the time that Addyman and Hill published their description of 32/134 (1969, 71), when the only others known were from Old Erringham, Sussex (Evison 1966) and Totternhoe, Bedfordshire (Dunstable Library and Museum 1925–6, fig 9), apart from a few examples from graves (eg Alfriston and Highdown, Sussex: Welch 1983, 74–5; Burton-on-Trent, Staffordshire: Baldwin Brown 1915, pl XXXVII, 6). Although a well-known continental brooch form attributed to the sixth to ninth centuries (Hübener 1972, Karte 1–6 and Capelle 1976, figs 45–7 for distribution maps of the principal different types), it seems likely that the quantity found in England indicates some manufacture here, at least of the type with circular terminals (Hübener's Group 1), such as 15/1 and 32/134, and the unexpanded type (Group 9), such as 254/811 (cf Hattat 1987, 383). This seems to be borne out by the discovery of one at Norwich on which casting flashes show that it was unfinished (Williams 1988, 63 and fig 55 no 3).

The Westgate example suggests that the fashion for them continued into the tenth century, a pattern borne out by the recent report of two from the City of London (Pritchard 1991, 143–4) and two from York's Coppergate (Roesdahl et al 1981, YTC 6). One from Norwich's Fishergate was in an early eleventh-century context (Williams 1994, 14 and fig 9 no 2). In Hamwic, 32/134 is from a pit that also contained a Type 23b sceat, which indicates a date in the eighth century. Their absence from cemeteries in Hampshire and the Isle of Wight perhaps shows that the fashion for them had not spread this far west before the end of the seventh century.

B. Disc-brooches (fig 1)

31 1653 (fig 1)
Lead alloy. Within a border of two beaded lines, a bird in relief pecks at a cross. Hatched lines within a segmental field above the bird. Remains of hinge-lugs and catch-plate on the back. Perforated in two places.
Diam 20mm
Context 5682

258 331 (fig 1)
Silver-gilt on electrum sheet over a lead-tin solder layer attached to a bronze plate (Conservation Lab Rep). The front is very corroded, but appears to have a bird in relief within a beaded- and plain-line

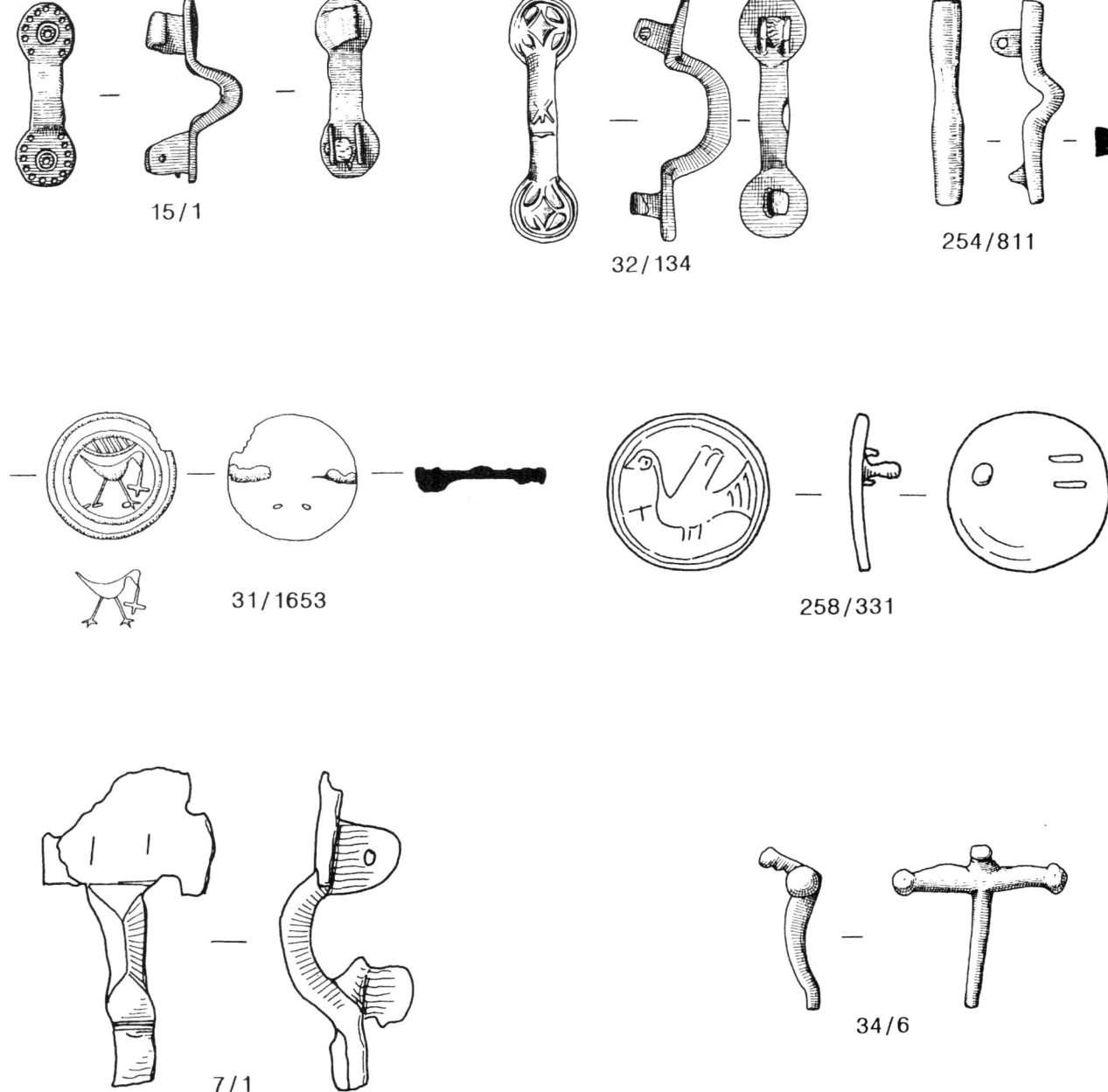

Figure 1. Brooches: equal-arm bow-, disc-, small-long and Roman bow-. Scale 1:1

border. The bird has a long neck, curved at the top to form the head, with a raised dot for an eye. A barred, rectangular wing is raised at 45° to the body, there is a barred, fan-shaped tail and a single, bent leg. There might be a cross in front of the body. The back has a catch-plate and broken lugs for a pin.
Diam 24mm
Context 17297

The only two disc-brooches identified from Saxon Southampton both have birds as their principal ornament, one certainly and the other probably pecking at crosses. This design is reminiscent of some varieties of the Series H Type 49 sceattas, which have a cross in the curve of a bird's neck and beak (eg Metcalf 1988, pl 4, nos 71–4). The birds' bodies on the coins are sinuous and flowing, however, not bulbous, and they do not have fan-shaped tails, although their splayed claws provide a better parallel to those on the brooches. The birds' bodies are closer to those on some earlier sceattas, such as Series B and E (Stuart 1984, 9–10) or the rare Series Q (*ibid*, 16). The Series H Type 49 sceattas are usually attributed to a Southampton mint, and since the two brooches appear to share a unique basic design, they may also be Southampton products, using a motif which may have become part of a local idiom.

Coins are imitated on such base-metal disc-brooches as that from Boxmoor, Hertfordshire, on which there is a copy of a ninth-century gold *solidus* (Wilson 1964, 35 n 1), but none has previously been associated with the eighth-century silver sceatta currency. This would, indeed, seem to support arguments that the sceattas were used for commercial transactions and were not regarded as prestigious. Their occasional appearance in early eighth-century graves may indicate wergild or tokens of similar payments, for they were very rarely pierced and never mounted for suspension on necklaces, unlike gold coins. The design of two standing figures flanking a cross on a gold pendant from Compton Verney, Warwickshire, has recently been compared to the eighth-century Series N sceattas (MacGregor and Bolick 1993, 154 and no 23.7), but their design is of two figures holding staves. The Compton Verney motif is more like some sixth- or seventh-century Merovingian *trientes* (eg Haith 1991, no 34e), and the pendant seems more appropriately attributed to the seventh than to the eighth century. If correct, this would restore the two Hamwic brooches to their unique position as the only objects recognised as copying sceatta designs.

Disc-brooches of the later sixth and seventh centuries are usually considered a product of Kentish influence, and are occasional finds in Hampshire (eg the Winnall II cemetery: Meaney and Hawkes 1970, 33–6 and pl II; and a surface find from Ampfield: Denford 1986). In silver, they are well known from ninth-century hoards, but base-metal examples are usually without such context-associations and are less datable from stylistic evidence – one from Thetford being an exception (Goodall 1984, 68 and fig 109, no 2, and the parallel cited for it, Wilson 1964, no 17). The absence of further examples from Southampton may be an indication that the Kentish fashion was not generally adopted for base-metal designs, and that disc-brooches were not in fact very widely worn in the eighth century. Their absence from Anglian York supports this conclusion (Rogers 1993), but an alternative possibility is considered below in the Discussion.

C. Small-long brooch (fig 1)

7 1 (fig 1)
Leaded bronze (XRF analysis, table 5). Square, notched, broken headplate, triangular-sectioned bow, grooved at junction with the slightly wider foot. Remains of a swivel-loop (not hinge-lugs) and catch-plate on the back.
L 50mm
Context F55, 1

This brooch is of a type of which there are examples from Sussex cemeteries at Alfriston and Highdown; they have been attributed to the first half of the sixth century (Welch 1983, 66–7; see also Leeds's distribution map, 1945, fig 12). Other types of small-long brooch include recently published cemetery discoveries from Collingbourne Ducis, Wiltshire (Gingell 1975/6, 94–7), Portway, Andover, Hampshire (Cook and Dacre 1985, 80) and Alton, Hampshire (Evison 1988, 8). Their absence from the Isle of Wight and from Droxford could indicate that small-long brooches were not generally worn in the south coast's 'Jutish' area in the sixth century. The Southampton example may not have come from the immediate locality, therefore, which may reduce slightly the likelihood of its having arrived as scrap for recycling. It is very worn, and it is not impossible that it had survived in use for long enough to have been virtually an antique when discarded. There is some support for this in the discovery of one at Chichester (Welch 1983, 66–7 and fig 126a), like Saxon Southampton a site from which there is otherwise no sixth-century material, with occupation perhaps restarting in the eighth century (Munby 1984, 322–3), but that brooch was from a modern suburb, not the walled core.

D. **Roman bow-brooch** (fig 1)

34 6 (fig 1)
Bronze (XRF analysis, table 5). T-shaped type, only upper part present.
W (extant) 22mm
Context Pit 155

Whereas it is possible that the small-long brooch, 7/1, was not brought into Southampton for scrap, that is the most likely explanation of the presence of a broken, first- or second-century Nauheim Derivative brooch (cf Hull 1967, fig 14, no 55). Like the Roman coins, it could have been foraged from the Bitterne area. Presumably it is only a coincidence that a very similar one was found at the Droxford cemetery (Aldsworth 1978, fig 31, no 1), but such finds from cemeteries make it possible that scavengings were as likely to be reused – as ornaments if not as brooches – as recycled; this would help to account for at least some of those found in Anglian York, which seem rather many to be casual losses by agricultural workers (Rogers 1993, 1357–8 and, *contra*, 1439).

BUCKLES AND BUCKLE-FITTINGS (fig 2)

4 6 (fig 2) Pin
Copper alloy. Bent strip.
L 16mm
Context F2

13 2 (fig 2) Frame and pin
Gunmetal (loop) and leaded gunmetal (pin) (XRF analysis, table 5). Cast, semi-circular frame with intermittent incised grooves. Heavy, cast pin.
W 34mm
Context F60, probably a grave (Morton 1992, 131)
Published Holdsworth 1976, 42 and pl VI A

15 281 (fig 2) Frame and pin
Copper alloy (frame) and iron (pin). Rectangular frame.
W 16mm
Context F52

15 289 (not illus) ?Frame
Copper alloy. Rectangular, broken.
W 19mm
Context F2

20 9 (fig 2) Frame, pin and plate
Brass (all parts) (XRF analysis, table 5). Oval frame, with double-sided, broken, rectangular plate wrapped over the bar. Two rivets.
W 17mm (frame), L overall 17mm
Context F288, a grave
Published Hinton 1980, 74

20 28 (not illus) Frame and plate
Copper alloy. Frame shape uncertain, plate rectangular, broken. Two rivets. Iron corrosion in the frame may indicate an iron pin. Now mislaid.
W (frame) 17mm
Context 183, a grave
Published Hinton 1980, 73–4

23 10 (fig 2) ?Plate
Copper alloy. Broken and twisted sub-rectangular sheet with two attachment holes, and slot ?for pin.
W 22mm
Context 6829 (F10/11 surface)

31 13 (fig 2) ?Pin
Copper alloy. Broken wire.
L (extant) 20mm
Context 4608

31 2642 (not illus) Pin
Copper alloy. Hammered strip.
L 25mm
Context 4636 (spit 6 BNW)

32 87 (fig 2) Plate
Tin bronze (AML). Rectangular, with three attachment holes, and slot ?for pin.
W 21mm
Context F157, 11

169 318 (fig 2) Frame and pin
Leaded brass (both) (XRF analysis, table 5). Oval frame made from bent wire, with unjoined ends.
W 18mm
Context 9884

169 2323 (not illus) ?Pin
Copper alloy. Flattened wire, with a loop at one end.
L *c* 30mm
Context 10467

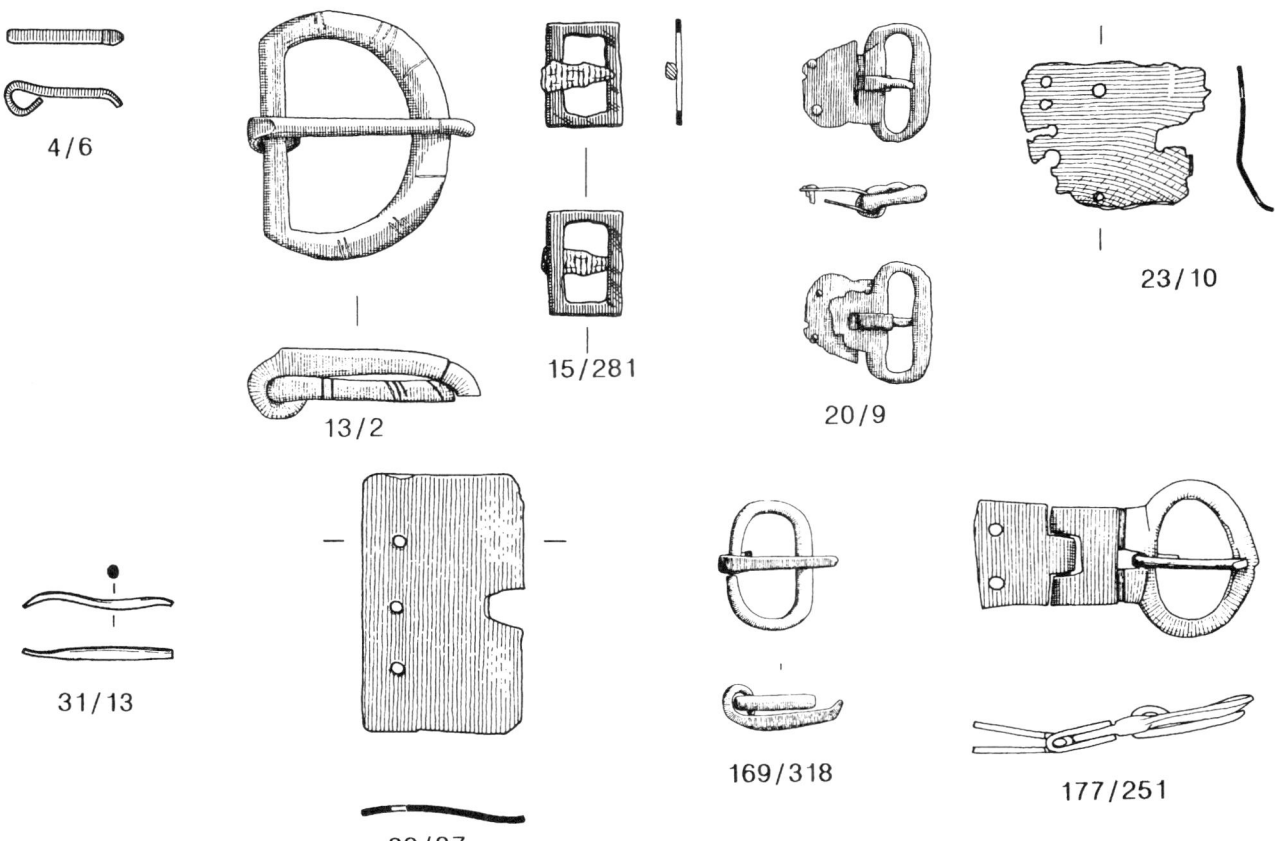

Figure 2. Buckles and buckle-fittings. Scale 1:1

177 251 (fig 2) Frame, pin and plate, with two hinge-plates
Copper alloy. Oval frame with attached rectangular plate, overlain by a sleeve, ?soldered on, which holds a hinge-bar on which swivels another rectangular plate with two attachment holes.
L *c* 42mm
Context 240

Although buckles are, after knives, the commonest objects in seventh-century graves, they are more often made of iron than of copper alloy; there are none in the latter metal at Winnall, for instance (Meaney and Hawkes 1970), although there was one in the Brook Street cemetery in Winchester (Hinton 1990A, no 1097), and four at Snells Corner, Horndean, Hampshire (Knocker 1956, 135–6). Two of the Saxon Southampton examples are from graves at site SOU 20, in both of which there were weapons, including a scramasax that has been identified as an eighth-century weapon of continental type (Evison, VI, cited in Morton 1992, 52). Both the sizes and the small attached plates of the buckles are similar to that from Brook Street, attributed to the seventh or early eighth century. Other examples from mid-Saxon sites include one from Cowage Farm, near Malmesbury (Hinchliffe 1986, 247–9). The rectangular frame of 15/281 has a silver parallel in the strap-slide in the Trewhiddle hoard, deposited *c* 868 (Wilson 1964, no 101) and in a few cemeteries, such as Chessell Down, Isle of Wight, Grave 37, though in that example the pin is more massive and elaborate (Arnold 1982, fig 8, 37iii). The D-framed 13/2, with its transverse lines, is recorded as from a grave, but may have been residual in the fill rather than originally associated with it (Morton 1992, 131–2, F60). This would mean that the buckle-frame pre-dates site SOU 13's latest phases; although dating is not precise, it is perhaps therefore more likely to be eighth than ninth century (*ibid*, 141). The arrangement of the plate fittings on 177/251 is unusual, but fixed plates were in use by the ninth century (eg Rogers 1993, nos 5311–3; Hinton 1990A, no 1098 etc), so perhaps it is not a later medieval intrusion.

There are not very many buckles or associated parts from Hamwic, so their number gives some support to the idea that belts, when worn, were fairly loose fitting, and that pins were more usually used to fasten costume. Copper-alloy buckles could also have been used with riding equipment, such as spurs. None of those from Hamwic was associated with any of the strap-ends, of which there are many more; so it seems likely that the two were not usually worn or used together.

CHAIN

5 61 (not illus)
Copper alloy. Very corroded length of figure-of-eight links.
Not measurable
Context F17

8 26 (not illus)
Copper alloy. Broken strands of figure-of-eight links.
L 8mm
Context F48, 11

Lengths of chain are often found associated with linked pins, and as there are two examples of this use from Saxon Southampton, catalogued below (30/266 and 254/1370), the two unassociated lengths of chain have been classed as personal items.

FINGER-RINGS (fig 3)

31 653 (fig 3)
Brass, mercury-gilded on front and back (XRF analysis, table 5). Circular-sectioned, untapering round hoop soldered or welded to back of bezel (but not splayed to strengthen the join). Lozenge-shaped bezel with a knop at each point. On the bezel, a 'chip-carved' open circle within an open star: twisted-wire S-scrolls in the fields, and a plain wire border. The back unornamented.
Diam (hoop) 27mm; Ht (bezel) 43mm
Context 5237

36 103 (fig 3)
Brass (XRF analysis, table 5), mercury-gilded (AML). Massive, swelling hoop with slight mid-rib approaching a small oval (now empty) setting.
Diam 26mm
Context Pit 9 (floor)

Although finger-rings, often quite elaborate and in precious metals, became more frequently used after the sixth century, partly at least as a result of Mediterranean influence, the Saxon Southampton material suggests that they were not much copied in base metals, since only two such rings can be positively identified: one plain example, 33/86 (see Rings and loops), might be another. The extent to which they were actually worn on the finger is called into doubt by the large number of plainer, usually wire or band rings found in pagan graves on necklaces, or associated with belts, or used as dress-fasteners (Fisher 1979); a recent mid-Saxon

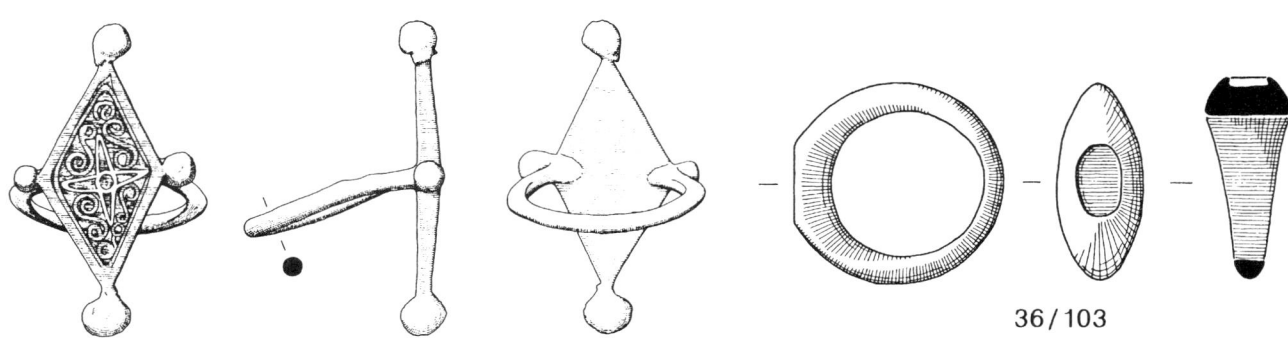

31/653   36/103

Figure 3.   Finger-rings.   Scale 1:1

discovery in a grave at Exeter was alongside the upper part of the skeleton's right arm (Graham-Campbell 1982A, 366 and pl L11c). The absence from Southampton of any recognisable examples of finger- (or ear-) rings with knotted or overlapping ends, as found in local cemeteries such as Winnall (Meaney and Hawkes 1970, 37–8 and fig 9) and Snell's Corner, Horndean (Knocker 1956, 135), may suggest that these types were out of fashion in the eighth and ninth centuries, but occurrence of the former type, and of penannular examples, at Anglian York (Rogers 1993, 1370–4) calls in question the value of placing too much weight on arguments from absence.

Of the two copper-alloy rings from Saxon Southampton, the more elaborate, 31/653, has two recently published parallels. One is of silver, with gold foil and wires, and a green glass setting; it has a lozenge-shaped flat bezel, with two knops at each point. Although from Iona Abbey, Scotland, it is thought to be of Anglo-Saxon workmanship (Webster 1995; Graham-Campbell 1995, 147 and pl 68, b). The other is a gold and chalcedony ring from Hitchin, Hertfordshire (Webster 1995). No continental parallels have been been recognised.

Although both the Iona and Hitchin rings may be tenth century, their dating is not so exact as to preclude an earlier date for Southampton's 31/653. This has filigree scrolls similar to those on strap-end 15/4 (see fig 16), and it is shown below that mercury-gilding was practised within Hamwic (Oddy, below). There is therefore no reason to doubt that the Southampton ring was made in England, which strengthens the case that the Iona and Hitchin rings are indeed Anglo-Saxon.

The other ring, 36/103, is of the 'expanded bezel' Roman type occasionally found in later graves (Fisher 1979, type E), and in consequence it is difficult to know if it is actually a Roman one picked up either as an ornament or for melting down, in the same way that a few other Roman objects reached Southampton (eg the brooch 34/6, and coins – see Scales and weights), or if it was made in the eighth or ninth century. Rings of this massive, swelling shape were current in the latter century (eg the Bologna ring: Bruce-Mitford 1956, 181 and pl XXII, B–D), but not with a small setting holding a gem or – more probably in this case – a glass bead. The mercury-gilding perhaps makes a mid-Saxon origin a little more likely, however.

It is just possible that the silver-mounted glass roundel, 169/2960, discussed below as a mount, is the broken-off bezel of a finger-ring (see Wamers 1986, fig 42).

HOOKED TAGS (fig 4)

31 668 (fig 4)
Copper alloy. Semi-circular plate with two attachment holes. Hook broken.
L 24mm
Context 5283

31 1482 (not illus) ?Hooked tag
Copper alloy. Circular plate, broken, with possible scar where hook protruded.
Diam 12mm
Context 4073, 1

32 170 (fig 4)
Leaded gunmetal (XRF analysis, table 5) with tin or lead coating on the front (AML). Discoid plate, with attachment holes in two projecting lugs, one broken, decorated with crudely incised border lines and cabling around a now unrecognisable central design.
L c 25mm
Context F347 general clearance
Published Addyman and Hill 1969, 70 and fig 27, 6

36 112 (fig 4)
Copper alloy. Sub-triangular plate with a single attachment hole.
L 26mm
Context Pit 15

36 190 (fig 4) ?Hooked tag
Copper alloy. Ring-and-dot decoration. Both ends broken. Perforations at top.
Extant L 13mm
Context 29, 5

38 39 (fig 4)
Copper alloy. Triangular plate with two attachment holes. Hook broken.
L 26 mm
Context Pit 50, 1

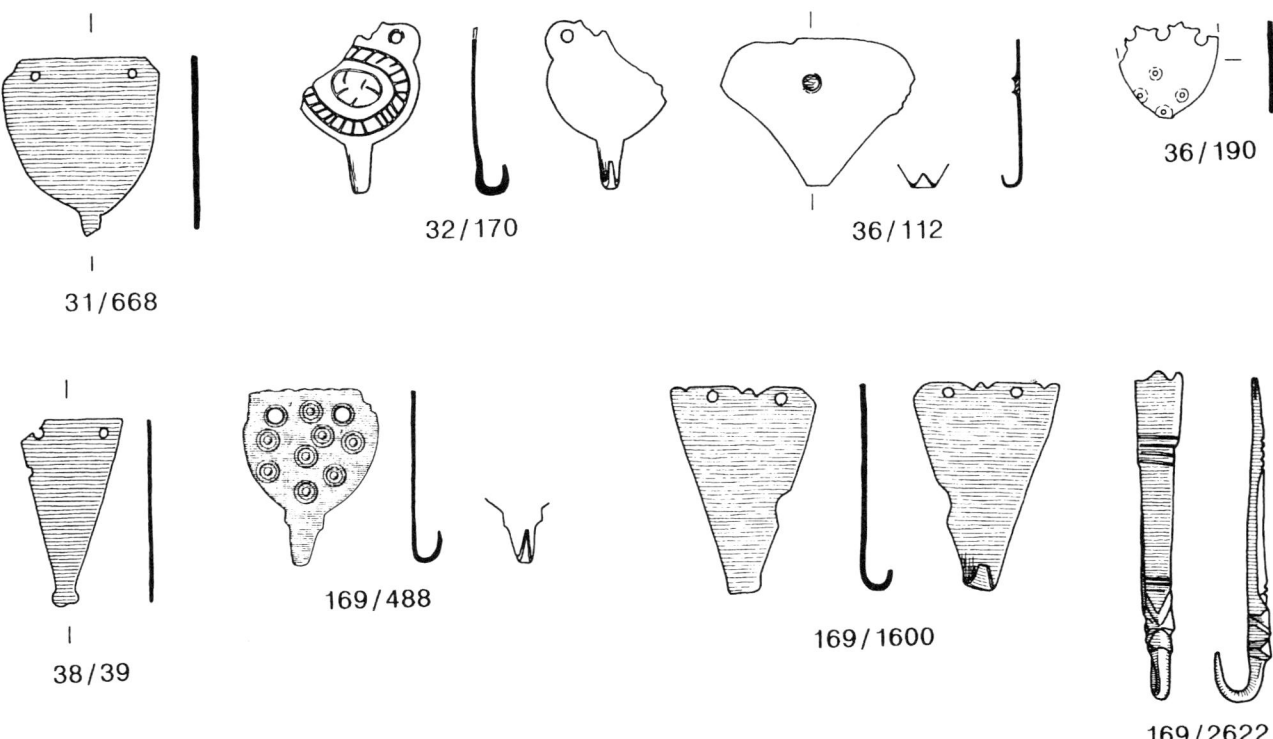

Figure 4. Hooked tags. Scale 1:1

169 488 (fig 4)
Leaded brass (XRF analysis, table 5). Semi-circular plate with nicked, straight top. Two attachment holes. Eight punched ring-and-dot ornaments on the front.
L 24mm
Context 8818

169 1600 (fig 4)
Tin bronze coated with tin or tin-lead alloy (AML). Triangular plate with nicked top. Two attachment holes. Undecorated except for white-metal coating, the front being scored diagonally, perhaps to aid adhesion.
L 28mm
Context 12200

169 2622 (fig 4)
Leaded brass (XRF analysis, table 5). Straight-sided, square-sectioned shaft with grooves dividing the unornamented centre from the slightly flaring split end which is now broken across the two attachment holes, and from the terminal, a vestigial animal mask holding a short hook in its mouth.
L 45mm
Context 12987

Introduced apparently in the seventh century (Dickinson 1973), hooked tags remained in use into the eleventh – the best late dating still being an execution cemetery at Meon Hill, Hampshire, where one was found in the fill of a grave next to a skeleton buried with a coin of Edward the Confessor (Liddell 1933, 154); another is from a grave about 20 feet (6m) from a skeleton which had six Edward the Confessor coins with it (Gray Hill 1937, 249). The Southampton examples add no information to the little that is known of their use: two fine silver tags from Winchester are usually referred to as garter-hooks because they were found around the knees of a skeleton (Hinton 1990B, no 1407), but it must be a possibility that these fastened a bag or purse, since Graham-Campbell has shown this almost certainly to have been the use of a pair found in Rome with coins of the 940s and inscribed with the name of Pope Marinus, 942–6 (Graham-Campbell and Okasha 1991); consequently the term 'garment hooks' is better avoided (*contra* Rogers 1993, 1359).

Although they are so common in England, hooked tags are infrequently found on continental sites; there is one from Birka

(Graham-Campbell 1982B, 146–7), one with ring-and-dot ornament from Haithabu (Capelle 1970, Abb 4.2), but apparently none from either Domburg (eg Capelle 1976) or Dorestad (eg Roes 1965). In the latter two cases, their absence may in part be a consequence of the difficulty of recovery of rather thin base metals in sheet form in acid soils, which may account for their relative paucity at Southampton (another possible example is published below as a Mount, 32/197). Their apparent absence from the prolific site at Cottam and Cowlam, where soil conditions seem beneficent (Haldenby 1990, 1992) is surprising, however, unless it can be taken to indicate that they were either less common in the eighth and earlier part of the ninth centuries than in the next two hundred years – or that the later ones were more likely to be cast, or cut from thicker sheets, and therefore have a better chance of survival – the thickness of most of those from Winchester suggests this (Hinton 1990B, no 1409 *et al*).

One of the Southampton tags, 169/488, has ring-and-dot decoration, which is quite common, and both 32/170 and 169/1600 had coatings to make them sparkle. The (broken) 38/39 may not be a hooked tag, despite its irregular shape and attachment holes: tags do not usually swell out at the bottom. The only unusual tag is 169/2622, with its narrow, straight-sided shaft, which appears to be the first of this type recorded. It is very like the two-riveted strap-ends recorded below, and it is perhaps surprising that such an obvious adaptation has not been seen before. Its suggested context date, *c* 850–*c* 900, accords very well with such strap-ends. A less certain example, 254/1149, is included among the strap-ends, below: although its elongated neck suggests that it was always intended to be formed into a hook, the curve is poorly executed and does not make the tight angle that is usual with tags.

LOOPS AND DISTRIBUTORS (fig 5)

31 254 (fig 5)
Copper alloy. One parallel-sided plate, one shorter and rounded, with one attachment hole in each.
L 42mm
Context 4644

31 1391 (fig 5)
Leaded bronze (XRF analysis, table 5). One parallel-sided plate, one shorter and rounded, with two attachment holes.
L 33mm
Context 5373

31 1647 (fig 5)
Bronze (XRF analysis, table 5). One tapering plate, one shorter and rounded, with two attachment holes.
L 24mm
Context 6182

31 1869 (fig 5)
Copper alloy. Broken.
L (extant) 16mm
Context 5261

31 2630 (fig 5)
Copper alloy. Tapering plates, with ?one attachment hole.
L 24mm
Context 4699 (F2008, 6)

32 173 (fig 5)
Copper alloy. Broken.
L (extant) 17mm
Context F554

39 42 (fig 5)
Copper alloy. Parallel-sided plates, with two attachment holes.
L 25mm
Context F70

169 238 (fig 5)
Leaded bronze (XRF analysis, table 5). Wire, twisted to form two loops.
L 35mm
Context 8629

169 1515 (fig 5)
Leaded bronze (XRF analysis, table 5). Slightly tapering plates, with two attachment holes.
L 30mm
Context 8765

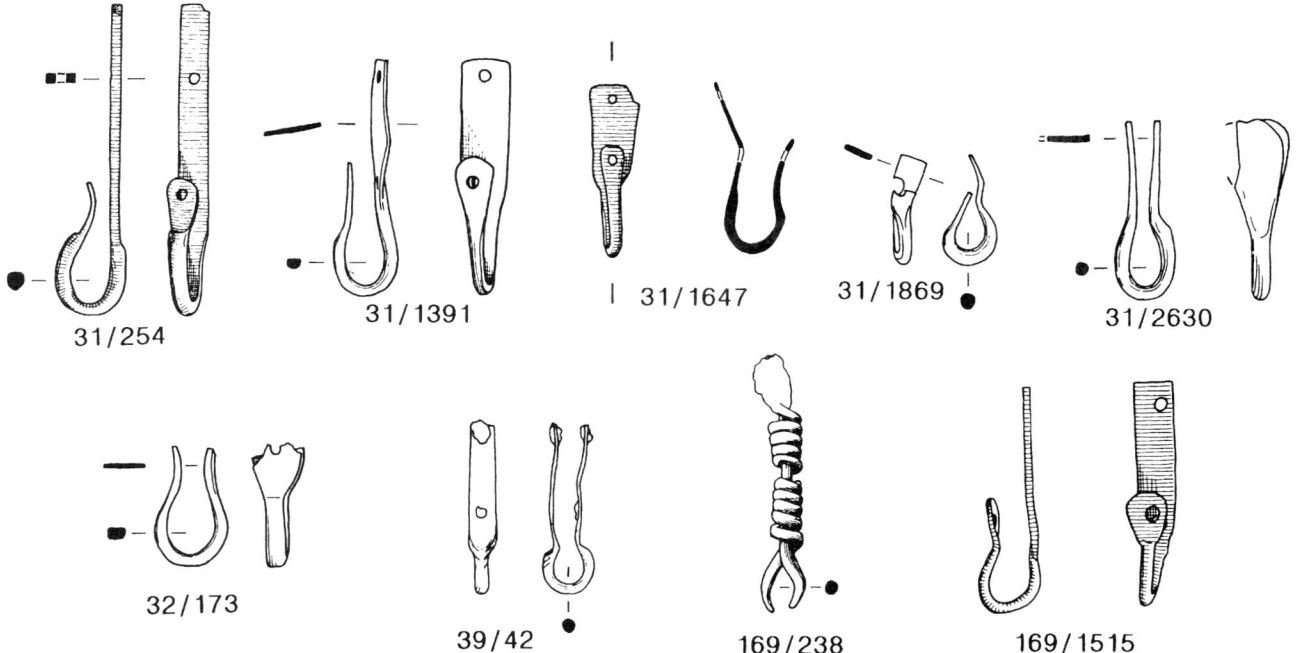

Figure 5.   Loops and distributors.   Scale 1:1

The majority of these objects have open loops with one straight-sided plate, and one that is either straight or shorter and discoid, pierced by attachment holes, nearly always presumably for metal rivets. They were 'made from a rod of circular section, bent in two over another rod of circular section to form a semi-circular loop, and the ends were hammered flat' (Tweddle 1992, 991), a description of fittings on the Anglian helmet found in Coppergate, York, on which loops were used to hold the cheek-pieces to the mail curtain. This is seemingly the only known *in situ* use of such loops, in copper alloy or in iron. One with a wire ring in its loop was found inside, but not attached to, the hanging-bowl at St Paul-in-the-Bail, Lincoln (Bruce-Mitford 1993, pl 6, 3). Something similar can be seen on the rims of an occasional bucket or pail (Baldwin Brown 1915, vol 4, pl CLII, nos 5, 8 and 9), but such loops are not usually part of the handle fittings of these vessels (Stamper 1977). An iron loop from a woman's grave at Horndean, Hampshire, was compared by Knocker to one from Shudy Camps, Cambridgeshire, which was attached to a length of chain, and was taken to have been used to help suspend a wooden vessel (Knocker 1956, 145 and fig 15, S, 28 no 3). Such loops are now, however, more usually taken as being used 'to suspend objects from belts or girdles' (Rogers 1993, 1352). Those from Droxford, for example, are in contexts that suggest suspension from belts worn at the waist – that in grave 21 had a bone bag-mouth at its end (Aldsworth 1978, figs 10 and 25) and that in grave 30 may have carried a knife (*ibid*, figs 10 and 27), both at the ends of iron chains (for a reconstruction, see Wamers 1986, Abb 5). This also seems likely to have been the function of a complex found in grave 14 at Watchfield, the recorded location between the skeleton's legs suggesting slight disturbance by animals or road-grading machinery (Scull 1992, 167 and ills 30 and 31, 83.33). There are two pairs of interlocked iron loops at West Stow, one of them joined to a D-shaped loop, identified as strap-distributors/separators (West 1985, fig 60, no 5; fig 129, no 2), and, more locally, there is one from Cowdery's Down (Crowther 1983, 251 and fig 72, no 42). Anglian York has yielded some iron, but not copper alloy, examples (Rogers 1993, 1352–3).

The Hamwic examples unfortunately do not throw further light on the uses that these loops had, and none has clear indications of former attachment to wood, metal, leather or textile. Nor is it obvious why some have two long plates, but several have one that is shorter and rounded, allowing only one rivet to link them. Nevertheless, the use of at least some of them to attach to belts from which festoons of objects could be hung is perhaps supported by 169/238, which may well also have served this purpose. It is closely matched by an attachment fitting that ended a chain from which dangled a 'work-box' or 'amulet-capsule', probably of the second half of the seventh century, found in the King Harry Lane cemetery outside St Albans, Hertfordshire (Stead and Rigby 1989, 222–3 and fig 79, grave 10, no 1).

PENDANTS (fig 6)

13 1 (fig 6) ?Châtelaine
Leaded bronze (XRF analysis, table 5). Broken openwork fitting from which were originally suspended, by figure-of-eight links, three pendants, each a straight shaft, initially round in section but becoming square with a row of dots down each side.
L (of pendants) 52mm
Context: at junction of F88, a grave, and F145 where F145 cut F88 (see Morton 1992, 133–4)

23 5 (fig 6) ?Pendant
Copper alloy. Shafted object with triangular ends, a broken-off attachment hole in one, ring-and-dot ornament in the other. Transverse lines at the necks.
L 53mm
Context 6821 (F7, 5)

24 821 (fig 6) ?Pendant
Leaded gunmetal (AML). Flat strip, one end widening and perforated, the other triangular with slight grooving.
L 45mm
Context 7959

This category is an artificial one, covering a miscellany of objects united only by having single perforations. The most curious is 13/1, which might possibly be a symbolic châtelaine like the more recognisable ones that occur in graves. A Swedish burial provides a slight and remote analogue, a group of four miniature staves attached to a ring, possibly transmogrifications of a symbol of 'Hercules's club' (Holmqvist 1979, 119). Single 'clubs' occur in English graves (Meaney 1981, 162–6). The Hamwic example may well have been a grave deposit: its context is not quite certain – it

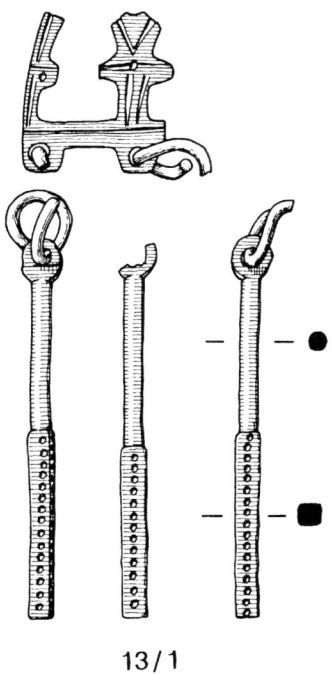

13/1

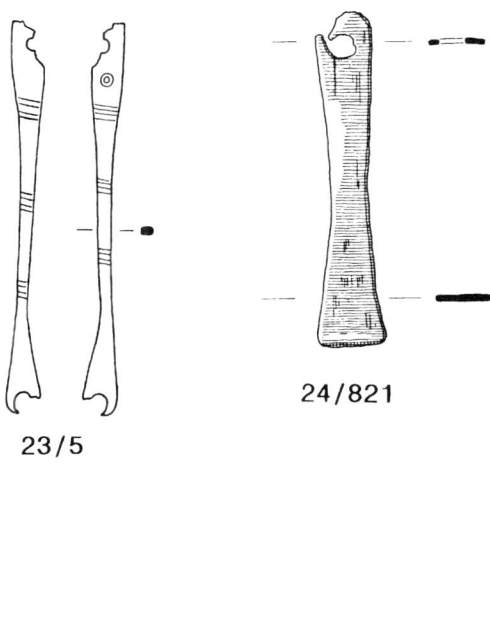

23/5

24/821

Figure 6. Pendants. Scale 1:1

was either from the right shoulder of a male skeleton, or from a pit which had cut through that skeleton's grave (SOU 13, F88) and which might therefore have contained objects disturbed from that or other graves during its digging. The burials at the sites are not closely dated, but are probably later seventh (if any in Hamwic are that early) or eighth century, with the grave F88 coming quite late in the sequence (Morton 1992, 130–1). If indeed a ritual deposit, the object suggests late continuance of the practice of deposition despite proximity to a building identified as a church.

No use is suggested for the other objects: 23/5 and 24/821 might be toilet items, but seem a little too broad at the ends. A very similar object, 349/80 (fig 18), has been included amongst Tweezers and other toilet implements as much to draw attention to such problems of identification as from any sense of conviction.

PINS (figs 7–13)
BY DAVID A HINTON AND ALISON L PARSONS
Introduction

The pins have been classified according to the shapes and styles of their heads (A: spherical; B: polyhedral (including cuboid and similar forms); C: bi-conical; D: spiral; E: disc; F: rhomboid; G: ring; H: oval; I: linked; J: miscellaneous; K: headless). Some of these, such as the disc-headed type E, are already standard names, and two, ring-headed, type G, and linked, type I, therefore fit uneasily into this categorisation; it seemed preferable to retain established nomenclature, however. Sub-divisions within these types are based firstly on decorative finish on the heads (a: undecorated; b: wrythen, that is, with swirling grooves; c: ring-and-dot; d: various); secondly on the absence (1) or presence (2) of an annular collar or collars at the junction of the head and shaft; and thirdly on the shaft itself (i: straight; ii: distinctly swelling, usually in the lower part; iii: hipped, that is, thickened near the point so as to create a distinct ridge). Inevitably there are some pins which are too decayed or broken for full classification, and many where the classifications, particularly of the shafts, are not clear-cut.

Any type of head may of course have existed with any combination of the sub-divisions, but not all potential combinations have yet been found in the Hamwic excavations. The classification has facilitated sorting of the pins, and may be helpful for other assemblages. It was originally devised in the hope that, for instance, a particular type of head and shaft might correlate, but no obvious patterns have emerged.

Collars on pins may be primarily decorative, though very few are given the distinction of cabling or grooving. They may also have been functional, providing a seating for a thread at the top of the pin's shaft. Some pins which lack collars have grooves, or at least a constriction, between shaft and head, which may have been intentional, to help to keep threads in place, or may have been fortuitously caused during manufacture. The latter is more likely to happen if heads were separately fitted, especially if the top of the shaft narrowed so that it could be fitted into the head. Oddy discusses (below) a wire-rolling process which would have involved separate attachment. It is very difficult to be sure of the manufacturing process in every case, though some pins appear to have been cast.

Lengths are given for each pin, but many are probably or certainly lacking at least parts of their tips. Pins with broken-off shafts have been catalogued as having straight shafts if the extant length shows no swelling or hipping.

Type A: Spherical-headed pins (figs 7–8)
Aa WITH SPHERICAL, UNDECORATED HEADS
1i. Without collars and with straight (or broken) shafts

8 19 (not illus)
Leaded bronze (XRF analysis, table 4).
L 27mm
Context, Level B, depth 11cm

8 38 (not illus)
Copper alloy.
L 21mm
Context F48, 2

24 822 (fig 7)
Leaded bronze (XRF analysis, table 4).
L 54mm
Context 9065

31   2644   (not illus)
Copper alloy. Broken.
Extant L 6mm
Context 5682

32   157   (not illus)
Bronze (XRF analysis, table 4).
Extant L 46mm
Context 20, 7

169   341   (not illus)
Leaded bronze (XRF analysis, table 4).
L 63mm
Context 9864

177   595   (not illus)
Copper alloy.
L 54mm
Context 731

1ii. Without collars and with swelling shafts

15   287   (not illus)
Leaded gunmetal (XRF analysis, table 4).
L 51mm
Context F49, 1

26   666   (not illus)
Leaded gunmetal (XRF analysis, table 4).
L 56mm
Context F3030, 3

30   442   (not illus)
Bronze (XRF analysis, table 4).
L 55mm
Context Unstratified

31   982   (not illus)
Leaded gunmetal (XRF analysis, table 4).
L 63mm
Context 5682

32   459   (fig 7)
Bronze (XRF analysis, table 4). Head misshapen. Distorted at junction.
L 59mm
Context not known
Published Addyman and Hill 1969, 68 and fig 26, 2

169   1503   (not illus)
Leaded bronze (XRF analysis, table 4).
L 52mm
Context 8766

169   1698   (fig 7)
Brass (XRF analysis, table 4).
L 65mm
Context 11961

184   124   (not illus)
Copper alloy. Grooved at shaft/head junction.
L 45mm
Context 161

258   181   (fig 7)
Silver, with traces of gold and copper (AML XRF analysis). Incised lines below head.
L 52mm
Context 15483

2i. With ring collars and straight shafts

24   3   (not illus)
Brass (XRF analysis, table 4).
L 53mm
Context 1400

32   163   (not illus)
Leaded bronze (XRF analysis, table 4).
L 35mm
Context F366

169   2568   (not illus)
Bronze (XRF analysis, table 4).
L 34mm
Context 12745

2ii. With ring collars and swelling shafts

5   3   (fig 7)
Leaded bronze (XRF analysis, table 4).
L 44mm
Context General clearance

20   8   (fig 7)
Leaded bronze (XRF analysis, table 4).
L 58mm
Context F131, 1

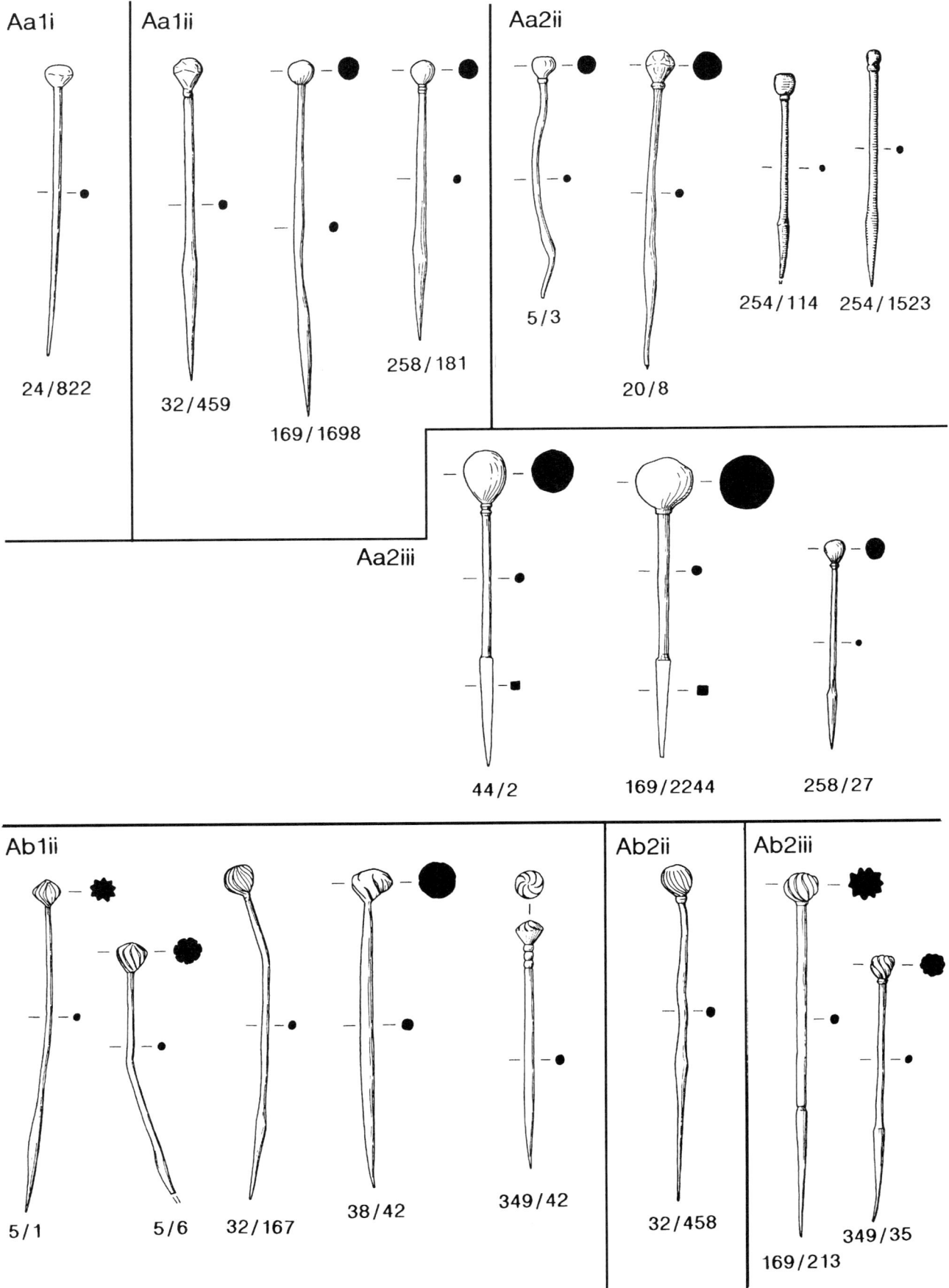

26 624 (not illus)
Silver, debased with copper (XRF analysis, table 4).
L 41mm
Context 5128, 3

39 45 (not illus)
Leaded bronze (XRF analysis, table 4).
L 58mm
Context Pit 66A, 1

169 748 (not illus)
Silver (XRF analysis, table 4). Double collar.
L 39mm
Context 8822

169 2499 (not illus)
Leaded bronze (XRF analysis, table 4).
L 65mm
Context 12819

177 567 (not illus)
Copper alloy.
L 45mm
Context 315

254 114 (fig 7)
Copper alloy.
L 36mm
Context 370
Published Hinton 1993C, no 8

254 1523 (fig 7)
Copper alloy.
L 43mm
Context 3847
Published Hinton 1993C, no 9

258 310 (not illus)
Copper alloy.
L 53mm
Context 16878

2iii. With ring collars and hipped shafts

31 1466 (not illus)
Silver, debased with copper (XRF analysis, table 4).
L 52mm
Context 5748/5952

44 2 (fig 7)
Copper alloy. Double collar.
L 58mm
Context Unstratified
Published Addyman and Hill 1969, 68 and fig 26, 3

99 25 (not illus)
Brass (XRF analysis, table 4).
L 47mm
Context 223

169 1409 (not illus)
Silver (XRF analysis, table 4).
L 42mm
Context 12094

169 2244 (fig 7)
Silver (XRF analysis, table 4). Large head.
L 57mm
Context 12482

177 234 (not illus)
Copper alloy.
L 55mm
Context 147

258 27 (fig 7)
Base silver, with gold, zinc, lead and copper impurities (AML XRF analysis).
L 39mm
Context 14885

Figure 7.   Pins: Type A, spherical-headed. Aa 1i: spherical, undecorated head without collar and with straight shaft; Aa 1ii: spherical, undecorated heads without collars and with swelling shafts; Aa 2ii: spherical, undecorated heads, with ring collars and swelling shafts; Aa 2iii: spherical, undecorated heads with ring collars and hipped shafts; Ab 1ii: wrythen-decorated spherical heads, without collars and with swelling shafts; Ab 2ii: wrythen-decorated spherical heads, with ring collars and swelling shafts; Ab 2iii: wrythen-decorated spherical heads, with ring collars and hipped shafts.   Scale 1:1

Ab. WITH WRYTHEN-DECORATED SPHERICAL HEADS (fig 7)

1i. Without collars and with straight shafts

169 6   (not illus)
Leaded bronze (XRF analysis, table 4).
L 29mm
Context 8421

1ii. Without collars and with swelling shafts

5 1   (fig 7)
Leaded bronze (XRF analysis, table 4).
L 57mm
Context F16

5 6   (fig 7)
Leaded bronze (XRF analysis, table 4).
L 46mm
Context F11, 1

26 144   (not illus)
Leaded bronze (XRF analysis, table 4).
L 43mm
Context 49

26 398   (not illus)
Leaded bronze (XRF analysis, table 4).
L 52mm
Context 94

31 11   (not illus)
Leaded bronze (XRF analysis, table 4).
L 62mm
Context Unstratified

32 167   (fig 7)
Leaded bronze (XRF analysis, table 4). Girth groove at head/shaft junction.
L 63mm
Context F366

38 42   (fig 7)
Leaded bronze (XRF analysis, table 4).
L 59mm
Context F53, 1

169 2998   (not illus)
Leaded gunmetal (XRF analysis, table 4).
L 55mm
Context 10774

349 42   (fig 7)
Copper alloy. Three grooves at neck/shaft junction.
L 46mm
Context 0173

1iii. Without collar and with hipped shaft

30 330   (not illus)
Leaded bronze (XRF analysis, table 4).
L 57mm
Context 3571

2ii. With ring collars and swelling shafts

24 14   (not illus)
Leaded bronze (XRF analysis, table 4).
L 49mm
Context 14025

32 458   (fig 7)
Leaded bronze (XRF analysis, table 4).
L 62mm
Context not known
Published Addyman and Hill 1969, 68 and fig 26, 9

35 5   (not illus)
Leaded bronze (XRF analysis, table 4).
L 62mm
Context Pit 128

169 1   (not illus)
Leaded bronze (XRF analysis, table 4).
L 52mm
Context 8419

177 562   (not illus)
Copper alloy. Gold-coloured line along shaft.
L 45mm
Context 311

2iii. With ring collars and hipped shafts

20   1   (not illus)
Leaded bronze (XRF analysis, table 4). Decorated on upper half of head only.
L 40mm
Context F70

31   1025   (not illus)
Leaded bronze (XRF analysis, table 4). Decorated on upper half of head only.
L 55mm
Context 3034, 2

169   213   (fig 7)
Leaded bronze (XRF analysis, table 4).
L 67mm
Context 8835

177   629   (not illus)
Copper alloy. Head misshapen.
L 67mm
Context 636

349   35   (fig 7)
Copper alloy.
L 49mm
Context 0115

Ac.   WITH SPHERICAL HEADS, DECORATED WITH RING-AND-DOT ORNAMENT (fig 8)
1i.   Without collar and with straight shaft

31   1247   (not illus)
Lead-alloy head, iron shaft.
L 57mm
Context 5888

1ii.   Without collar and with swelling shaft

24   24   (fig 8)
Leaded bronze (XRF analysis, table 4).
L 56mm
Context 7521

2ii.   With ring collars and swelling shafts

30   72   (not illus)
Leaded bronze (XRF analysis, table 4).
L 73mm
Context Unstratified

31   672   (fig 8)
Leaded bronze (XRF analysis, table 4).
L 57mm
Context Trench 3, unstratified

32   162   (not illus)
Leaded brass (XRF analysis, table 4).
L 47mm
Context F307, 3

32   420   (fig 8)
Leaded bronze (XRF analysis, table 4).
L 47mm
Context Unstratified

Ad.   WITH SPHERICAL HEADS, VARIOUSLY DECORATED (fig 8)
2ii.   With ring collars and swelling shafts

31   1464   (fig 8)
Silver. 'Pineapple' decoration on head.
L 61mm
Context 5460

254   115   (fig 8)
Silver. 'Pineapple' decoration on head. Grooved in hip position.
L 69mm
Context 370
Published Hinton 1993C, no 10

254   1613   (fig 8)
Silver. 'Pineapple' decoration on head.
L 64mm
Context 4175
Published Hinton 1993C, no 11

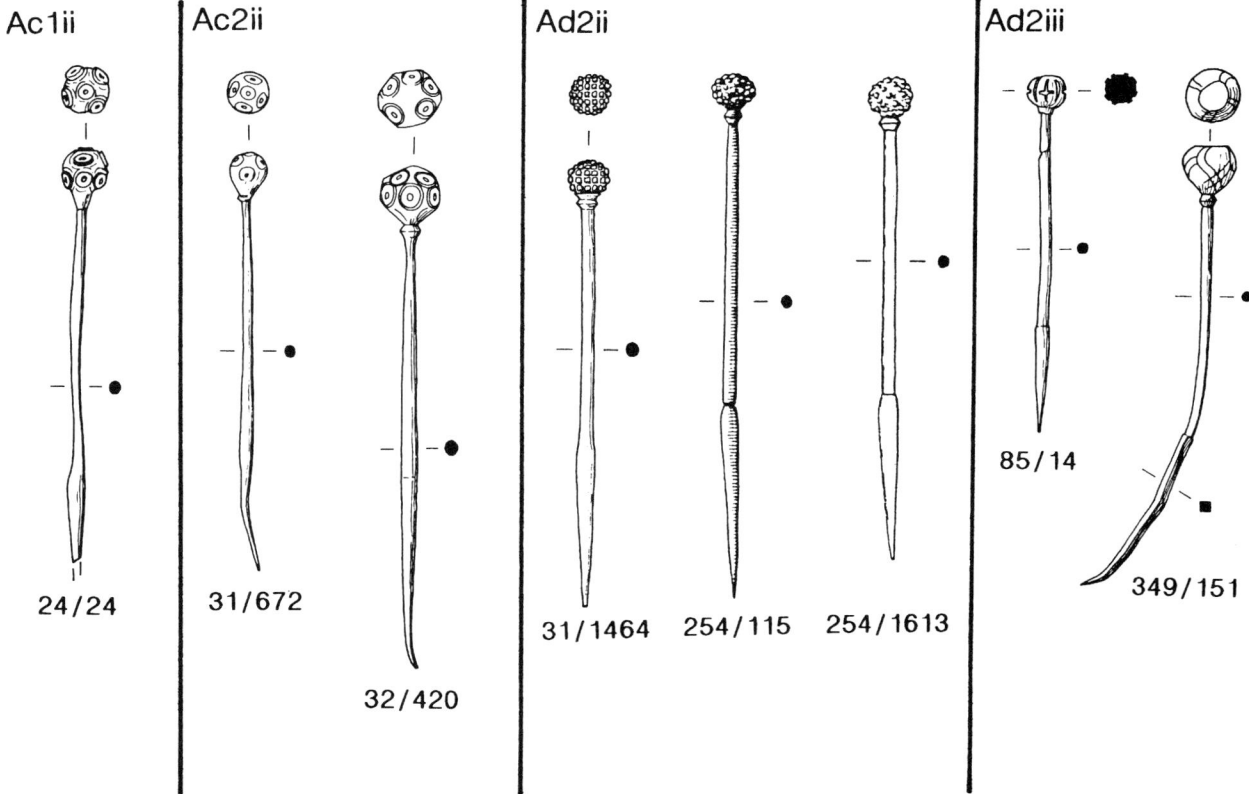

Figure 8. Pins: Type A, spherical-headed. Ac 2ii: spherical heads decorated with ring-and-dot, with ring collars and swelling shafts; Ad 2ii: spherical heads, variously decorated, with ring collars and swelling shafts. Scale 1:1

2iii. With ring collar and hipped shafts

36 347 (not illus)
Copper alloy. Criss-cross grooving on head, ring collar.
L 44mm
Context not known
Published Maitland Muller 1950, 128–9. Currently mislaid, described from publication

85 14 (fig 8)
Bronze, mercury-gilded (XRF analysis, table 4). Head divided by counter-sunk vertical lines into four sections, each containing a cross. Ring collar.
L 61mm
Context not known

349 151 (fig 8)
Copper alloy. Criss-cross grooving on flat-topped head.
L 63mm
Context 400

Discussion of Type A: Spherical-headed pins
(figs 7–8)
This is the commonest type of pin from Saxon Southampton, with about half being decorated. They come with and without collars, with all three shaft types and in various alloys. It is a common type also at a range of sites in England (eg York: Waterman 1959, fig 11, 9; Whitby Abbey: Peers and Radford 1943, fig 14, various), including some local to Southampton (eg Chalton: Champion 1977, 369; Winchester, one silver and two copper alloy from Cathedral Green: Biddle 1990B, nos 1430, 1434 and 1438; Aldbourne, Wiltshire: Robinson 1994), and on the continent (Domburg: Capelle 1976, Taf. 13 and 14; Dorestad: Roes 1965, pl 5, no 45). Wrythen and ring-and-dot decoration also occurs on this type at these and other sites.

Ten of the seventy-one pins classified here as spherical-headed are in an alloy of silver, including three (of type Ad) which have more elaborate decoration than most. It has been suggested that the two from site 254 may have been worn as a pair (Hinton 1993C, nos 10 and 11). The use of mercury-gilding on 85/14 suggests that it also had more than run-of-the-mill status.

It is noted below, by Wilthew, that a very substantial majority of the decorated spherical-headed pins are of leaded bronze, whereas the undecorated ones are in a range of alloys.

Type B: Polyhedral-headed pins (fig 9)
Ba. WITH POLYHEDRAL, UNDECORATED HEADS
1i. Without collars and with straight shafts

8   33   (not illus)
Copper alloy.
L 20mm
Context F7, 7

169   915   (not illus)
Leaded bronze (XRF analysis, table 4). Head very small. Grooved at junction of head and shaft.
L 45mm
Context 11283

2i. With ring collars and straight shafts

35   34   (not illus)
Leaded brass (XRF analysis, table 4).
L 61mm
Context Pit 128

169   442   (fig 9)
Leaded brass (XRF analysis, table 4). Girth grooves on shaft.
L 58mm
Context 10128

2ii. With ring collars and swelling shafts

31   1563   (not illus)
Brass (XRF analysis, table 4). Small head.
L 47mm
Context 5916

258   270   (not illus)
Copper alloy.
L 55mm
Context 16199

2iii. With ring collars and hipped shafts

4   4   (fig 9)
Brass (XRF analysis, table 4).
L 56mm
Context General clearance

24   23   (fig 9)
Leaded gunmetal (XRF analysis, table 4). The collar wrythen.
L 56mm
Context 7837/8251

32   456   (fig 9)
Brass (XRF analysis, table 4).
L 50mm
Context not known
Published Addyman and Hill 1969, 68 and fig 26, 5

36   97   (fig 9)
Leaded bronze (XRF analysis, table 4). The collar wrythen.
L 70mm
Context Pit 40

Bb. WITH POLYHEDRAL HEADS, DECORATED WITH A SINGLE RING-AND-DOT DECORATION ON THE FOUR FACES UNLESS DESCRIBED OTHERWISE (fig 9)
1i. Without collars and with straight shafts

15   6   (fig 9)
Leaded bronze (XRF analysis, table 4). Ring-and-dot also on upper facets.
L 25mm
Context F52, 1

23   1   (not illus)
Copper alloy.
L 54mm
Context 6839

31   1258   (not illus)
Leaded bronze (XRF analysis table, 4). Small head.
L 32mm
Context Unstratified

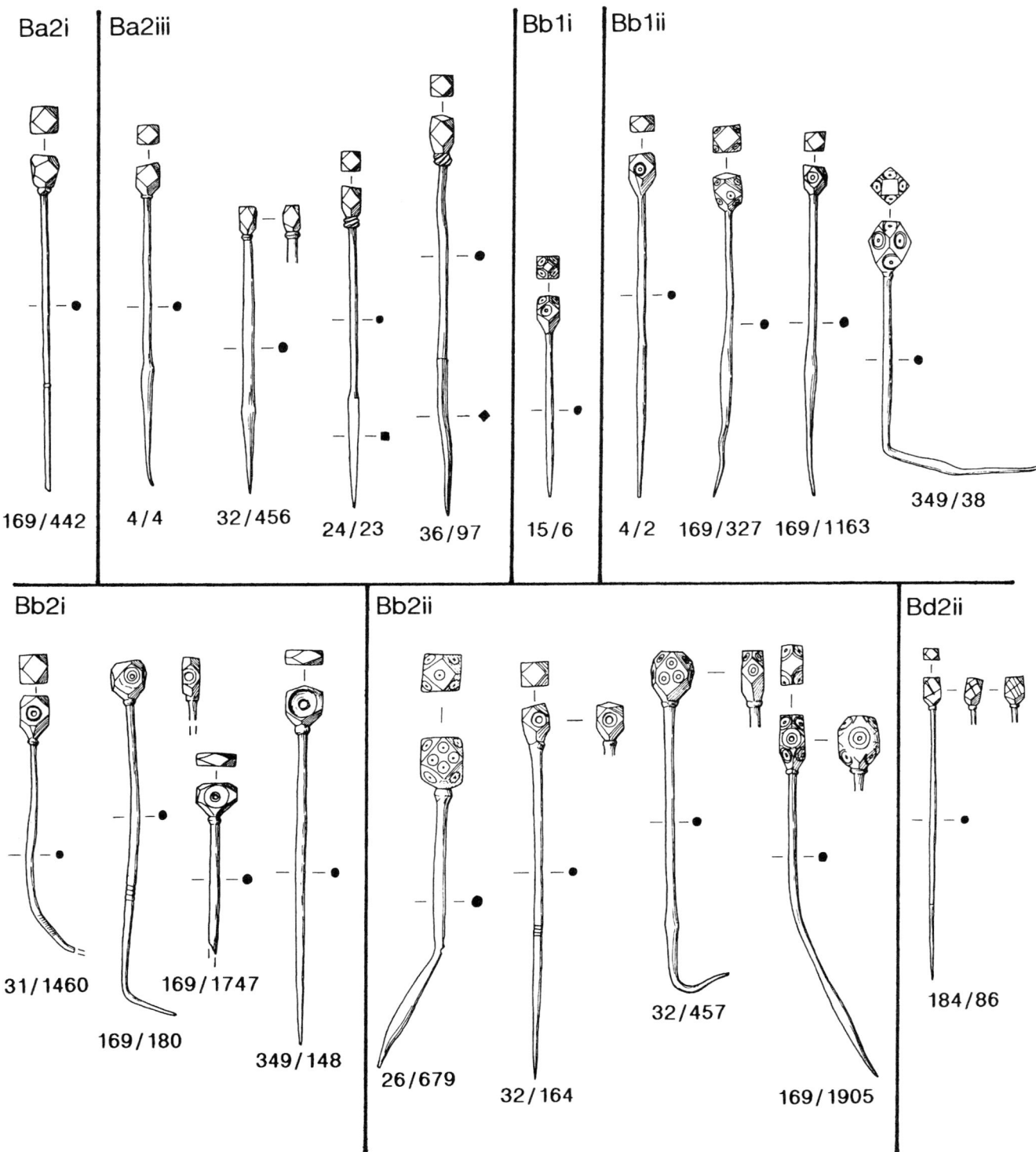

Figure 9. Pins: Type B, polyhedral-headed. Ba 2i: polyhedral, undecorated heads with ring collars and straight shafts; Ba 2iii: polyhedral, undecorated heads with ring collars and hipped shafts; Bb 1i: polyhedral heads decorated with ring-and-dot, without collars and with straight shafts; Bb 1ii: polyhedral heads decorated with ring-and-dot, without collars and with swelling shafts; Bb 2i: polyhedral heads decorated with ring-and-dot, with ring collars and straight shafts; Bb 2ii: polyhedral heads decorated with ring-and-dot, with ring collars and swelling shafts; Bd 2ii: polyhedral heads, variously decorated, with ring collars and swelling shafts. Scale 1:1

CATALOGUE

169 1286 (not illus)
Leaded bronze (XRF analysis, table 4).
L 37mm
Context 11896

258 138 (not illus)
Copper alloy.
L 16mm
Context 15353

1ii. Without collars and with swelling shafts

4 2 (fig 9)
Leaded bronze (XRF analysis, table 4).
L 50mm
Context General clearance

30 66 (not illus)
Copper alloy.
L 64mm
Context 3594

169 327 (fig 9)
Leaded bronze (XRF analysis, table 4). Ring-and-dot also on upper and lower facets.
L 57mm
Context 9885

169 817 (not illus)
Leaded bronze (XRF analysis, table 4). Ring-and-dot also on upper facets.
L 60mm
Context 11008

169 1163 (fig 9)
Leaded bronze (XRF analysis, table 4).
L 58mm
Context 8409

177 4 (not illus)
Copper alloy (XRF analysis, table 4). Counter-sunk cross on top.
L 48mm
Context 101

258 400 (not illus)
Copper alloy.
L 60mm
Context 18994

349 38 (fig 9)
Copper alloy. Ring-and-dot on all facets.
L 68mm
Context 109

1iii. Without collar and with hipped shaft

258 260 (not illus)
Copper alloy. Misshapen head.
L 64mm
Context 14828

2i. With ring collars and straight shafts

24 2 (not illus)
Brass (XRF analysis, table 4).
L 58mm
Context 14025

24 819 (not illus)
Leaded gunmetal (XRF analysis, table 4). Non-cuboid head. Ring-and-dot on two faces only.
L 36mm
Context 7521

31 677 (not illus)
Leaded bronze (XRF analysis, table 4).
L 42mm
Context Trench 3, Unstratified

31 1434 (not illus)
Leaded bronze (XRF analysis, table 4).
L 48mm
Context Unstratified

31 1460 (fig 9)
Leaded gunmetal (XRF analysis, table 4).
L 46mm
Context 5941

31 1562 (not illus)
Leaded bronze (XRF analysis, table 4). Ring-and-dot also on upper and lower facets and on top.
L 24mm
Context 6068

169   180   (fig 9)
Leaded brass (XRF analysis, table 4). Girth rings incised on shaft.
L 70mm
Context 8712

169   1747   (fig 9)
Leaded brass (XRF analysis, table 4). Ring-and-dot on two faces only.
L 31mm
Context 12310

169   2469   (not illus)
Leaded gunmetal (XRF analysis, table 4). Shaft grooved.
L 60mm
Context 12805

349   148   (fig 9)
Copper alloy. Flattened head.
L 61mm
Context 401

2ii. With ring collars and swelling shafts

15   218   (not illus)
Leaded bronze (XRF analysis, table 4). Ring-and-dot also on top.
L 63mm
Context F1, 1

23   4   (not illus)
Leaded bronze (XRF analysis, table 4). Ring-and-dot also on upper facets.
L 55mm
Context 6838

24   13   (not illus)
Leaded brass (XRF analysis, table 4).
L 60mm
Context 8015

26   679   (fig 9)
Leaded bronze (XRF analysis, table 4). Four rings-and-dots on each face, one on upper facets and top.
L 58mm
Context 229

30   161   (not illus)
Leaded bronze (XRF analysis, table 4).
L 50mm
Context 3293

31   157   (not illus)
Leaded bronze (XRF analysis, table 4). Grooved shaft.
L 53mm
Context 4801

31   1058   (not illus)
Bronze (XRF analysis, table 4).
L 64mm
Context 5748/5952

31   1428   (not illus)
Leaded bronze (XRF analysis, table 4). Ring-and-dot also on upper facets.
L 52mm
Context Unstratified

31   1487   (not illus)
Leaded bronze (XRF analysis, table 4).
L 57mm
Context 6068

31   1645   (not illus)
Leaded bronze (XRF analysis, table 4). Ring-and-dot also on upper and lower facets.
L 62mm
Context 6254

32   164   (fig 9)
Leaded brass (XRF analysis, table 4). Girth grooves on shaft.
L 65mm
Context F342/2

32   165   (not illus)
Leaded gunmetal (XRF analysis, table 4).
L 86mm
Context F375A

32 457 (fig 9)
Leaded bronze (XRF analysis, table 4). Three rings-and-dots on each face, one on each upper facet.
L 68mm
Context not known
Published Addyman and Hill 1969, 68 and fig 26, 8

169 245 (not illus)
Gunmetal (XRF analysis, table 4).
L 62mm
Context 9718

169 1905 (fig 9)
Leaded bronze (XRF analysis, table 4). Ring-and-dot decoration also on upper and lower facets.
L 65mm
Context 11995

169 2955 (not illus)
Leaded bronze (XRF analysis, table 4).
L 54mm
Context 8779

Bd. WITH POLYHEDRAL HEADS, VARIOUSLY DECORATED (fig 9)
1i. Without collar and with straight shaft

31 1567 (not illus)
Leaded bronze (XRF analysis, table 4). Small head with a crude counter-sunk cross on each face.
Extant L 25mm
Context 6024

2ii. With ring collar and swelling shaft

184 86 (fig 9)
Copper alloy. Grooves on head. Shaft broken.
L 53mm
Context 235

Discussion of Type B: Polyhedral-headed pins (fig 9)
Slightly less common than the spherical type, the polyhedral head presumably involved more difficulty in creating a mould, or in filing of the head to create sharply defined facets. The flat surfaces lend themselves to ring-and-dot decoration, so that a higher proportion of this type is decorated.

They are represented at the same sorts of site as the spherical-headed (York: Waterman 1959, fig 11, 7 and 12; Whitby: Peers and Radford 1943, fig 14 various; Chalton: Champion 1977, 369; Winchester, both Cathedral Green: one silver, one copper alloy, Biddle 1990B, nos 1432, 1433; Portchester: Hinton and Welch 1976, fig 139, 54; Domburg: Capelle 1976 Taf. 12 and 13; Dorestad: Roes 1965, pl 5, no 40). There is a pin from the Droxford cemetery which has a small polyhedral head, but its grooved neck and long shaft distinguish it from the Hamwic examples (Aldsworth 1978, fig 31, 35). More comparable is one with a slightly larger head and a shaft of a length like Hamwic's pins from a cremation at Alton, but even this has grooves at the neck/shaft junction rather than the collar normally used at Hamwic when that junction is embellished, and the excavator considered it a Roman type (Evison 1988, 12 and fig 41, cremation 24, 4).

None of the fifty-three polyhedral-headed pins is in any metal other than a copper alloy, nor has any been noted as having been gilded, even 31/1567 (of type Bd), which has counter-sunk crosses like the mercury-gilded Ad2iii type, 85/14. That two of those with hipped shafts, 24/23 and 36/97 (type Ba2iii), also have wrythen collars is an indication that slightly more care went into the making of that type of shaft.

Type C: Bi-conical-headed pins (fig 10)
Ca. WITH BI-CONICAL, UNDECORATED HEADS
1i. Without collars and with straight shafts

20 3 (fig 10)
Brass (XRF analysis, table 4).
L c 48mm
Context F131, 1

24 826 (not illus)
Brass (XRF analysis, table 4). Dome-topped head.
L 74mm
Context Unstratified

169 1605 (not illus)
Leaded brass (XRF analysis, table 4). Flat median band around head.
L 10mm
Context 11634

258 118 (not illus)
Copper alloy.
L 42mm
Context 15101

1ii. Without collars and with swelling shafts

24 830 (not illus)
Copper alloy. Flat-topped head.
L 53mm
Context 13935

39 44 (fig 10)
Bronze (XRF analysis, table 4). Flat-topped head.
L 55mm
Context Pit 68, 1

169 555 (not illus)
Leaded bronze (XRF analysis, table 4).
L 47mm
Context 10361

169 616 (not illus)
Leaded bronze (XRF analysis, table 4). Domed head.
L 48mm
Context 10383

169 1867 (not illus)
Leaded gunmetal (XRF analysis, table 4). Flat-topped head. Shaft grooved near tip.
L 40mm
Context 12356

1iii. Without collars and with hipped shafts

11 1 (fig 10)
Bronze (XRF analysis, table 4). Dome-topped head. Grooved at head/shaft junction.
L 52mm
Context F49

32 168 (not illus)
Leaded bronze (XRF analysis, table 4). Dome-topped head.
L 45mm
Context F484

2i. With ring collars and straight shafts

24 18 (not illus)
Brass (XRF analysis, table 4).
L 31mm
Context GR 413.96/542.82

26 300 (fig 10)
Brass (XRF analysis, table 4). Flat median band around head.
L 63mm
Context 513

26 765 (not illus)
Brass (XRF analysis, table 4). Flat median band around head.
L 32mm
Context 224

30 68 (not illus)
Leaded gunmetal (XRF analysis, table 4). Flat-topped head.
L 37mm
Context 3569

30 99 (not illus)
Brass (XRF analysis, table 4). Flat median band around head.
L 67mm
Context 4290

31 600 (not illus)
Brass (XRF analysis, table 4).
L 45mm
Context 5237

31 2102 (not illus)
Leaded bronze (XRF analysis, table 4).
L 38mm
Context 5261

32 161 (not illus)
Brass (XRF analysis, table 4).
L 60mm
Context F375

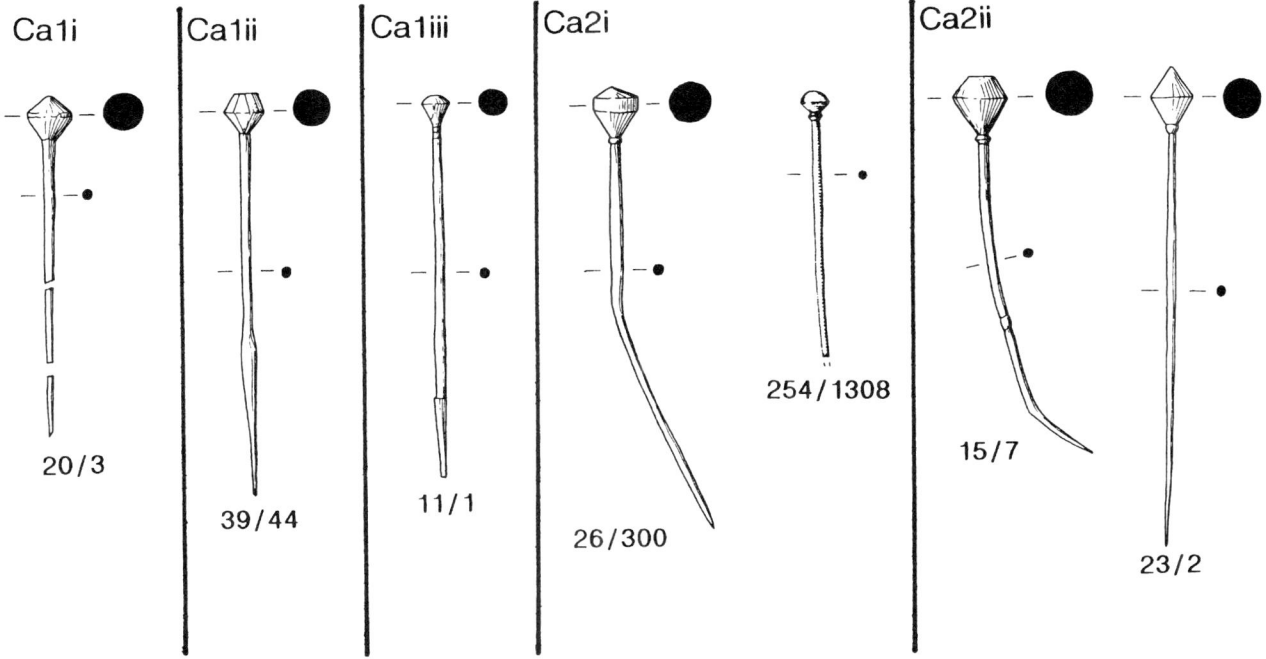

Figure 10. Pins: Type C, bi-conical-headed. Ca 1i: bi-conical, undecorated heads, without collars and with straight shafts; Ca 1ii: bi-conical, undecorated heads, without collars and with swelling shafts; Ca 1iii: bi-conical, undecorated heads, without collars and with hipped shafts; Ca 2i: bi-conical, undecorated heads, with ring collars and straight shafts; Ca 2ii: bi-conical, undecorated heads, with ring collars and swelling shafts. Scale 1:1

36 95 (not illus)
Leaded bronze (XRF analysis, table 4). Domed head.
L 32mm
Context Pit 43

169 21 (not illus)
Leaded bronze (XRF analysis, table 4). Domed head. Flat median band around head.
L 44mm
Context 8468

169 1973 (not illus)
Leaded brass (XRF analysis, table 4). Flat median band around head.
L 32mm
Context 12382

169 2390 (not illus)
Leaded brass (XRF analysis, table 4).
L 32mm
Context 12313

254 1308 (fig 10)
Copper alloy.
L 35mm
Context 2916

2ii. With ring collars and swelling shafts

15 7 (fig 10)
Leaded bronze (XRF analysis, table 4). Flat-topped head. Girth grooves on shaft.
L 52mm
Context F42

23 2 (fig 10)
Brass (XRF analysis, table 4).
L 65mm
Context 6819

31 574 (not illus)
Leaded bronze (XRF analysis, table 4).
L 64mm
Context 5249

169 2376 (not illus)
Leaded bronze (XRF analysis, table 4). Flat-topped head.
L 55mm
Context 12387

2iii. With ring collars and hipped shafts

26 393 (not illus)
Leaded brass (XRF analysis, table 4).
L 58mm
Context 233

32 160 (not illus)
Leaded gunmetal (XRF analysis, table 4). The upper cone grooved.
L 45mm
Context F358, General clearance

Discussion of Type C: Bi-conical-headed pins (fig 10)
By including in this category a few which have a flat band around the middle, the bi-conical heads become the third most frequent of the Saxon Southampton types. They do not have ring-and-dot decoration, although a few have counter-sunk grooves of various kinds. They are also widespread (York: Waterman 1959, fig 11, 8; Whitby: Peers and Radford 1943, fig 14, two examples; Chalton: Champion 1977, 369; Winchester: Biddle 1990B, no 1447; Domburg: Capelle 1976, Taf. 13 and 14; Dorestad: Roes 1965, pl 5, no 42), but they seem to be less numerous generally than types A and B, both in Hamwic and elsewhere.

Of the thirty listed, none is of a metal other than a copper alloy, and none even has a wrythen collar.

Type D: Spiral-headed pins (fig 11)
Da. SPIRAL-HEADED
1i. Without collars and with straight shafts

31 520 (fig 11)
Leaded bronze (XRF analysis, table 4). Grooved at head/shaft junction on one side. Corroded shaft.
L 75mm
Context 4932

31 1648 (fig 11)
Leaded bronze (XRF analysis, table 4).
L 30mm
Context 6254

169 914 (fig 11)
Leaded bronze (XRF analysis, table 4).
L 55mm
Context 11283

169 1408 (fig 11)
Leaded bronze (XRF analysis, table 4).
L 29mm
Context 12094

169 2418 (not illus)
Leaded bronze (XRF analysis, table 4).
L 47mm
Context 12539

177 652 (fig 11)
Copper alloy.
L 32mm
Context 799

254 107 (fig 11)
Copper alloy.
L 57mm
Context 299 (post-Saxon)
Published Hinton 1993C, no 7

254 144 (fig 11)
Copper alloy.
L 54mm
Context 272
Published Hinton 1993C, no 5

254 1679 (fig 11)
Copper alloy.
L 52mm
Context 4400
Published Hinton 1993C, no 6

1ii. Without collars and with swelling shafts

31 1644 (fig 11)
Leaded bronze (XRF analysis, table 4).
L 53mm
Context 6182

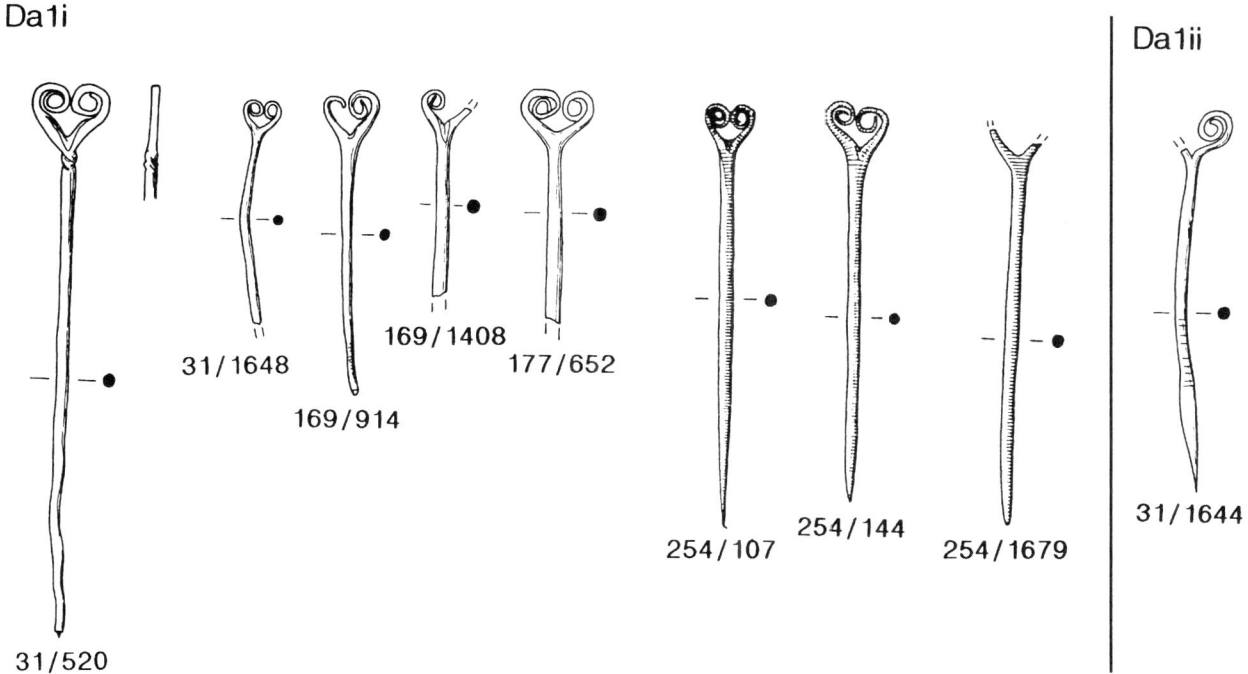

Figure 11. Pins: Type D, spiral-headed. Da 1i: spiral heads, without further decoration, without collars and with straight shafts; Da 1ii: spiral heads, without collars and with swelling shafts. Scale 1:1

32 171 (not illus)
Leaded bronze (XRF analysis, table 4).
L 50mm
Context F305, General clearance

Discussion of Type D: Spiral-headed pins (fig 11)
Saxon Southampton has yielded eleven recognisable examples of a type of pin which, unlike the three types so far described, has been found in a number of Anglo-Saxon cemeteries. None from Saxon Southampton is from a grave, but the distribution shows that several are from sites where burials were found. There is of course always the possibility that others are from sites contiguous to as yet unidentified cemeteries.

The spiral-headed pins from Hamwic that have been examined metallurgically are all made of leaded bronze (see above, 'Manufacturing and Technology'), so care went into selection of the alloys. Care would also have been needed to create the spirals. This seems to give these pins a greater significance than the three commonest types, which is borne out by the use of silver for the pair from Eccles, Kent (Detsicas and Hawkes 1973, 283), and for one from Brandon, Suffolk (Webster 1991, no 66h – labelled g in the photograph). The spiral heads are delicate, implying delicate use, and a few, like the Eccles pair, are recorded from positions on skeletons which make it likely that they were being worn or used to secure shrouds rather than, for instance, being carried in bags. 'It is noteworthy that at Eccles, Kingsworthy and Bourton-on-the-Water spiral-headed pins were buried in pairs, and that at the latter [*sic*] site the excavators noted the remains of a thread which had perhaps joined them together' (Detsicas and Hawkes 1973, 283); although there is no definite pairing in Hamwic, two from Cook Street might be an example (Hinton, 1993C – though that report was written without knowledge of the third spiral-headed pin from that site and confuses the numbers – the likely pairing is 254/107 and 254/144, both from Trench 2); the two from Six Dials were found in different contexts, but close together.

Local to Southampton are the pair from Kingsworthy (Welch 1976, 212 states that they are bronze; they are still unpublished) and a single one from Portchester (*ibid*, 211–14, with distribution map). There is one from Domburg (Capelle 1976, Taf. 11, no 177), but none has been published from Dorestad (Roes 1965). At one time spiral-headed pins were thought to be fifth or sixth century in date, on the basis of finds made at Girton, Cambridgeshire, and elsewhere (Pretty 1972), but it is now accepted that they are not so early, and that Girton's is the only one for which even a sixth-century date can be claimed (Detsicas and Hawkes 1973, 283–4). The relative quantity from Saxon Southampton suggests that they were current well into the eighth century: they have not, however, been reported from contexts where residuality is precluded; one was found in York's Coppergate, but may be residual there; although it may take the type into the ninth or even the tenth century, further evidence would be welcome (Rogers 1993, 1363). As well as Brandon (Webster 1991, no 66h), Hartlepool (Jackson 1988, 182–3), Carlisle (Dickinson 1990), and Flixborough (Leahy 1991, nos 69j and k) have yielded newly published examples (one from Canterbury has out-turned spirals, and may not be part of the series: Sherlock and Woods 1988, fig 70, 86). Of these, Hartlepool was certainly a female house, and there is an assumption that these pins would have been worn by women, particularly when found in linked pairs. Few of the grave finds have come from cemeteries in which the skeletons have been specifically sexed, however, and it should perhaps not be taken for granted that the spiral-headed pins were specifically for female attire.

Type E: Disc-headed pins (fig 12)
Ed. DISC-HEADED, DECORATED
1i. Without collars and with straight shafts

169 568 (fig 12)
Leaded-bronze shaft, separate leaded-bronze sheet attached to head (XRF analysis, table 4). The head flat on one side, convex on the other, with a beaded collar. Grooved at head/shaft junction.
L 53mm
Context 10383

169 634 (fig 12)
Leaded-bronze shaft, bronze sheet on head (XRF analysis, table 4). As 169/568.
L 56mm
Context 10383

169 2959 (fig 12)
Tin-bronze with mercury-gilding and silver fitting (AML). 'Chip-carved' decoration on the front, unornamented on the back, but both sides gilded. The ungilded, copper-alloy round-sectioned shaft of the pin, now broken, hammered to a flat strip pierced by two rivet-holes; on the front, at the centre, a small square washer and a rivet of white metal, probably debased silver. Three other rivet-holes around the circumference of the disc; all four bored without respect for the pattern. They retain copper-alloy rivets with nicked heads, one of which holds a short, broken strip of white metal on the back. The design of the ornament is uncertain; seems to be knotted interlace, possibly zoomorphic.
Diam 35mm
Context 12462

Discussion of Type E: Disc-headed pins (fig 12)
Two small copper-alloy disc-headed Hamwic pins may be cheap copies of a form represented at the highest echelons of Anglo-Saxon society by gold examples, as at Roundway Down, Wiltshire (Youngs 1989, no 40). Those have cabochon garnets in their centres, with beaded wire frames: Hamwic 169/568 and 169/634 seem to imitate them by their convex centres, which Wilthew (below) has identified as separate elements, and their beaded borders. Unlike those from Roundway Down, they do not have attachment loops, but the upper parts of the shanks are grooved in the same way. They were found together in a pit, and had probably therefore been discarded, and before that worn, together. A local parallel in silver is the flat, disc-headed pin from a grave at Winnall, which has a loop on the back showing that, although found on its own, it was intended to be linked or sewn to something, presumably to make a pair (Meaney and Hawkes 1970, 12 and fig 9). No new discoveries of this type have been reported in recent local cemetery excavations, and it may have been a fashion which could not survive in quite this form beyond the end of the seventh century; as gold and garnets became increasingly difficult to obtain, pins of the Roundway Down type would have become increasingly rare, so there would have been no exemplars to copy in cheaper metals. The Hamwic pair may therefore be amongst the earliest of the town's artefacts, unlike the spiral-

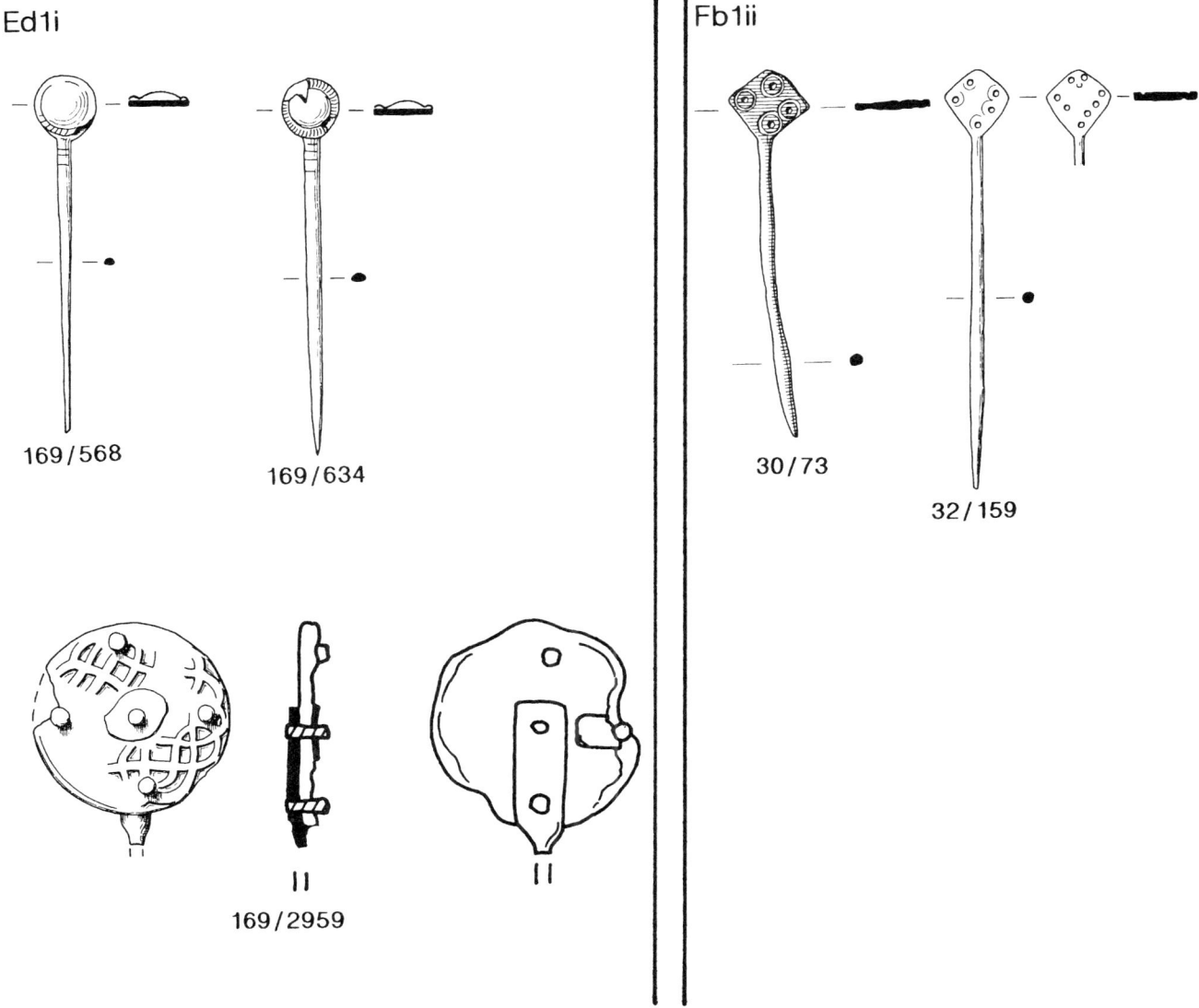

Figure 12. Pins: Type E, disc-headed. Ed 1i: discoid heads, decorated, without collars and with straight shafts.

Type F, rhomboid-headed. Fb 1ii: rhomboidal heads decorated with ring-and-dot, without collars and with swelling shafts. Scale 1:1

headed pins which appear in sufficient quantity here and elsewhere to justify slightly later dating.

Disc-headed pins did not cease to be produced, however. The heads tended to become larger, and the ranges from Brandon and elsewhere have shown that it is as though they took on a life of their own, with contorted beasts untrammelled by circular outlines, although discs probably remained the norm, with the linked silver-gilt suite from the River Witham still the apogee of survivals, despite the more recent discoveries (Webster 1991, no 184 and *passim*). Hamwic has nothing so grand, although 169/2959 is comparable in being gilt, although on copper, and in having its shaft riveted on to the head. The short broken strip on the Southampton piece could be the original pin, replaced when broken by one with a longer strip provided with a washer for extra security, despite the adverse effect that this had on the pattern. Such disregard for the pattern is seen again in the placing of the other rivet holes, and is seen also on the Witham pins, a head from Pontefract, Yorkshire (Bailey 1971) and the disc from Bolney, Bedfordshire (Smallridge 1969). 169/2959 is from a very late context, but is likely enough to be residual.

It is possible that some fragments listed under Mounts (fig 22) and Discs (fig 19) could be broken examples of disc-headed pins.

Type F: Rhomboid-headed pins (fig 12)
Fa. WITH RHOMBOID, UNDECORATED HEADS
1i. Without collars and with straight shafts

26   177   (not illus)
Leaded bronze (XRF analysis, table 4).
L 23mm
Context 655

254   1370: see below, Linked pins

1ii. Without collar and with swelling shaft

4   84   (not illus)
Leaded bronze (XRF analysis, table 4).
L 52mm
Context F101

Fb. WITH RHOMBOID HEADS, DECORATED WITH RING-AND-DOT ORNAMENT
1ii. Without collars and with swelling shafts

30   73   (fig 12)
Bronze (XRF analysis, table 4).
L 55mm
Context 3540

32   159   (fig 12)
Leaded bronze (XRF analysis, table 4).
L 62mm
Context F307, 1

Discussion of Type F: Rhomboid-headed pins (fig 12)
This small group has a type of head that is easy to make, but was clearly not regarded as fashionable. It is not much found elsewhere, either; a recent suggestion sees the type as a precursor in York of a more elaborate, Anglo-Scandinavian knopped head (Rogers 1993, 1363), a type found in London (Pritchard 1991, 150), but not in Winchester or Southampton.

Type G: Ring-headed pins (fig 13)
Ga. RING-HEADED
1ii. Without collar and with swelling shaft

30   328   (fig 13)
Silver, debased with copper (both shaft and ring: XRF analysis, table 4). The ring is a wire loop with knotted ends, passing through a loop at the top of an oval head. Below this is an oval knop.
L 60mm
Context 4524

2i. With collar and straight shaft

31   882   (fig 13)
Leaded gunmetal (shaft) and bronze (ring) (XRF analysis, table 4). Cast ring with unclosed ends, passing through a loop at the top of a short stem separated by a keeled ring collar from the straight shaft which has a flattened lower section.
L 113mm
Context 5570/5857

Discussion of Type G: Ring-headed pins (fig 13)
The first example in this category, the silver pin with a wire loop, 30/328, is quite likely to be one of the earliest of the Hamwic objects, for its parallels are from cemeteries such as Winnall II, at which two were worn as a linked pair (Meaney and Hawkes 1970, fig 9, grave 8 no 1; a single one was found in grave 7). Like the disc-headed, linked pins, they seem to have passed out of fashion as the mid-Saxon period progressed, since they seem to be absent not only from the rest of Southampton, but from other sites as well.

The other, much larger, ring-headed pin, 31/882, seems out of place in Southampton. Its parallels seem to be with the seventh- to ninth-century ringed pins of Ireland (eg Edwards 1990, 141–2 and fig 69, d), and the solidity of the metal seems to fit into a Celtic rather than a Saxon milieu. York has nothing like it from the Anglian Fishergate (Rogers 1993), but there are decorated examples from the later Anglo-Scandinavian areas (Waterman 1959, fig 11, nos 13 and 14). Irish examples seem to have been prototypes for a Scandinavian series (Fanning 1990; Liversage 1983). Is this pin evidence of an Irish merchant passing through Hamwic?

CATALOGUE

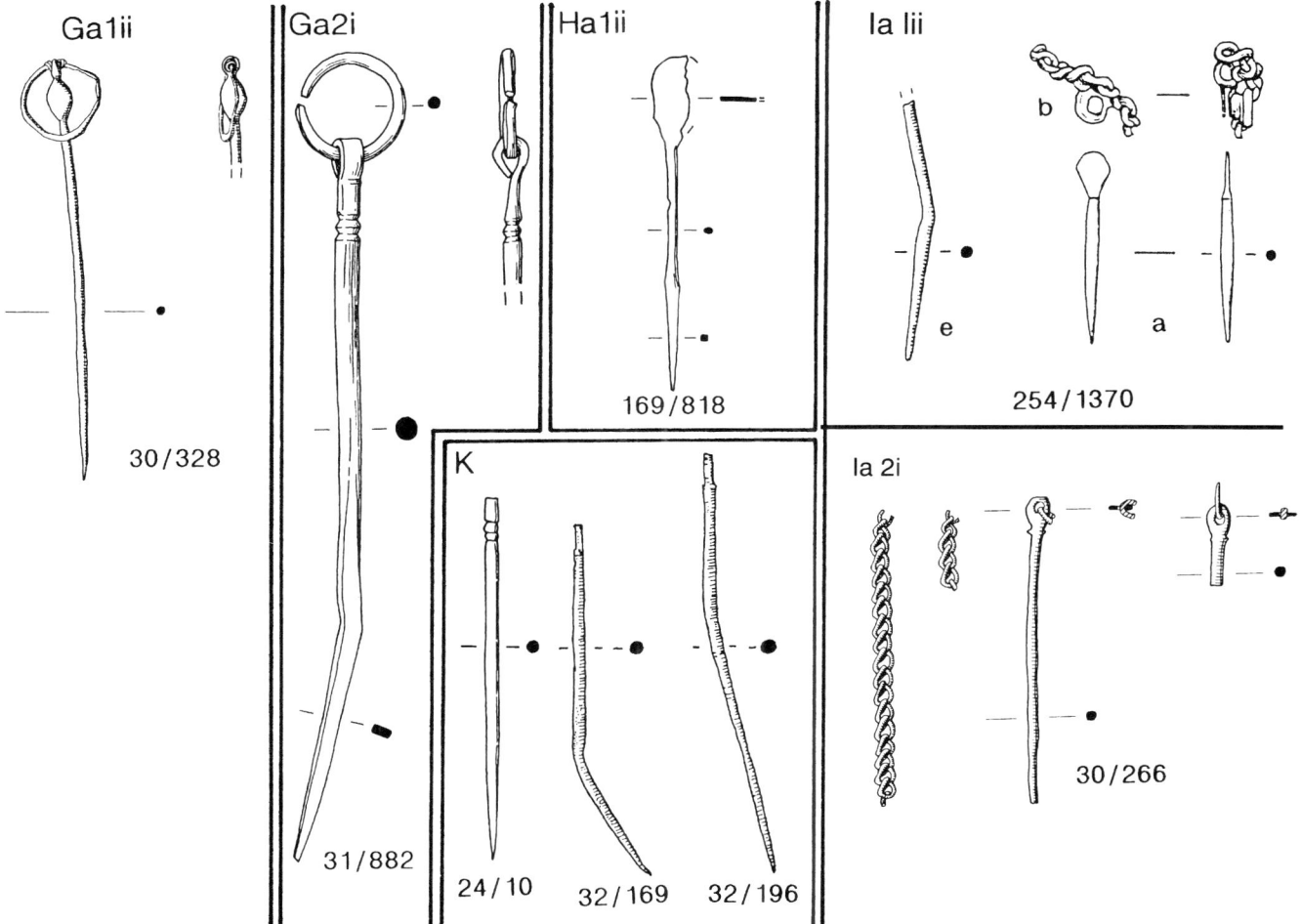

Figure 13. Pins: Type G, ring-headed. Ga 1ii: pierced heads with rings, without collars and with swelling shafts; Ga 2i: pierced heads with rings, with collars and with straight shafts.
Type H, oval-headed. Ha 1ii: oval, undecorated heads, without collars and with swelling shafts.
Type I, linked. Ia 1ii, linked pin suites, pins without collars and with swelling shafts; Ia 2i, linked suites, pins with collars and straight shafts.
Type K, headless.   Scale 1:1

Type H: Oval-headed pins (fig 13)
Ha. WITH OVAL HEAD, UNDECORATED
1ii. Without collar and with swelling shaft

169 818 (fig 13)
Bronze (XRF analysis, table 4).
L 47mm
Context 11008

Discussion of Type H: Oval-headed pins (fig 13)
The only example in this category may be misplaced, as its head seems to be damaged. Its shaft shows that it was a pin, however, and the present shape of its head conforms with none of the other shapes.

Type I: Linked pins (fig 13)
Ia. LINKED PINS
1ii. Without collar and with swelling shaft

254 1370 (fig 13)
Base silver, with glass, copper alloy, and (?)textile.
a) Base silver pin. Rhomboid, flat undecorated head, without collar and with slightly swelling shaft.
L 28mm

b) Glass and silver fitting. Flat, (?)colourless, circular glass surrounded by substance that could be textile, and a beaded silver collar.
Diam (glass) *c* 35mm
c) Chain (not illus). Copper alloy. Short length of figure-of-eight links, attached to b).
Extant L *c* 16mm, link L *c* 4mm
d) Chain. Disconnected length, as c).
e) Pin shaft. Copper alloy. Two lengths corroded together when found.
Extant L *c* 35mm
Context Grave 2962, near left shoulder of skeleton
Published Hinton 1993C, no 4

2i. With collars and straight shafts

30 266 (fig 13)
Copper alloy. Two of a pair or set, both with flattened, perforated heads and triangular collars between those and the straight shafts. The heads retain fragments of wire loops; a short three-strand plaited length survives separately. One shaft survives to a length of 43mm, but the other for only 10mm.
L (extant) 43mm
Context 4318

Discussion of Type I: Linked Pins (fig 13)
This is an unsatisfactory category, but is too well-established to replace: its use disguises the likelihood that other pins were worn in pairs or sets, such as 254/115 and 254/1613, 169/568 and 169/634, and 254/107 and 254/144. The short lengths of chain listed above (Chain, 5/61 and 8/26) could once have been used to link pins.

The two pins and associated chains, 30/266, were found close together though not actually joined; they were not in a grave, though could of course have been scattered from one. The closest local parallel is from a cemetery, however, at Collingbourne Ducis, Wiltshire, found with two sixth-century saucer-brooches (Gingell 1975/6, fig 19; their 'astragal' design does not seem to have finer dating limits: Dickinson 1993, 22–4).

The incomplete pin suite, 254/1370, came from the grave of a mature but unsexed skeleton, with which was also an iron knife. The two pins are of different alloys and might not have been made, or even used, as a pair; they were found near the skeleton's shoulder, so were presumably not being worn, but were placed in the grave as a deliberate act of deposition; the Winnall II grave 8 linked pin suite was in a similar position (Meaney and Hawkes 1970, fig 9), which hints at a common rite. The Winnall II parallel suggests that the Southampton set is late seventh or early eighth century, at the beginning of the Hamwic sequence. The little piece of glass in its silver collar presumably came from one of the pin's heads; it may be a cheap imitation of gold-and-garnet pin heads like those from Roundway Down (Youngs (ed), 1989, no 40).

Type J: Miscellaneous. Category created, but not used

Type K: Headless pins (fig 13)

23 6 (not illus)
Gunmetal (XRF analysis, table 4).
L 21mm
Context 6862

24 10 (fig 13)
Leaded bronze (XRF analysis, table 4). Girth grooves at head end.
L 52mm
Context 7547

32 169 (fig 13)
Copper alloy.
L 60mm
Context F554
Published Addyman and Hill 1969, fig 26, 13

32 196 (fig 13)
Copper alloy.
L 52mm
Context General clearance
Published Addyman and Hill 1969, fig 26, 12

39 41 (not illus)
Bronze (XRF analysis, table 4).
L 50mm
Context Pit 66A

Discussion of Type K: Headless pins (fig 13)
Addyman and Hill (1969, 68) suggested that some

pins were intended for use even though, having no head at the top of the shaft, they would have been awkward to handle and easily lost. Of course, many headless shanks would be accidental breakages, and some would be incomplete pins – the intention having been to solder a separate head on to them, with implications about manufacturing processes (discussed below by Oddy: see also Rogers 1993, 1366, with further references).

Wood or bone was identified adhering to some shafts at Shakenoak, Oxfordshire, and it was suggested that they were the teeth of heckles or wool-combs (Brodribb *et al* 1972, 158–61). Most copper alloys would be too soft for the purpose, however, and such teeth would have needed to be stouter at the tops for mounting (eg Goodall 1990). A copper-alloy object from Abbots Worthy might have been such a tooth, but is almost certainly too long (Davies 1991, fig 32, 1). Similarly, use as awls is almost precluded for most such shafts because they would bend too easily.

Table 1 does not attempt to make a distinction between shafts that lack heads, and deliberately headless pins, as has recently been done in York, nor have solder traces been consistently noted (Rogers 1993, 1364–6). Nor have the shafts been classified as straight, swelling or hipped, as too little survives of many for definition to be possible. Fragments without points cannot normally be distinguished from other lengths of wire, and have been excluded, but many which are tapering are assumed to be pins that have had their points broken off.

PINS: DISCUSSION

Despite their number, the majority of the Hamwic pins are limited in their range. There is no great difference between the three most frequently found types of head, A–C, in size or decoration, nor in the different types of shaft. Lengths vary, but no one head type is consistently found with a short or a long shaft. It seems unlikely that these different heads were reserved for different functions, therefore.

Only the pin suite 254/1370 (fig 13) is certainly from a Hamwic grave, although many other pins could be from disturbed burials. Linked pins like the 254/1370 suite are found in a few seventh-century female graves – albeit apparently deposited in bags at Hamwic and Winnall, rather than being worn on costume. An elaborately grooved pin from Alton was found on the chest of a woman with sixth-century button brooches: Evison considers this type to derive from late Roman pins, and notes that they were worn as hair-pins on the Continent, but apparently as dress-fasteners in England (1988, 12). A simpler example came from Droxford, its precise context unknown (Aldsworth 1978, fig 31, no 35). A pin with a perforated head was found in a similar position in a female grave at Portway (Cook and Dacre 1985, 24). At Portway, there were rather more iron pins, and pins of various types are not uncommon in female graves, often with brooches (*ibid*, 88). Pins with unperforated heads – the vast majority of those from Hamwic – seem to have been a more infrequent component of female attire in the pagan period in the south of England, however, if grave goods are a true reflection of contemporary costume. The recent catalogue of the Ashmolean Museum's collection suggests that this is somewhat less true of areas other than the south of England (MacGregor and Bolick 1993, 183–9).

There is only one type of pin, the spiral-headed (fig 11), which occurs with any frequency both in Hamwic – and at other settlements of the eighth and ninth centuries – and in cemeteries. The linked and small disc-headed pins, such as 30/266 (fig 13) and 169/568 (fig 12), are a very small minority. None of the local cemeteries has a parallel for Hamwic's Types A, B and C – and the Ashmolean Museum houses only a single pin, of Type A, which would not look out of place in Southampton (MacGregor and Bolick 1993, 184 and 186, no 31.6, from Faversham, Kent, its associations unknown). In the same way, Southampton has none of the pins with perforated heads like those which figure largely in the Ashmolean and elsewhere. Whatever their purpose, these had become redundant by the eighth century – unless the ubiquitous pierced pigs' femurs had supplanted metal. As the parallels cited in the discussions of the various types show, this change was one that occurred throughout England. Similarly, there are fewer brooches and buckles: the obvious conclusion is that pins were the basic dress-fastener of the mid-Saxon period, the swelling and hipped shafts on many of them helping to prevent the pin from accidentally slipping out of position.

TABLE 1
Pins without heads: broken shafts or headless

5	59	31	965	99	24	169	1846	184	127
8	44	31	1488	99	83	169	2032	184	457
11	14	31	1822	99	120	169	2040	254	355
15	279	32	169	99	134	169	2140	254	1899
15	288	32	188	99	160	169	2206	254	2916
23	121	32	190	169	124	169	2362	254	3054
24	19	33	118	169	305	169	2459	254	3601
24	831	33	119	169	796	169	2460	254	4400
26	158	33	120	169	874	169	2537	258	83
26	160	34	82	169	933	169	2586	258	185
26	164	34	83	169	997	169	2704	258	218
30	10	34	85	169	1521	169	2862	258	226
30	65	34	86	169	1525	169	2984	258	293
30	84	34	97	169	1665	169	3623	349	118
30	118	35	14	169	1685	169	3649	349	153
30	361	36	134	169	1737	177	720	349	154

Table 1. Pins without heads: broken shafts or headless.

Some might perhaps have been hair-pins, but for that purpose thicker shafts and blunter points would seem appropriate. The collars on some may have helped to prevent threads from slipping, but the occasional incised girth grooves seem purposeless. That the pins are fairly slender has some implication for the weave of the textiles being worn, as the pins' shafts are not thick enough for an open weave, but are probably too thick for the finest woollens, let alone linens and silks.

Knowledge of everyday costume is not sufficient for assumptions to be made about whether the Hamwic pin types were more likely to be worn by men than by women in the mid-Saxon period (eg Owen-Crocker 1986, chapters 5 and 6). Recent finds from nunneries such as Barking Abbey have included a short, silver spherical-headed pin, elegant enough to suggest 'securing veiling on a headdress' (Webster 1991, 89, no 67e) and Hamwic's silver examples with 'pineapple' decoration (fig 8) are no less elegant – but not necessarily therefore more appropriate for women than for men. The much greater proportion of pins with large and elaborate, or animal, heads from sites with religious associations (eg also Brandon: *ibid*, 82–7; Flixborough: Leahy 1991, 94–101) may reflect differences in disposable wealth between Hamwic and those places. Even the seventh-century association of linked pins with women may reflect burial customs as much as differences between male and female use of pins. But in any case, they are exceptional and cannot prove a general rule; the spiral-headed Type D (fig 11) pins are not specifically sex-linked in graves, and are the only other type for which such associations can be discussed.

Because of the absence of types distinctive to Hamwic, or of pin moulds, the distribution of pins from Hamwic cannot be pursued, unlike the Helgö workshop products (Holmqvist 1972). This is discussed further in the concluding section, but it should be noted that the ubiquity of the principal pin types is an argument for a considerable degree of uniformity of material culture in mid-Saxon England. Most of the Hamwic pins would pass unremarked if placed in Anglian York's collection, although a few of York's would raise an eyebrow in Southampton (Rogers 1993, fig 662; nos 5363–5 are not obviously parallelled in Hamwic). For similar reasons, pins brought into Hamwic from elsewhere cannot be picked out, except 31/882 (fig 13). Indeed, there can be no absolute certainty that pins were made here, though the sheer quantity, and the evidence of copper-alloy working such as the fragments from the wire-folding process (Oddy, in Morton, below), make it highly unlikely that they were not. This is further supported by the occasional misshapen head that has been observed:

it cannot be assumed that such things were rejects, but no examples have been noted elsewhere, and it is perhaps unlikely that obviously faulty pieces would have been generally acceptable.

Apart from the spiral-headed Type D pins, in which the heads were formed by cutting and twisting the end of a shaft, pins could be made in two ways, either by casting head and shaft in a mould, or by making the two elements separately and soldering them together. Traces of solder have been noticed on some shafts, but equally on many pins no weld can be discerned. Despite the absence of moulds, therefore, it is assumed that many pins were cast. Evidence that some were made in two separate pieces is more direct. Pin shafts are the most likely intended use of much of the folded wire produced at SOU site 8 (see Oddy in Morton, below); although the surviving fragments are not as long as the average pin shaft, further processing would have resulted in acceptable lengths and diameters. (An object reported to be an iron 'draw plate' from site SOU 16 (Holdworth 1976, 43) has been re-identified as part of a wool-comb (Morton 1992, 160); in any case, there is some doubt over whether such 'draw plates' were used for making non-ferrous wire (Whitfield 1990, 22–6).) Pins where the heads are of different alloy composition from the shafts would be further evidence, but none was noted (Wilthew, below). Pins with heads of different materials altogether are, of course, even more clear-cut examples, but Hamwic has produced only one certain example, 31/1247, which has a lead-alloy head on an iron shaft, and is thus not relevant to copper-alloy production. Nor has Hamwic produced any with a copper-alloy shaft and a glass head (cf Winchester, Type C, Biddle 1990B, 557) – nor have any glass heads separated from shafts been reported, which suggests that this is a Roman or a late Saxon, but not a mid-Saxon, type of pin.

Only in three pin types can distribution within Hamwic be recognised as having any significance. The Type D spiral-headed pins are found throughout the town, but they have tended to be found in the lower levels of pits, and in areas like Cook Street, SOU 254, with cemeteries. Despite the Coppergate example, therefore, they do seem likely to be seventh- or eighth-century rather than later. If it is correct to see the wearing of Type E disc-headed pins like 169/568 and 169/634 (fig 12) as a fashion that did not long outlast the seventh century, that pair is a good indication that the northern part of Hamwic was in use little if at all later than the rest of the town (cf Morton 1992, 39).

There is no concentration of pins or a particular type of pin within Hamwic to suggest production within a particular zone. Wilthew notes (below) the logic of presuming that a specific choice of alloy for a specific type of pin, which he recognises for the decorated Type A spherical-headed pins and for the Type D spiral-headed pins, indicates workshops at particular places specialising in particular products. This may, however, be because it was known that certain mixtures were better for certain types – to take a clear impression in the former case, or to cut and bend in the latter. As with the metalworking evidence generally, there are some sites which have yielded certain types of pin and not others, but this is likely to be simply a reflection of the size of the site, the amount of Saxon material that was derived from it, and its date.

STRAP-ENDS (figs 14–17)
Introduction
Strap-ends of various sorts are relatively common finds. Those from Saxon Southampton have been divided into five different categories; a more rigid classification could probably be made, but the range is so wide that it might serve to confuse rather than to clarify.

The perforations which enabled the strap-ends to be attached, either to leather or fabric, have been described as rivet-holes since in some cases rivets survive; the characteristic split end would be superfluous if attachment had been by sewing, as the hooked tags demonstrate. No doubt, however, many were sewn into place at later stages of their use as rivets dropped out.

A. Single-riveted, with narrow shafts, small triangular split ends and spherical terminals (fig 14)

15 5 (fig 14)
Copper alloy. Circular-sectioned shaft with oblique grooving.
L 46mm
Context F44

24 17 (fig 14)
Copper alloy. Circular-sectioned shaft. Terminal missing.
L (extant) 35mm
Context 14064

24 25 (fig 14)
Copper alloy. Flat shaft with oblique grooves. Double-sphere terminal.
L 52mm
Context 7475

24 824 (fig 14)
Copper alloy. Circular-sectioned shaft, now very bent.
L c 60mm
Context 9422

31 910 (fig 14)
Copper alloy. Flat shaft.
L 52mm
Context 5622

32 316 (fig 14)
Copper alloy. Flat, lozenge-shaped shaft.
L 54mm
Context not known
Published Addyman and Hill 1969, 68 and fig 27, 1

32 317 (fig 14)
Copper alloy. Flat, lozenge-shaped shaft.
L 47mm
Context not known
Published Addyman and Hill 1969, 68 and fig 27, 2

33 89 (fig 14)
Silver, debased with copper etc (XRF analysis, table 5).
L (extant) 34mm
Context F2, post-medieval disturbance of Saxon features

36 99 (fig 14)
Silver, with copper etc (XRF analysis, table 5). Flat shaft. Split end broken.
L (extant) 40mm
Context Pit 15, 9

44 1 (fig 14)
Copper alloy. Flat shaft.
L 54mm
Context Unstratified

177 53 (fig 14)
Copper alloy. Criss-cross grooves incised into shaft. Rivet extant.
L 43mm
Context 117 T2

The relatively large number of very narrow strap-ends or lace-tags with spherical terminals from Saxon Southampton (31/622, below, may be another, broken at the end) contrasts with their paucity in other places. One or two may have been identified elsewhere as toilet implements, but, as the Hamwic tweezers show, these were usually suspended on wire loops, not on rivets such as survive in 15/5 and others in the group – ear-scoops, the implements most like them in shape, would have spoon-like ends. Addyman and Hill (1969, 68) compared the two which they published, 32/316 and 32/317, to one from Maxey (Addyman 1964, fig 17, 1), but that is double-riveted and has a series of knops rather than a sphere at its end: it is more like Southampton's 30/177, below. Grave 10, Winnall II (Meaney and Hawkes 1970, 12 and fig 9) yielded a split-ended single-riveted tag, but the shaft was made from a rolled sheet and has a pointed end; two other rolled sheet fragments, from Grave 5, may also have been tags (*ibid*, 10 and fig 8), but the parallels cited (*ibid*, 39) are not quite the same as those from Southampton, lacking the distinctive spherical terminal. A closer parallel is from Snell's Corner, Horndean, in that it was cast, not made from sheet metal, but it is shorter than those from Southampton, and has a spatulate terminal (Knocker 1956, fig 11, S, 18, 1). Further afield, there is one from Glastonbury (Carr 1985, 52–3, no 93).

The Winnall and Horndean grave finds were from near the feet and ankles of skeletons, which suggests their use as lace-tags worn with shoes or gartering. The Southampton ones may indicate survival of this fashion, with more elaborately finished objects having preference. Their length seems rather extreme for use with footwear, however. Unfortunately they are not from contexts which give any indication of their function.

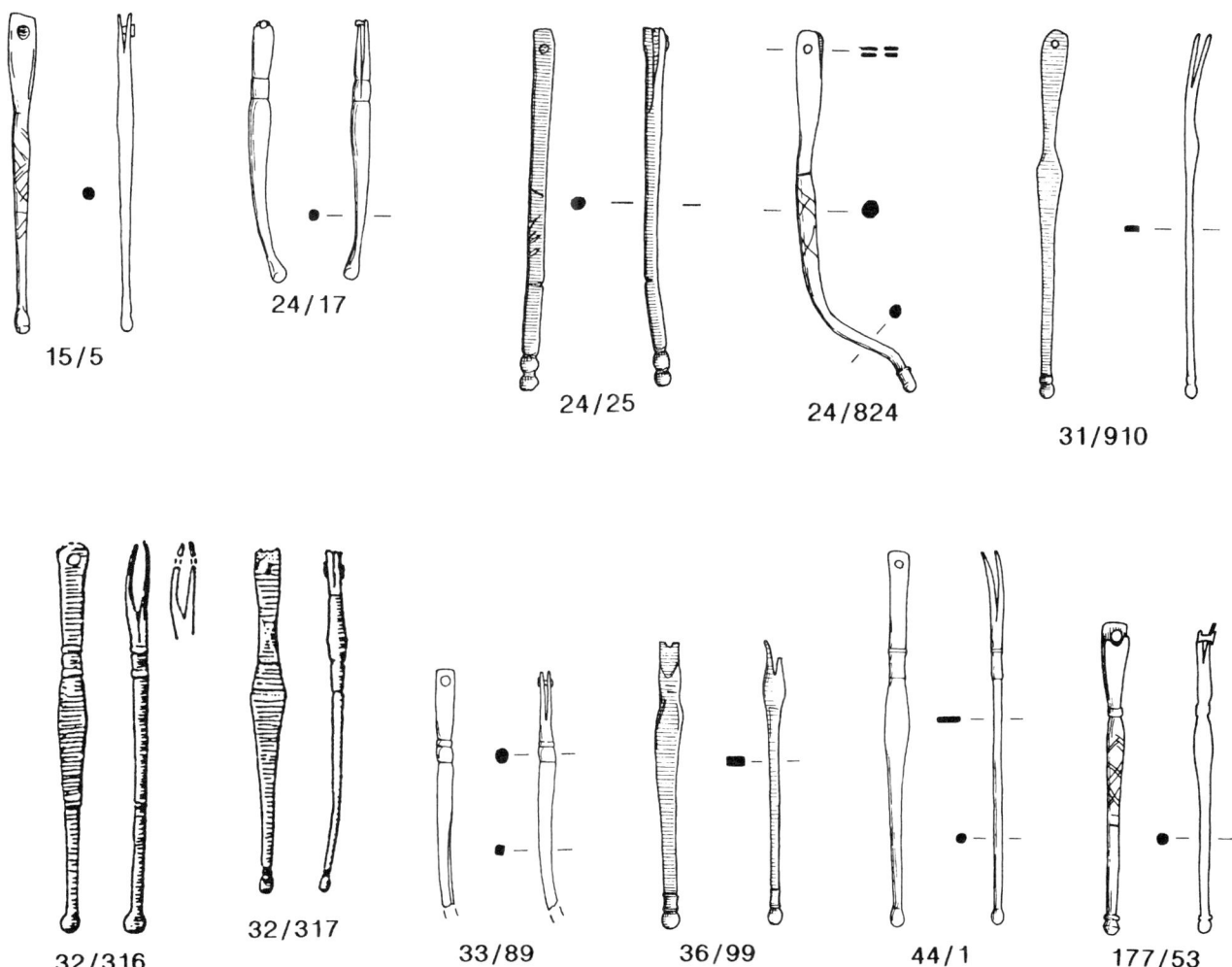

Figure 14. Strap-ends: Type A, single-riveted with narrow shafts, small triangular split ends and spherical terminals. Scale 1:1

B. Single-riveted, with various terminals
(fig 15)

5 71 (fig 15)
Silver, with copper and lead (XRF analysis, table 5). Concave-sectioned shaft, broken. One of a pair, or set, with 5 72.
L (extant) 24mm
Context F27
Published Hinton 1980, fig 13, 1 no 2

5 72 (fig 15)
As 5/71, and from same context.
L (extant) 27mm
Context F27
Published Hinton 1980, fig 13, 1 no 3

20 2 (fig 15)
Copper alloy. Flat shaft. Rounded terminal.
L 38mm
Context F116

24 4 (fig 15)
Copper alloy. Broken.
L (extant) *c* 25mm
Context 14802

24 5 (fig 15)
Copper alloy. Flat shaft with transverse grooves. Rounded terminal.
L 45mm
Context 13963

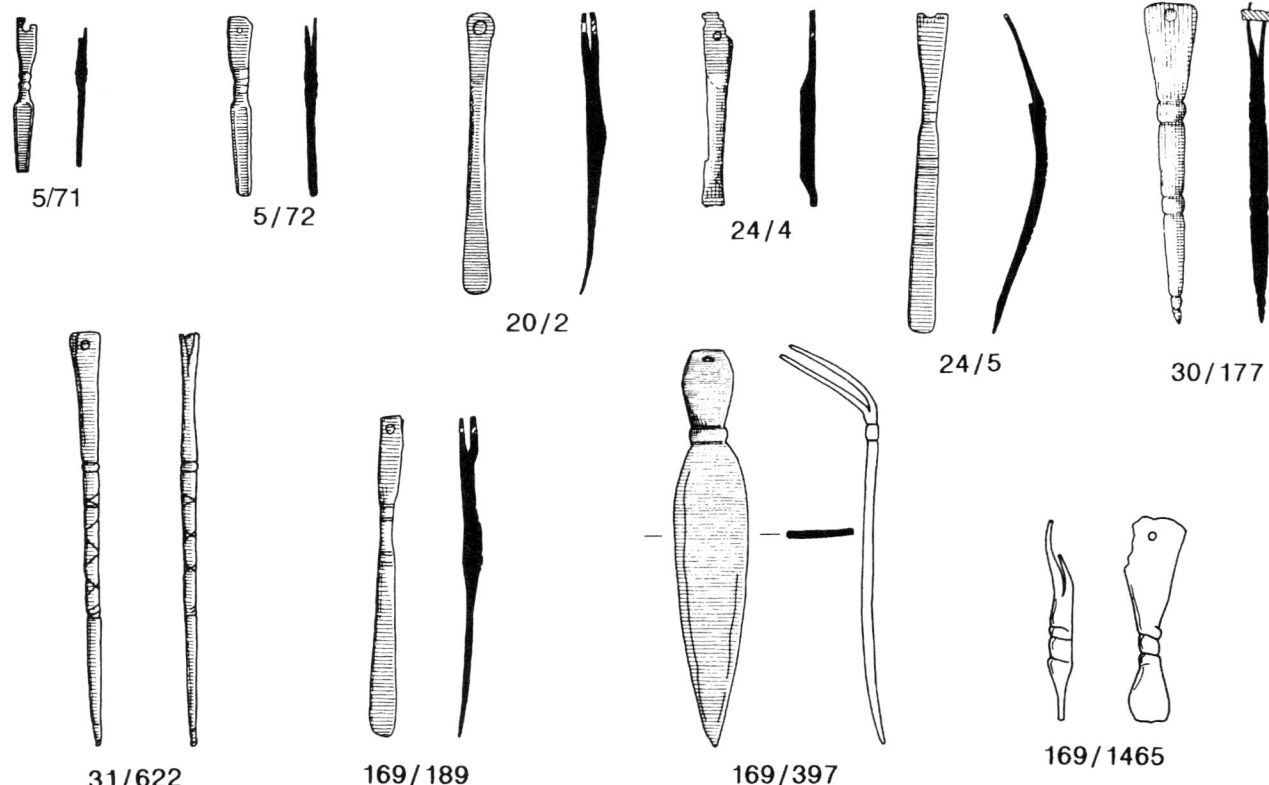

Figure 15. Strap-ends: Type B, single-riveted, with various terminals. Scale 1:1

30 177 (fig 15)
Leaded bronze (XRF analysis, table 5). Circular-sectioned, tapering shaft with knops. Pointed terminal.
L 44mm
Context 3293

31 622 (fig 15)
Copper alloy. Circular-sectioned shaft with transverse and oblique grooves. Terminal broken, probably pointed like 30/177, but may have been rounded.
L (extant) 57mm
Context 5273

169 189 (fig 15)
Copper alloy.
L 44mm
Context 8733

169 397 (fig 15)
Leaded brass, possibly with silver gilding on inlay (XRF analysis, table 5). Leaf-shaped shaft with border lines. Split end concave-sided. Now bent.
L c 60mm
Context 8568

169 1465 (fig 15)
Copper alloy. Broken.
L (extant) 28mm
Context 11961

Most of the other single-riveted strap-ends probably served the same purpose or purposes as those with spherical terminals – 31/622 may indeed be one of those, with its end broken off. The two broader-shafted examples, 169/397 and 169/1465, presumably fitted broader straps, and suggest more robust use; the former has a sixth- or early seventh-century parallel at Kingston-by-Lewes, Sussex (Welch 1983, 217 and 70a). A recently published single-riveted strap-end is from Hartlepool monastery, which flourished in the seventh century and is the date attributed to the strap-end (Jackson 1988, no 2).

C. Double-riveted, with flat, convex-sided shafts, animal-mask terminals and plain reverses (fig 16)

15 4 (fig 16)
Brass, with some lead (XRF analysis, table 5). On

the shaft, crude, silver wire S-scrolls set in a lead compound (cerussite: $PbCO_3$), with traces of ?enamel but not of niello (report by S La Niece).
L 39mm
Context F31, 1

24 834 (fig 16)
Leaded gunmetal (XRF analysis, table 5). Sunken, void field in shaft. Incised leaf pattern by split end. Terminal broken.
L (extant) 34mm
Context 7521

26 181 (fig 16)
Leaded brass (XRF analysis, table 5). 'Inlaid with what is now metallic silver, [possibly] decomposed from silver sulphide niello' (report by S La Niece). Cross pattern on the shaft, with Trewhiddle-style animals in two of the four fields, and plant ornament in the other two.
L 38mm
Context 655

32 172 (fig 16)
Leaded brass (XRF analysis, table 5), perhaps enamelled but almost certainly not nielloed as XRF analysis showed a total absence of silver (report by S La Niece). Traces of a plant pattern with vestigial animals or leaves in the fields on the shaft.
L 44mm
Context F307
Published Addyman and Hill 1969, 70 and fig 27, 3

32 455 (fig 16)
Copper alloy. White metallic silver inlay, possibly decomposed silver sulphide niello, on the shaft (report by S La Niece). Nicked edges. X-ray photograph reveals knot-interlace pattern in the field.
L 49mm
Context not known
Published Addyman and Hill 1969, 70 and fig 27, 4.

169 1270 (fig 16)
Brass (XRF analysis, table 5). Inlaid with silver sulphide niello (report by S La Niece). Plant pattern in the field, vestigial leaf pattern by split end.
L 41mm
Context 11887

169 2169 (fig 16)
Brass (XRF analysis, table 5). 'Inlaid, with what has corroded to silver sulphide: [possibly] decomposed from silver sulphide niello' (report by S La Niece). Billeted border, with interlace, perhaps zoomorphic, in the field. Crude, incised leaf pattern by split end. Animal mask with incised ears and leaf pattern on the forehead. Leather surviving in the split end, but no rivets.
L 57mm
Context 12482

254 1149 (fig 16)
Copper alloy. Stylised leaf ornament at the split end, contoured animal in a notched frame, grooved, bent neck and narrow, three-dimensional animal-mask terminal. Traces of red enamel in the frame.
L 55mm
Context 3301
Published Hinton 1993C, no 1

In contrast to the single-riveted strap-ends, there is no lack of information from other sites about the double-riveted, convex-sided strap-ends which terminate in animal masks that range from the elaborate, like 26/181, to the vestigial, like 15/4. Whether the 'comma-like' ears that feature on so many had as much fascination for their wearers as for their twentieth-century students is a moot point. It is remarkable, however, that this strap-end type should almost invariably end in an animal head, as though it was felt that this was the only appropriate terminal; it is difficult to believe that deeper meanings were involved.

The double-riveted strap-ends, like the single-riveted, appear to have their origins in the seventh century (Evison 1976, 247), though they do not feature in cemeteries close to Southampton. The Hamwic examples do not seem to have any with features that may be early in the series as a whole, such as incised-line decoration, and none is from an early context. The type seems to have remained current into the tenth century and perhaps into the eleventh (Hinton 1990C, 502), but there do not seem to be contexts to demonstrate that, as there seem to be for the hooked tags discussed above. Indeed, their absence so far from the Test-side successor of the mid-Saxon port is one pointer

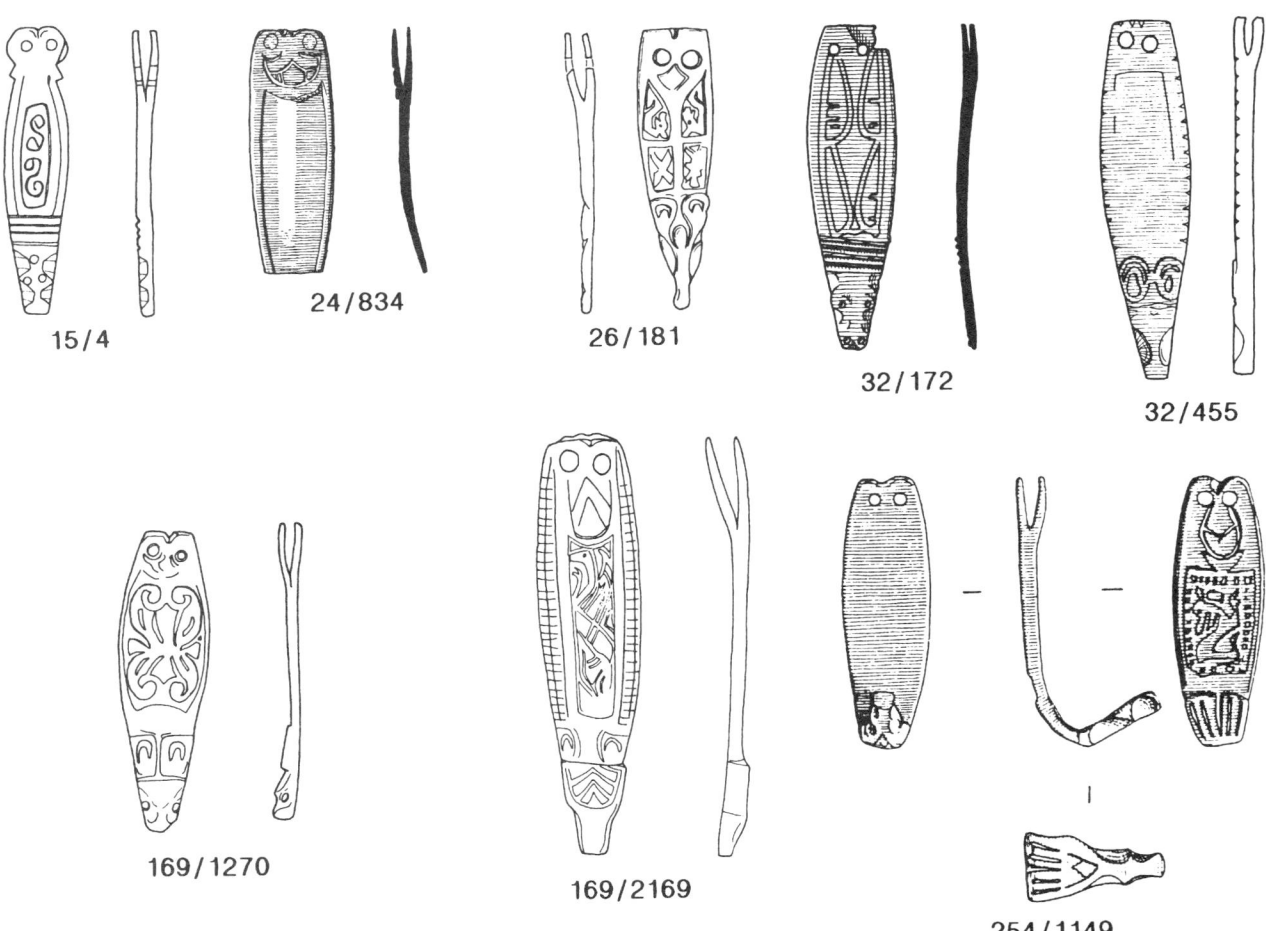

Figure 16. Strap-ends: Type C, double-riveted, with flat, convex-sided shafts, animal-mask terminals and plain reverses. Scale 1:1

towards declining use. A *floruit* of the type in the ninth century is shown by their appearance in such hoards as Sevington, Wiltshire (Wilson 1964, nos 71–7), the dates of which are suggested by coins, and run from the 840s to the 870s in southern England, later in the north.

Several of the Southampton strap-ends have variations of the Trewhiddle style's contorted animals and plants (26/181, 32/172, 254/1149), and the knot-interlace now only visible on X-ray photographs of 32/455 is also a common-place. (X-rays were not available to Addyman and Hill when they argued that 32/455 is a workshop 'blank', similar to some from Sevington (1969, 68–70), and they could not see the pattern on the shaft or the second rivet-hole. Nevertheless, its thickness might suggest that it had not been finished, if strap-ends cast in moulds – there is one from Carlisle (Taylor and Webster 1984) – were filed down before use. Corrosion also obscures 169/2169, which seems to have had a more elaborate, interlaced creature, rather like one from Halstock, Dorset (Keen 1986, no 6). 169/1270 has a form of symmetrical plant with lobed leaves, similar to those on a ring from Poslingford, Suffolk (Wilson 1964, 33 and no 61). The most unusual is 15/4 with its S-scroll silver wires, which are reminiscent of those on the finger-ring, 31/653; no published parallels for the scrolls have been noted, though there are unpublished examples at Bawsey, Norfolk (S Margeson, pers comm). Although it has one of the most stylised animal masks, there is more shaping of the split end, a sign of its quality.

Four of the strap-ends are reported as having traces of sulphide or of its corrosion, indicating niello work. Three had enamel inlay, which is now increasingly reported, and may be one of the earliest instances of enamel's spreading use: other Wessex examples are from Poundbury, Dorset (Keen 1986, no 7) and Trowbridge, Wiltshire (Hinton 1993B, 83).

D. Double-riveted, with various shafts (fig 17)

11 3 (fig 17)
Leaded gunmetal (XRF analysis, table 5). Flat, triangular-sided shaft with no division between shaft and split end. Beaded edge; field not visibly ornamented, but possible inlay visible on X-ray. Vestigial animal-mask terminal.
L 33mm
Context F66

32 166 (fig 17)
Copper alloy. Slightly tapering shaft with grooves (identification not certain).
L (extant) 32mm
Context F342, 2

169 2037 (fig 17)
Leaded gunmetal (XRF analysis, table 5). Straight-sided, unornamented shaft plano-convex in section, with triangular split end and vestigial animal-mask terminal.
L 32mm
Context 11961

258 80 (fig 17)
Copper alloy. Undecorated, short shaft.
L 29mm
Context 14925

Of the cast strap-ends, the narrow, straight-sided shaft is generally less common than the convex-sided, so the two certain and one less certain examples, 169/2037, 258/80 and 32/166, are probably about representative proportionally, both in Wessex (Keen 1986, fig 2; Hinton and Welch 1976, no 52) and further afield (eg Haldenby 1990, fig 4 and 1992, fig 3; Rogers 1993, fig 652). A hooked tag, 169/2622 (fig 4), has a shaft of this type. The triangular-sided 11/3 is presumably an occasional variant of the convex type.

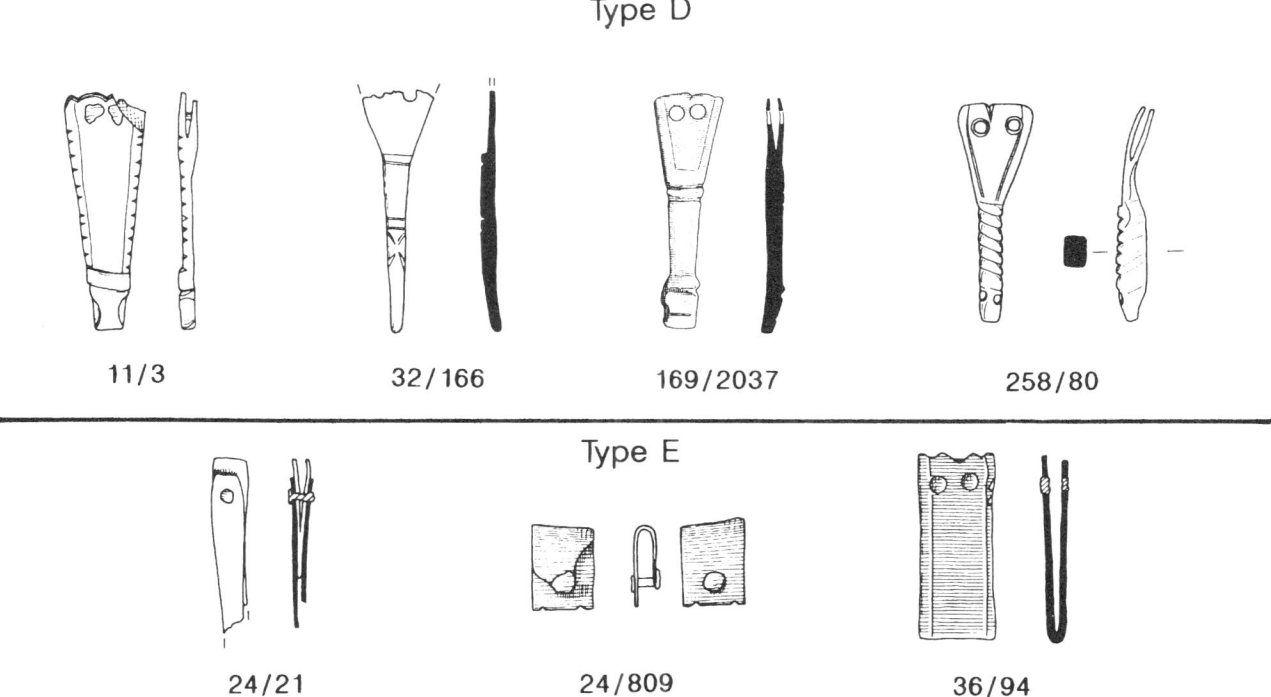

Figure 17. Strap-ends: Type D, double-riveted, with various shafts. Type E, folded and other sheet-metal strap-ends. Scale 1:1

E. Folded and other sheet-metal strap-ends (fig 17)

24 21 (fig 17)
Copper alloy. Single rivet, holding two thin plates to a split strip (identification not certain).
L (extant) 22mm
Context 7766

24 809 (fig 17)
Copper alloy. Single rivet-hole, with copper-alloy rivet.
L 11mm
Context 14064

36 94 (fig 17)
Copper alloy. Two rivet-holes.
L 25mm
Context Pit 29, 3

Although all these objects could have been edge-bindings on the rims of wooden or leather objects, like some catalogued below in Mounts, the extra degree of finishing, albeit no more than small notches, on 24/809 and 36/94, suggests that they could have been intended to be worn on costume items such as belts. 24/21 is perhaps a lace-tag end, as its aperture is so narrow at the rivet.

TWEEZERS AND OTHER TOILET IMPLEMENTS (fig 18)

4 5 (fig 18)
Bronze (XRF analysis, table 5). Stirrup-shaped terminals with inturned ends and incised cross- and border-lines. Transverse lines on shaft. Unthickened loop.
L 64mm
Context F4, 17

24 12 (fig 18)
Brass, with silver loop (XRF analysis, table 5). Slightly flaring, straight-ended terminals expanding to shaft. Loop apparently cast. Now very distorted.
L c 85mm
Context 14721

31 101 (fig 18)
Leaded bronze (XRF analysis, table 5). Straight-sided flat strip.
L c 42mm
Context 4803

38 40 (fig 18)
Bronze (XRF analysis, table 5). Triangular terminals with inturned ends and ring-and-dot ornament. Unthickened loop.
L 58mm
Context Pit 53, 3

39 40 (fig 18)
Copper alloy. Flaring terminals with ring-and-dot and incised-border lines. Broken.
L (extant) 45mm
Context Pit 66A, 6

99 75 (fig 18)
Bronze (XRF analysis, table 5). Triangular terminals with inturned ends and V-shaped projections at junction with shaft, on which is ring-and-dot ornament. Unthickened loop, containing remains of wire ring.
L 56mm
Context 556

169 2548 (fig 18)
Leaded bronze (tweezers), bronze (ring) (XRF analysis, table 5). Triangular terminals with inturned ends. Incised transverse and crossed lines on the shafts. Loop thickened and grooved, and containing a wire ring with twisted-knot ends. Broken.
L 56mm; Diam (of wire ring) 15mm
Context 12964

258 102 (fig 18)
Copper alloy. Flaring terminals with border lines. Loop thickened, containing a wire ring with twisted end-knots.
L 58mm   Diam (of wire ring) 13mm
Context 15013

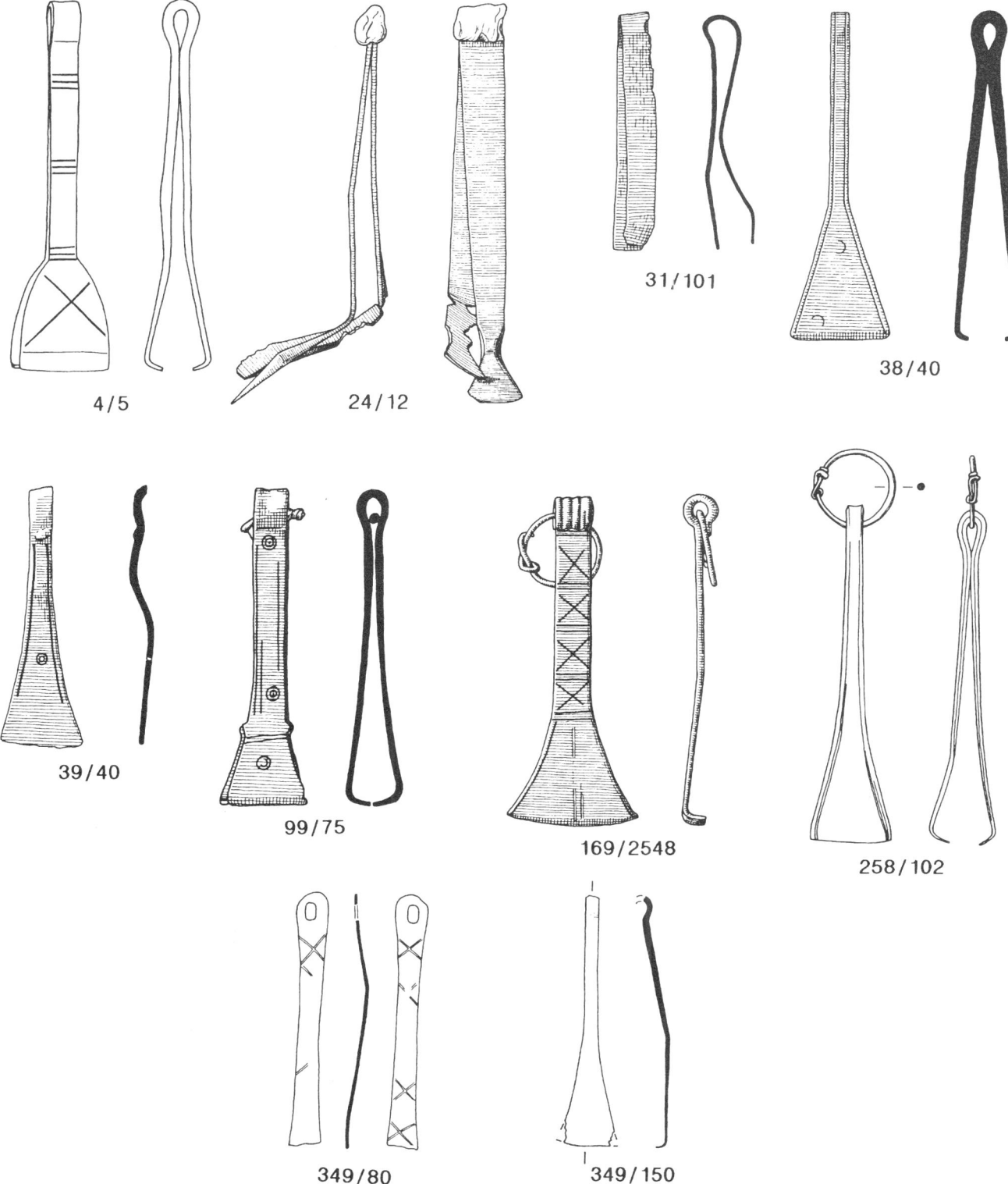

Figure 18. Tweezers and other toilet implements. Scale 1:1

349 80 (fig 18) ?toilet implement
Copper alloy. Waisted strip, with attachment hole at one end, the other end broken. One face incised with a series of crossed oblique lines.
L (Extant) 43mm
Context 0263

349 150 (fig 18) ?broken tweezers
Copper alloy. Bent sheet with inturned end. Undecorated. Broken.
L 43mm
Context 401

Tweezers are amongst the very few objects which are relatively often found both in cemeteries and in settlements: Hampshire examples of the former include Droxford (Aldsworth 1978, 137 and fig 34, nos 33 and 34), Portway (Cook and Dacre 1985, 91) and Alton (Evison 1988, 24); of the latter Abbots Worthy (Davies 1991, 40 and fig 32 no 2) and Chalton (Champion 1977, 369). Although usually found in male graves in the upper Thames Valley (Scull 1992, 236), at Portway and Alton they were equally divided between males and females, although the unpublished Kingsworthy cemetery is said to have them only in male graves (Davies 1991, 40). There is no discernible difference between those found in cemeteries and those found in occupation debris, so that there is no reason to think that some were specially made for funerary deposit. They are also more often found on their own in graves, rather than with other toilet implements such as ear-scoops and tooth-picks, so it is not as surprising that none has been found at Hamwic with anything else on the same ring as that no other types of object for personal use of this sort have been recognised. It is assumed that tweezers were indeed mainly for cosmetic use, to remove hairs, but may occasionally have been pressed into service to remove splinters (Webster 1991, 85) or for sewing (Rogers 1993, 1388).

The Southampton tweezers are mostly cast, and reasonably well finished; the few made from cut sheet are plainer, as would be expected (349/150 and 31/101, which is so crude that the identification is uncertain). None has the heavy facetting said to characterise some Roman and early Anglo-Saxon tweezers (Scull 1992, 236), which may serve to confirm that dating but which may also have implications for interpreting such Roman objects as have been found in Hamwic – that by and large they were collected as scrap metal, not for reuse to serve their original function. None has the slide often seen on later medieval tweezers, which supports the suggestion that these were a tenth-century innovation (Biddle 1990D, 690), probably to serve as clips.

One implement which appears to have been a pair of tweezers, 24/12, is very differently made from the others, apparently having a silver-alloy top to solder together two separate cast strips: these have thickened but not inturned ends, and are now very bent. They may have had different use from the other pairs, but have some similarity to a pair from Reculver, Kent (Wilson 1964, no 62). Object 349/80 might be a nail-cleaner, but the identification is far from certain; a somewhat similar object, 24/821 (fig 6), has been classified above as a pendant.

FITTINGS

DISCS (fig 19)

38 44 (fig 19) Disc
Copper alloy. Flat disc with projecting top and T-shaped opening, as though an escutcheon plate, but the absence of rivet-holes makes that identification unlikely.
Diam 24mm
Context Pit 60, 1B

169 549 (not illus)
Copper alloy. Unornamented. One perforation near the irregular circumference. Broken.
Diam c 29mm
Context 8891

169 2831 (fig 19)
Leaded gunmetal (XRF analysis, table 5). Unornamented. One perforation near the irregular circumference.
Diam 17mm
Context 12332

CATALOGUE

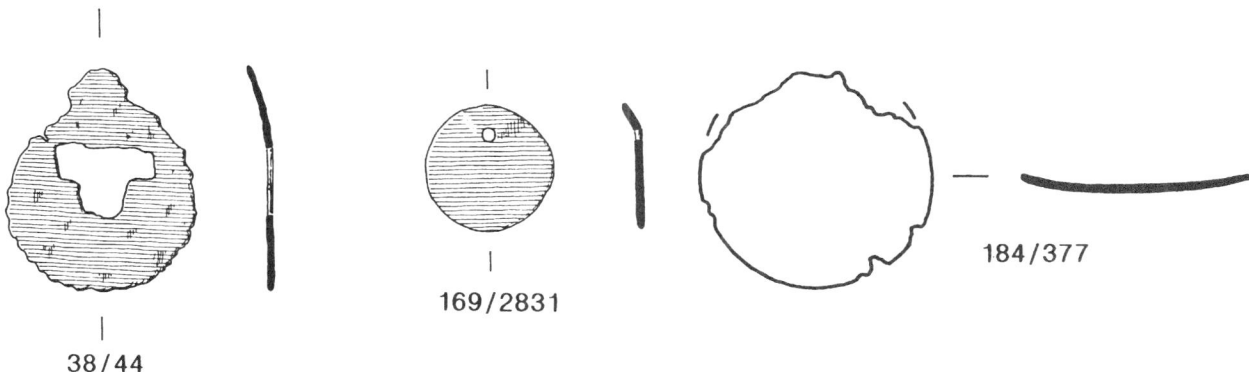

Figure 19. Discs. Scale 1:1

184 377 (fig 19)
Copper alloy. Slightly convex. No attachment holes or perforations visible, but edges decayed.
Diam 30mm
Context 1158

The reasons for categorising small discs separately from Mounts are, firstly, that an object like 169/2831 might have been a pendant, worn like the pierced Roman coins found in many graves, and, secondly, that it picks out two discs that might possibly be scale-pans (see below), although 169/2831 appears only to have a single perforation, for suspension, and 184/377 has none at all, but does have the concave section that a pan would usually have.

There are fragments in the Mounts which might have been discs (eg 26/145 and 26/193, fig 22) and, for completeness, Disc-headed pins (fig 12) should be mentioned.

HOOKS AND HANDLES (fig 20)
A. Double-ended hooks

30 178 (fig 20)
Copper (XRF analysis, table 5). Flat bar perforated in two places (one perforation having split the top), with moulded top and a sharp hook at each end.
L 21mm
Context 3357

34 8 (fig 20)
Brass (XRF analysis, table 5). Flat bar perforated in the centre, with lozenge faceting on the top and a sharp hook at each end.
L 23mm
Context SB1

Double-ended hooks with a central perforation have been recorded at a number of continental sites from the seventh century onwards. Some have chains linked to the perforations, and at least one had a brooch at the other end (Roes 1954). On the basis that they would not have been strong enough to stand up to very much strain, it has been suggested that they were shroud-hooks (Audin 1955). Some may have been, but others may have been for everyday use, as garment-fasteners or to give extra security to an insecure brooch on a weakly-sprung pin. They have sharply inturned hooks rather like the harbicks, of iron or copper alloy, used to hold cloth while its nap was sheared (Goodall and Keene 1990, 239-40), but their arms are a little shorter, and there would have been no use for the central perforations. The harbicks do, however, show that such hooks could be expected to have robust usage.

One double-ended hook is from a cemetery at the site thought to be Quentovic (Leman 1981, 938, 943 and fig 6), another from a Merovingian cemetery at Giberville, Normandy (Pilet et Alduc-le Bagousse 1990, pl 22, grave 228 no 1), and there are some further south at the Herpes cemetery (BM 1923, fig 196). They also occur on occupation sites, however, with dates into the ninth century; in cemeteries, they are mostly in female graves (Musée national 1988, 190-1). To the north, they occur at Dorestad (Roes 1965, 16 and pl III). One of the two from Southampton, 34/8, came from a linear feature which cut through a pit which in turn cut through human burials, suggesting a disturbed cemetery, attributable to the early eighth century (Morton 1992, 194); the other, 30/178, has no demonstrable links with burials, having come from a pit with contents that suggest a mid-eighth-/mid-ninth-century range (Morton, pers comm).

Until recently, the Southampton hooks appeared to be the only ones found in England. Another has, however, now been reported from Norwich; although from an eleventh- or twelfth-century context, it is from the Cathedral Close, and 'may be pre-Conquest, perhaps even middle Saxon' (Margeson 1993, 19 and fig 9, no 79), a perceptive identification which Saxon Southampton would seem to confirm. There is no known cemetery in the immediate area (S Margeson, pers comm). The Norwich discovery weakens the case that these hooks show the singular overseas connections of Saxon Southampton. It is perhaps more reasonable now to record that their usage in cemeteries like Herpes and Giberville, which have evidence of English contacts (Pilet et Auduc-le Bagousse 1990, 34–5), makes it a little surprising that such hooks have not been found more frequently in 'Final Phase' and subsequent cemeteries on this side of the Channel.

B. Miscellaneous hooks and handles (fig 20)

5 67 (fig 20) Hook or handle
Leaded bronze (XRF analysis, table 5). One end looped, the other cut into a flange.
L 39mm
Context F22

5 73 (fig 20) Handle
Copper alloy. Broken shaft with ring containing iron corrosion.
Diam 18mm
Context F21

30 493 (fig 20) Hook or handle
Copper alloy. Rectangular-sectioned rod, one end turned into a hook. Broken.
L (extant) 70mm
Context 4445/7764

31 919 (fig 20) Hook or handle
Copper alloy. Flat, bent, and broken strip tapering to a hooked end.
L (extant) c 130mm
Context 5646

31 1324 (fig 20) ?Hook
Copper alloy. Round wire, twisted apparently deliberately to form hook.
L (extant) 46mm
Context 5932

33 83 (not illus) Hook or handle
Copper alloy. Circular-sectioned wire, with closed loops at each end.
L c 140mm
Context F50

33 84 (fig 20) Hook or handle
Copper alloy. Shaft square-sectioned at one end, round at the other, with loops set at 90°.
W 65mm
Context F54

39 43 (fig 20) Hook or handle
Leaded bronze (XRF analysis, table 5). Square-sectioned rod having ring-and-dot ornament grouped in threes on two sides, and a carefully made loop at one end, the other end broken.
L (extant) c 120mm
Context Pit 70

169 1447 (fig 20) Hook, handle, or needle
Copper alloy. Solid rod, lozenge-sectioned, becoming socketed and perforated in one place at one end, close to which is a second perforation through the solid part. The other end forms an L-shaped point.
L c 80mm
Context 11961

169 1585 (fig 20) Hook
Copper alloy. Round wire, apparently deliberately bent to form a hook. Broken.
W (extant) 50mm
Context 12147

169 1611 (fig 20) Hook or handle
Copper alloy. Rectangular-sectioned, broken, curved bar, one end bent into a hook.
W (extant) 66mm
Context 12200

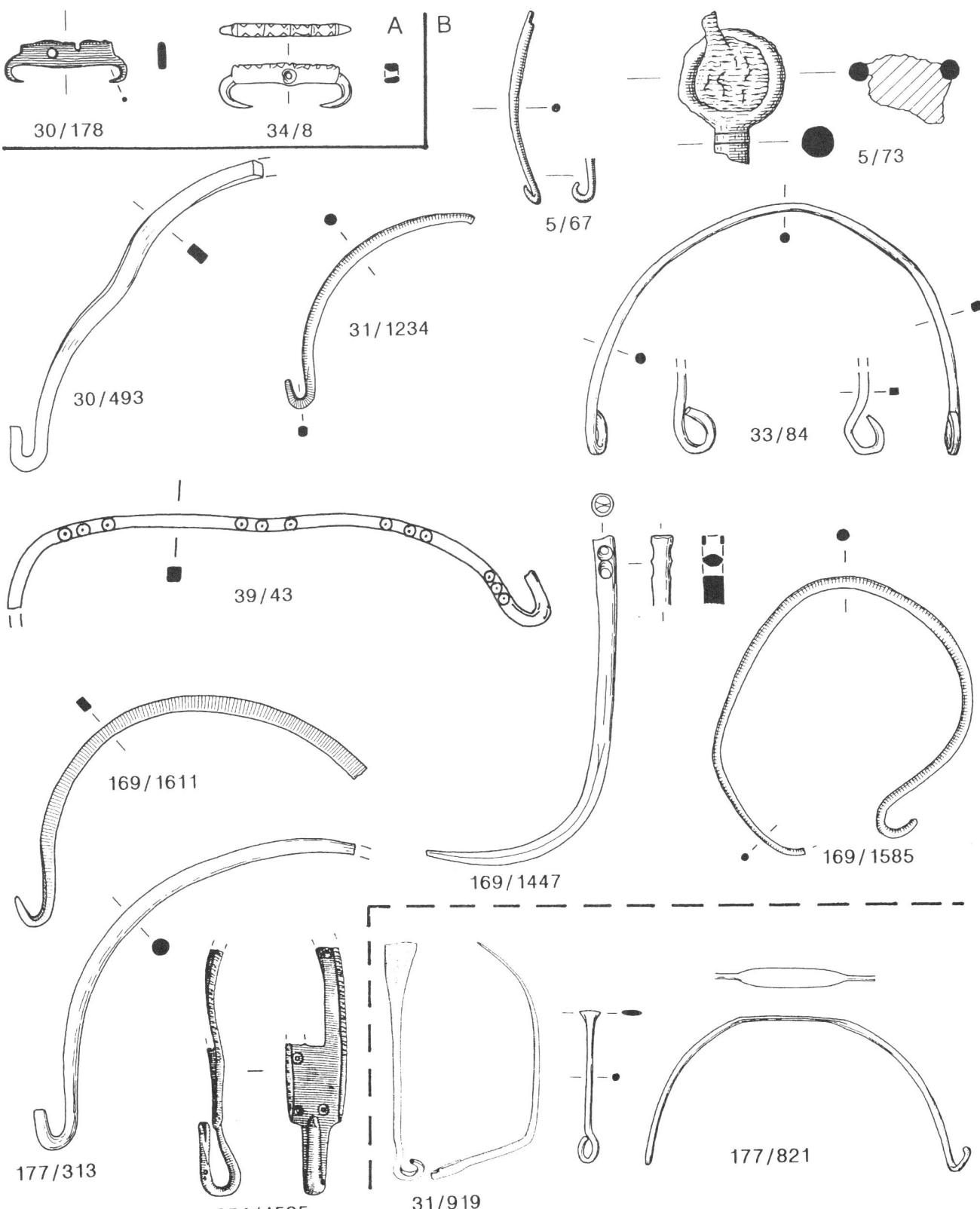

Figure 20. Hooks and handles. A, double-ended; B, miscellaneous. Scale 1:1, except 177/821, 1:2

177 313 (fig 20) Handle
Copper alloy. Corroded.
L (extant) 76mm
Context 277

177 821 (fig 20) Handle
Copper alloy. Top hammered flat. One loop twisted out of shape.
W 110mm
Context 954

254 1595 (fig 20) Hook
Copper alloy. Slightly tapering, nearly closed loop with stylised animal-head terminal, attached to a flat plate with ring-and-dot ornament and a grooved-line border, with a piece deliberately cut from it, and broken at the end.
L (extant) 43mm
Context 3145
Published Hinton 1993C, no 2

Other pieces of wire or rod that appear to have been deliberately bent into hooks include: 4/42, 5/68, 30/493, 31/789, 31/1324, 36/104, and 169/1585.

It is not possible to make a confident distinction between a hook and a broken handle with an open loop, so this category is inevitably something of a miscellany. Hooked tags have been treated separately, above, as has a split-ended hook which seems likely to have been a strap-end.

The most distinctive object in the category is 254/1595, which has a neatly made animal's head as its terminal. It may have been fitted to something like a casket which had some importance for its owner, or have been a swivel for a handle on a pail (and has been drawn as though in that position). Object 169/1447 might be a curved needle for embroidery, rather than a hook.

The simplest hooks or handles are merely wires bent to shape, such as 5/67. More substantial are rods or bars, like 30/493, on which the loop would probably have had to be formed by heating it to make it pliable. Object 33/84 is an example of a complete handle, perhaps from a pail. Object 177/821 is broken, but seems to have been similar: its flattened top may explain 31/919.

A rather different handle is the cast loop, 5/73, which may be part of a key, but has been included here as it may have come from some other object, most Saxon keys having ovoid loops.

KEYS AND LOCKS (fig 21)

36 96 (fig 21) Key
Leaded bronze (XRF analysis, table 5). Loop broken, hollow shank, ward with three rectangular slots and three flanged prongs.
W (wards) 11mm
Context General clearance, trench B

Although two copper-alloy keys were among the only five metal objects from Saxon Southampton illustrated in 1857 by Charles Roach Smith (1857, and Addyman and Hill 1969, pl VIIIe), only one example has been positively identified from all the subsequent excavations, although 5/73 (fig 20), catalogued as a handle, may be a broken key. There are, of course, many more iron keys; copper-alloy ones are usually assumed to have been used to lock caskets and boxes. The complicated ward of 36/96 is not unlike no 2 in Roach Smith's illustration, but has a longer shank. Another with projecting prongs like 36/96's is in the British Museum, without provenance (Wilson 1964, no 140). Copper-alloy keys were probably not often used in the mid-Saxon period: there is one from Brandon, Suffolk (Webster 1991, no 66q), but the only one from Anglian York may be Roman (Rogers 1993, 1422–3).

An object of iron and copper alloy, 36/117 (fig 26) in Other Identified Objects as a bell, might possibly be a padlock, as these were sometimes plated (eg Rogers 1993, 1422), but there seems to be no early parallel for the shape.

MOUNTS, STUDS AND ATTACHMENTS (fig 22)

4 7 (fig 22) Binding-strip/hinge fitting
Gunmetal (XRF analysis, table 5). Flat sheet, now twisted. Two sub-rectangular terminals with attachment holes in which is iron corrosion.
W 14mm
Context General clearance

5 2 (fig 22) ?Mount
Brass (XRF analysis, table 5). Oval, with incised

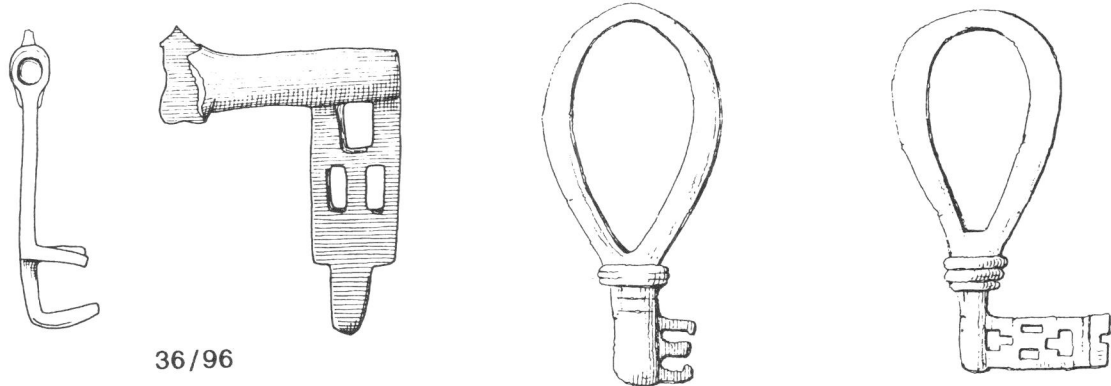

Figure 21. Keys. 36/96, Scale 1:1; two drawings reproduced from Smith 1857, at published size, probably approximately 1:1

pattern of cross or flower with central circle and four pear-shaped arms within a border to which segmental space-fillers append.
L (orig) *c* 38mm
Context F16, 17
Published Hinton 1980, 73 and fig 13, 1, no 1

5 5 (fig 22) Binding-strip
Copper alloy. Pentagonal-sectioned, broken shaft with circular terminal and attachment hole.
L (extant) 50mm
Context not known

15 2 (fig 22) Binding-strip
Leaded gunmetal (XRF analysis, table 5). Segmental-sectioned, broken shaft with trefoil end, collars, and two attachment holes.
L (extant) 33mm
Context General clearance

15 3 (fig 22) Mount
Tin bronze, mercury-gilded (AML). Broken, flat fragments with curvilinear, ?plant, filigree ornament in relief.
W (extant) 16mm
Context F54, 1

24 9 (fig 22) Binding-strip
Copper alloy. Flat strip with girth grooves.
L (extant) 78mm
Context 9440

24 832 (fig 22) Binding-strip
Copper alloy. Broken, tapering strip, bent into a right angle. Ring-and-dot ornament on top and one side.
L (extant) 22mm
Context 7766

26 145 (fig 22) Mount
Leaded gunmetal (XRF analysis, table 5). Flat fragment with 'chip-carved' interlace knot in relief.
L (extant) 15mm
Context 94

26 193 (fig 22) Mount
Silver, debased with copper or copper alloy with silver plating (XRF analysis, table 5). Flat fragment with 'chip-carved' curvilinear plant scroll in relief.
L (extant) 15mm
Context 655

26 304 (not illus) ?Binding-strip
Lead. Flat strip with attachment hole.
L (extant) 34mm
Context 578

30 1 (fig 22) Edge-binding strip
Copper alloy. Flat sheet, folded over, with three attachment holes.
L 27mm
Context 3302

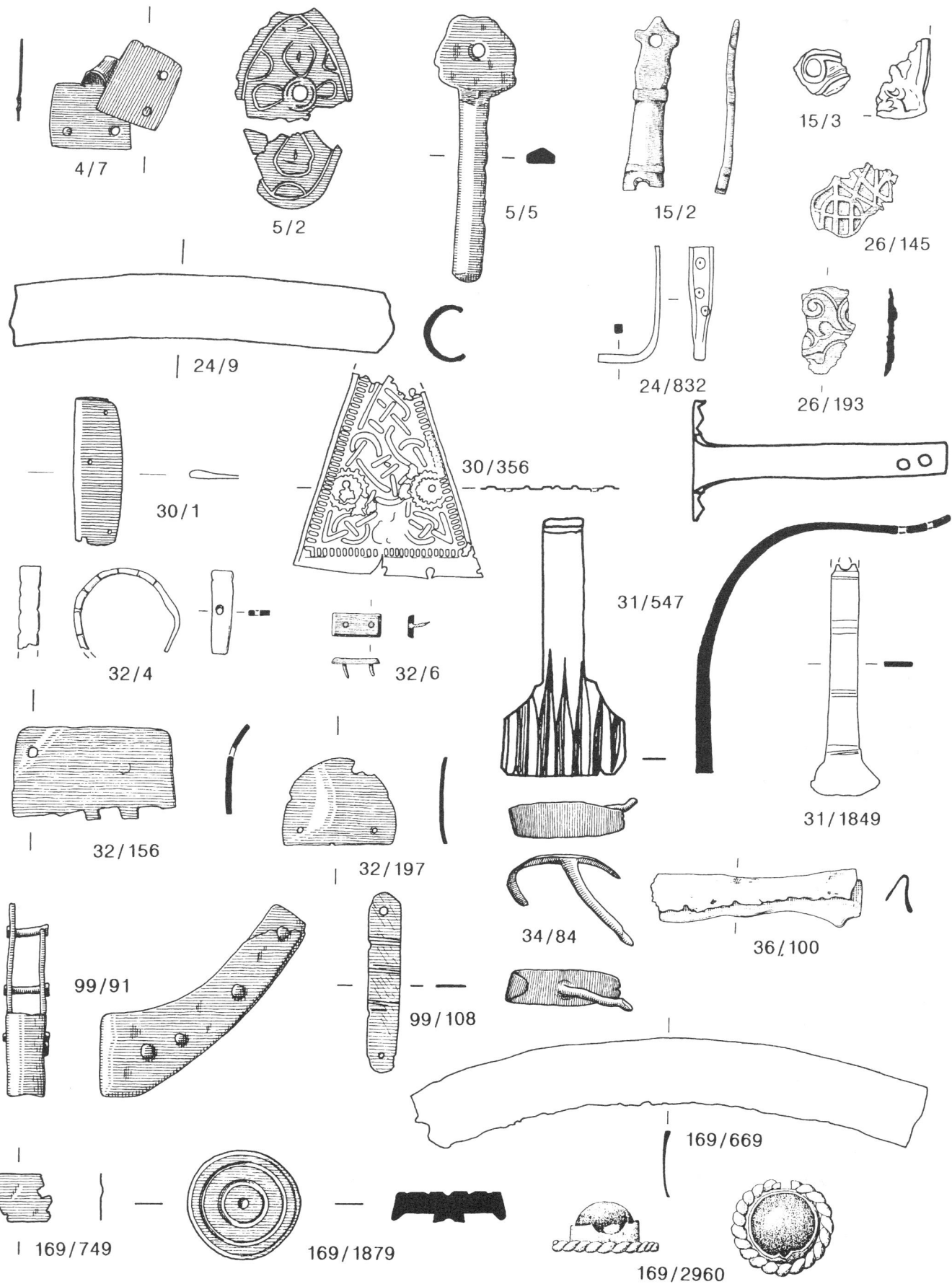

Figure 22. Mounts, studs and attachments. Scale 1:1

30 356 (fig 22) Mount
Bronze (XRF analysis, table 5). Thin, triangular flat sheet, the apex broken, with repoussé ornament: within a billeted border, unsymmetrical knot interlace, interrupted by two circles within which are attachment holes. There is another attachment hole in the short side.
W 35mm
Context 3544

31 547 (fig 22) Binding-strip
Brass (XRF analysis, table 5). Flat sheet, now bent, having notched head-plate with V-section grooves and two attachment holes at the other end.
L c 85mm
Context Unstratified

31 1849 (fig 22) ?Binding-strip
Copper alloy. Flat bar, broken, with circular terminal, transverse grooves and attachment hole.
L (extant) 45mm
Context 6182

32 4 (fig 22) Binding-ring
Copper alloy. Broken, flat, slightly tapering strip with engrailed edges and two attachment holes.
Diam c 20mm
Context F423   General clearance
Published Addyman and Hill 1969, 70 and fig 27, 10

32 6 (fig 22) Mount
Copper alloy. Rectangular bar with two rivets.
L 9mm
Context General clearance
Published Addyman and Hill 1969, 70 and fig 27, 8

32 156 (fig 22) ?Mount
Copper alloy. Flat, rectangular sheet with two crudely made lugs and an attachment hole.
L 30mm
Context General clearance

32 197 (fig 22) ?Mount
Copper alloy, ?with white metal coating. Broken, flat, semi-circular sheet with two attachment holes.
W 21mm
Context General clearance

34 84 (fig 22) Nail or tack
Copper (XRF analysis, table 5). Round shaft with long, strip head. Now bent.
L c 20mm
Context SB1, 1

36 100 (fig 22) ?Edge-binding strip
Copper alloy. Bent-over sheet. Crudely finished.
L (extant) 39mm
Context Pit 26

99 91 (fig 22) Edge-binding strip
Bronze (XRF analysis, table 5). Flat, curved sheet, folded over and held by four rivets.
L 49mm
Context 423

99 108 (fig 22) Mount
Copper alloy. Oval strip with two attachment holes and bands of transverse lines.
L 34mm
Context 540

169 145 (not illus) Edge-binding strip
Copper alloy. Fragment of flat, curved sheet, folded over.
L (extant) 16mm
Context 8613

169 669 (fig 22) ?Binding-strip
Leaded bronze (XRF analysis, table 5). Flat, broken, curved strip with attachment holes along lower edge.
L (extant) 95mm
Context 10566

169 749 (fig 22) Binding-strip
Brass, with tin plating (AML). Flat, lozenge-shaped sheet with attachment hole.
W 11mm
Context 10218

169 1879 (fig 22) Stud
Copper alloy. Cast disc with concentric circles and central dot incised in the top, a projecting stud on the back.
Diam 20mm
Context 12302

169   2960   (fig 22)   Mount
Silver and glass. Disc with a vertically set silver strip surrounded by a collar of two-plait twisted wire – the joins broken. In the setting, a flat-based, cabochon, red glass roundel (to be described in Hunter and Heyworth, forthcoming). Adhesive or filler was noted at its base during conservation by the Ancient Monuments Laboratory.
Diam 16mm
Context 12462

A wide range of metal mounts was fitted to Saxon objects made of wood, leather, metal and bone, for practical and for decorative purposes. Except for 169/2960 and 26/193, those from Saxon Southampton are of base metal, though some are gilt.

Cabled silver provides a decorative setting for the red glass roundel, 169/2960, which might have ornamented an object like the lost, probably eighth-century, Witham hanging-bowl (Bruce-Mitford 1993, pl 9) or the eighth- or ninth-century Gravesend cross (Wilson 1964, no 20). A blue glass stud, also in a silver setting, is one of the few finds from York's Coppergate attributed to the Anglian period (Hall 1984, 33–4 and pl 29). (169/2960 might possibly have been a finger-ring bezel, see above, or even have come from a disc-brooch of seventh-century Kentish composite type.) The precise metal of 26/193 is not certain, but it is the only other mount with a distinct silver content; its curvilinear pattern is probably some form of plant scroll. Like 26/145, it could be part of a disc-headed pin, or a brooch.

Two mounts have interlace ornament: 30/356 appears not to be a zoomorphic pattern, as it seems to be a continuous knot, and probably therefore did not contain a head in its broken top. Triangular mounts or vandykes occur on drinking horns, buckets and books: 30/356 seems too thin for use on the first of those and may have been on something that had less robust use. It was probably not from the head of a stylus (eg Webster 1991, nos 67k and 107c), as it is both too wide at the bottom, and has circular settings which show that it was tacked into place. Interlace also occurs on 26/145. Of the other decorated objects, the comparison of 5/2's pattern with the Minster Lovell jewel might be said to be a case of travelling hopefully rather than arriving (Hinton 1980, 73).

A number of the mounts were probably edge- or rim-binding strips from objects like wooden buckets (eg Speake 1989, figs 49–50) or from leather straps – some may have been strap-ends, cf 24/21 etc. Objects 15/2, and perhaps 5/5 and 31/1849, may be strips for nailing on to caskets of the sort more often seen in late eleventh- or twelfth-century contexts, but the possibility of an earlier date for some of them was opened by those from Portchester Castle, Hampshire (Hinton and Welch 1976, 217–9). 4/7 may be part of a hinge fitting from a box or casket. The nail, 34/84, is included here because its long head suggests that it had ornamental use, perhaps on a box. The short bar with two rivets, 32/6, might be a belt-stiffener, since such things were certainly used on leather belts in the Middle Ages, or it may be a repair strip as Addyman and Hill suggested (1969, 70). An 'attachment plate', similar to 32/6 except for a central perforation, from a grave presumed to be Anglo-Saxon, had 'traces of wood/bone' on its underside, suggesting that it was nailed to a box or casket: it was found at the monastic site at Breedon-on-the-Hill, Leicestershire, founded in the eighth century (Dornier 1977, 162 and fig 4, no 3). The use of 31/547 is uncertain: being unstratified, it may not be a Saxon object – a post-medieval pastry-cutter has been suggested; a similar doubt hangs over the solid casting 169/1879.

RINGS AND LOOPS (fig 23)

31   1266   (fig 23)   Loop
Copper alloy. Undecorated, cast strip.
Diam 14mm
Context Surface cleaning

33   86   (fig 23)   Loop
Brass (XRF analysis, table 5). Undecorated, untapered.
Diam 19mm
Context F42

36   101   (fig 23)   Loop
Copper alloy. Undecorated, cast, circular-sectioned strip.
Diam 11mm
Context Pit 18

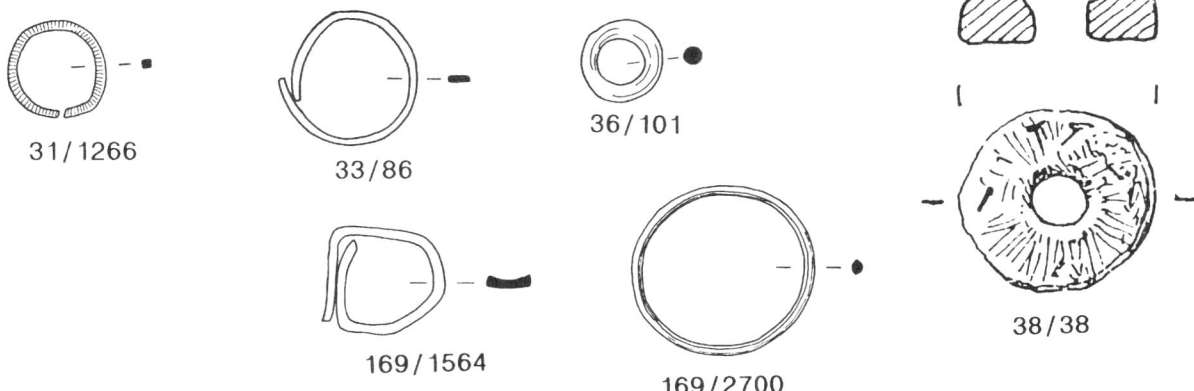

Figure 23.   Rings and loops.   Scale 1:1

38 38 (fig 23) Ring
Lead or pewter. Undecorated.
Diam *c* 26mm
Context Pit 56, 3
Published Addyman and Hill 1969, fig 28, no 2

169 1564 (fig 23) Loop
Lead or pewter. Undecorated, flat strip.
Diam *c* 26mm
Context 11411

169 2700 (fig 23) Ring
Brass (XRF analysis, table 5). Undecorated wire.
Diam 24mm
Context 12553

Simple rings had various uses, for instance as carrying-handles on boxes (eg Speake 1989, figs 25–6). Those categorised here cannot be ascribed to a particular use, and cannot be specifically identified as, for example, finger-rings – 169/2700 is a possibility for that function, but seems too simple. 38/38 might be a net-sinker, or a washer.

MISCELLANEOUS

'FORKS' AND 'SPOONS' (fig 24)

4 37 (fig 24) 'Spoon'
Copper alloy. Round-sectioned shaft with intermittent transverse grooves, scroll-ended hook at one end, slightly convex oval terminal at the other.
L 120mm
Context General clearance

24 7 (fig 24) 'Spoon'
Leaded bronze (XRF analysis, table 5). Flat shaft with intermittent transverse grooves, oval hole near one end, slightly convex leaf-shaped terminal at the other.
L 77mm
Context 13680

24 27 (fig 24) 'Spoon'
Bronze (XRF analysis, table 5). Round-sectioned and polygonal shaft with girth grooves and central, perforated boss, and flat, oval, now broken terminal at one end, the other end broken.
L (extant) 104mm
Context General clearance

26 593 (fig 24) 'Fork' and 'spoon'
Leaded bronze (XRF analysis, table 5). Round-sectioned shaft with collar knops, one end spatulate, the other bifurcated and pointed (one point now broken).
L (extant) 123mm
Context 590

31 869 (fig 24) ?'Fork' and 'spoon'
Copper or tin bronze with tin coating (AML). Very corroded, shafted object, spatulate at one end, perhaps bifurcated at the other.
L (extant) 53mm
Context 5261

The curious objects in this category are perhaps the most enigmatic from the Hamwic assemblage. Silver spoons are known in high-status seventh-century graves, such as Swallowcliffe and Sutton Hoo; the former was found with a capsule that might have been used to sprinkle scented liquids, perhaps to settle the dust on the floor in a gesture to be seen as appropriate in an aristocratic household before an important occasion (Speake 1989, 41–7). The Sutton Hoo spoons should be viewed as part of a set of silver tableware for ceremonial feasts (Werner 1992, 7–8). Those spoons, however, are in the Classical form, with an angle at the junction of stem and bowl. There may, therefore, be no direct connection between them, and their function, and the mid-Saxon examples.

Hamwic excavations have yielded six examples which certainly have spoon-like terminals, three being old finds (Roach Smith 1857, Addyman and Hill 1969, pl VIIIe); another, 26/593, has a flat, spatulate end, and one, 31/869, has a broken end that may have been spoon-like. Three, 26/593, 31/869 and Roach Smith's no 3, have two-pronged terminals; 24/27 is broken off and may have been a fourth. Two, 4/37 and Roach Smith's no 4, have a looped end, and two, 24/7 and Roach Smith's no 5, had a perforation near the end (the latter was broken, but the drawing clearly shows part of the hole). One, 24/27, has a central, perforated knop. The three with forked ends seem all to have had a form of spoon at the other end. This seems to imply that 'forks' did not have a separate existence, unlike 'spoons', and that provision for suspension was a convenience, though the unclosed loop of 4/37 – and probably of Roach Smith's no 4 – suggests that this was for immobile storage, since a châtelaine fitting for personal wear would have needed the extra security of a closed loop. In turn, this reduces the likelihood that the objects had the significance of personal association with a female house-ruler that the silver spoons in graves may have had.

A silver 'spoon' and 'fork' combination, and a silver double spoon were in the Sevington hoard, with coins of c 850 (Wilson 1964, nos 67 and 68). The hoard otherwise contained objects like strap-ends which give no clue to the likely use of the 'spoons' although Wilson preferred to see them as having a domestic rather than a Eucharistic function, and cited several parallels (*ibid*, 61–2); Meols, Cheshire, had also produced a copper-alloy spoon, with a short, pointed terminal (Bu'lock 1960, fig 3f), as had Whitby (Peers and Radford 1943, 60, no 63 and fig 12, no 7). Since then, several more bone spoons have been reported from later Saxon Winchester (Collis and Kjølbye-Biddle 1979); copper-alloy examples from West Stow, Suffolk (West 1985, fig 228, no 7) and Thetford, Norfolk (Goodall 1984, no 48), and a tin-coated iron double-ended spoon from York (Hall 1984, 60), are better parallels. More recently, some have been found at the site at Brandon, Suffolk, where some objects imply considerable ecclesiastical presence (Webster 1991, no 66p). There is a bone spoon from Flixborough (Leahy 1991, no 69s), but the most interesting new discovery seems to be that from Beverley, of a copper-alloy 'fork' with a (?broken) spatulate 'spoon' and interlace decoration on the shaft which suggests an object of some significance (Goodall 1991, 148, 151 and fig 115, no 616). None of these new examples throws further light on the function of the 'spoons' and 'forks', and although the last three are from sites with known or inferred churches, this is not proof of a ritual use. The quantity of those from Hamwic makes a routine domestic role their most likely explanation, the careful finishing of several perhaps suggesting that they were used at meals, and that they were thus on occasional display, which would help to explain why silver was preferred for the Sevington pair.

SCALES AND WEIGHTS (fig 25)

258 370 (fig 25) Scale-pan
Copper alloy. Convex disc with three suspension holes.
Diam 48mm
Context 15549

During the early Middle Ages, beam-balances were used to check small amounts of precious metals, and coins (Scull 1990, 183–5; Kruse 1992). At Hamwic, no balance arm and only a single scale-pan has been identified, although two objects listed above as discs (fig 19) cannot be completely ruled out. Beam-balances required small weights, to go in one of the scale-pans, and for this purpose

CATALOGUE

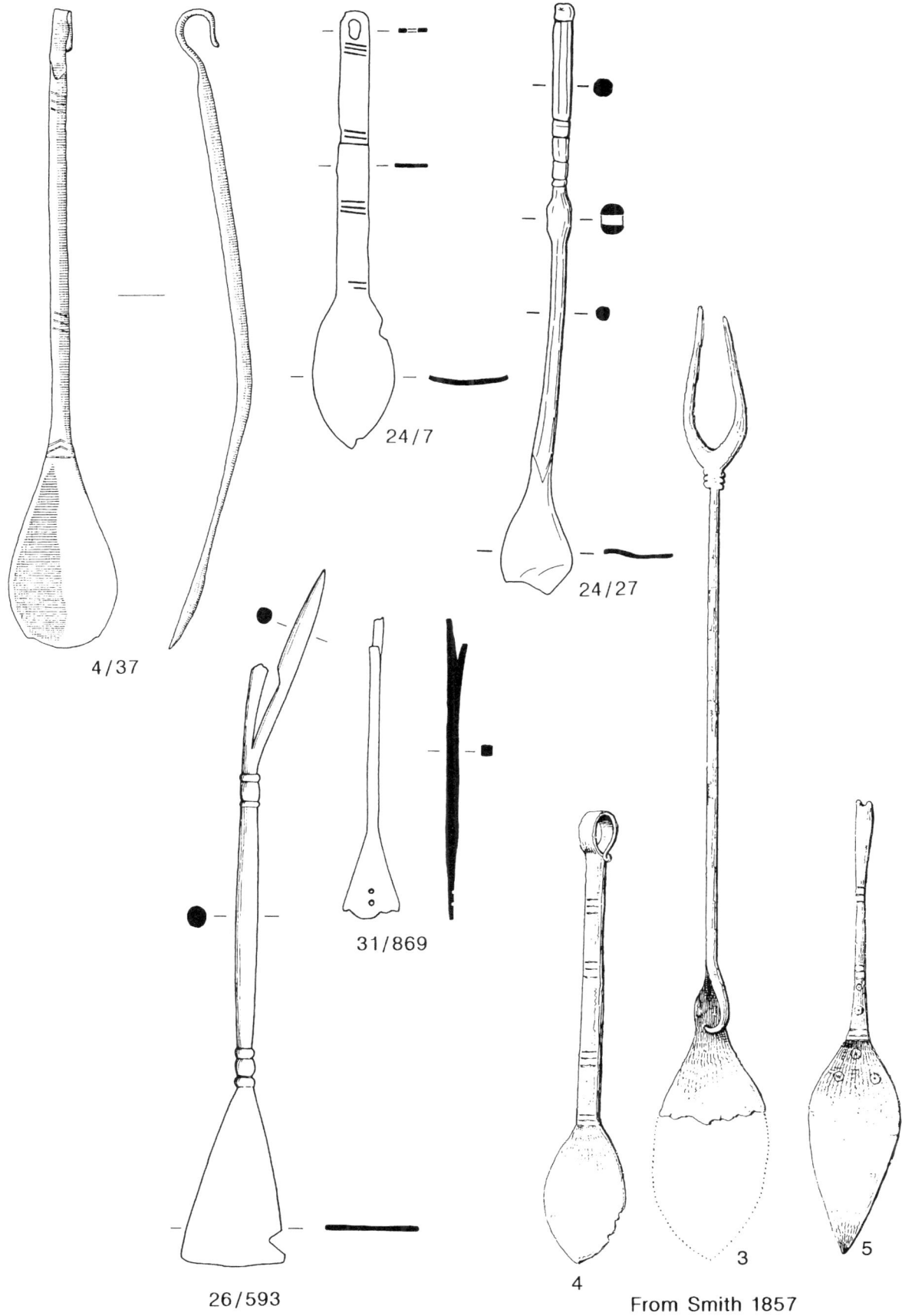

Figure 24. 'Forks' and 'spoons'. Scale 1:1 except three drawings reproduced from Smith 1857, at published size, probably approximately 1:1

Roman coins, sometimes punched with weight-marks, or filed to produce a specific weight-measure, were often utilised (White 1990, 140), as well as specially made metal blocks. None of the Hamwic copper-alloy or lead objects has identification marks such as occur on some of the known weights, and none of the amorphous 'ingots', such as 24/1 (fig 27), has the shape or finish which might suggest that it had functioned as a weight.

Weighing equipment was current as early as the sixth century in post-Roman England (Scull 1986; 1990) and there are several balance sets or parts of sets in seventh-century graves, mostly but not exclusively in Kent: a scale-pan was part of the content of the smith's grave at Tattershall Thorpe, Lincolnshire (Hinton 1993A, 156–60). A trading settlement, such as Hamwic is presumed to have been, might therefore have produced more direct evidence of the use of weighing equipment than seems to be the case. So, because of the inclusion of Roman coins in some of the known balance sets, the question of whether their use as weights at Hamwic could be recognised has been considered.

Enough Roman coins have been found in Hamwic for it to have been suggested that they could have been reused as a form of money (Metcalf 1988, 17). Other possibilities are that they functioned as counters or playing-pieces, which has been proposed for a pile of six third-century bronzes found in a tenth-century building in York (Hall 1986, 15); as none is pierced, or shows signs of having been set in a mount, use in jewellery at Hamwic seems precluded. Some may have been collected as scrap for recycling. But it might be possible to recognise some as having had reuse as weights, if a significant number conform to a set pattern.

There is no certainty about what weight system or systems may have been used in the Saxon period. Smith (1923) argued that 3.11g was a 'median weight value' in the Kentish sets, but this has been questioned by Scull, who argues that two systems were in use, both based on the seventh-century gold coin known as the *tremissis*; but while one system was based on the eight-*siliquae* (Byzantine) *tremissis* of c 1.52g, the other was based on the lighter seven-*siliquae* (Merovingian) *tremissis* of c 1.33g (1990, 190–1). He has also shown that a balance beam could achieve accuracy only within a 0.2g tolerance range (see also Kruse 1992, 86–8). Consequently, a coin found to weigh 1.35g, for instance, could be taken either as a 'good' weight for a 1.33g standard, or a 'bad' one for a 1.52g standard! Nor does that take any account of post-depositional deterioration. Only with higher weights do the variations become wide enough between the two systems to allow any useful discussion, so no account has been taken of the Hamwic Roman coins or fragments weighing less than 1g; this leaves twenty-five coins to be considered (Table 2).

If both 1.33g and 1.52g could be significant, any coin that falls in the range c 1.1g to c 1.7g must be considered as within the 'tolerance' zone of either the Byzantine or the Merovingian system. Similarly, doubling 1.33g and 1.52g gives 'tolerance' zones that span a range from c 2.4g to c 2.9g. Any coin that weighs between 1.7g and 2.4g can be discounted as having been part of a weight set. Only one (258/408) of the seventeen coins weighing less than 3g listed in Table 2 can thus be said not to have been used as a weight. The next 'tolerance' zone extends to c 3.3g, with a short gap to the start of the next at c 3.7g: only no 157 falls into that interlude. No other coin weighing less than 5g is actually excluded from one or other of the two weight systems. Consequently only two of the twenty-three lightest of the Hamwic Roman coins can be said positively not to have been weights, but that certainly does not mean that all or even any of the other twenty-one necessarily were! It has to be pointed out, for instance, that the 'exclusion' zones of 1.0 to 1.1g, 1.8g to 2.3g, 3.4g to 3.7g and 4.9g to 5.0g total only 1.4g, whilst the 'tolerance' zones total 2.6g. Nor does it take account of whether random collection of old Roman coins is likely to yield more which weigh between 1.1g and 1.7g than of heavier coins.

Some support for the idea that Roman coins were specially selected as weights comes from nos 163 and 176, which weigh 1.33g and 1.34g respectively, which are clearly candidates for quite accurate seven-*siliquae* units. Number 162, at 1.52g, could be an accurate eight-*siliquae* unit, and no 173, at 1.56g is close enough. Expressing the weights of all the coins in the 1g–2g range as a bar chart, however (Table 3), shows that these are not

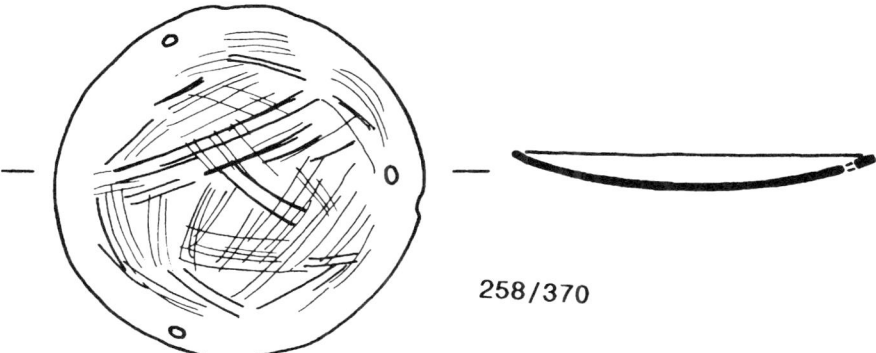

Figure 25.   Scale-pan.   Scale 1:1

distinctive: the absence of any coins weighing between 1.28g and 1.33g particularly reduces confidence that 1.33g was a 'target' (cf Metcalf 1993, 39: more of the English finds of *tremisses* are in that band than in any other). Similarly, no 158, at 3.10g, is very close to Smith's 'target' of 3.11g; but the bar chart (Table 3) demonstrates that there are none otherwise close to it. It now becomes useful to consider the weights in the various assemblages from graves (Scull 1990, tables), from which it becomes clear that very few indeed of those below 4g are at all close to any 'targets', although many can be fitted into a 1.33g unit system if deviations of up to 0.2g are allowed. It seems, therefore, that although most of the Roman coins from Saxon Southampton which weigh between 1g and 5g could have been used as weights, even those which seem to be good candidates may just have been random acquisitions. Nevertheless, a little comfort may be derived from no 163, which has an edge which looks as if it was deliberately cut, as though to reduce its weight (to 1.33g, an exact 'target'): it also has fairly clear extant designs, unlike many. It is not the only one that has been cut; four others have certainly been treated in this way (nos 119, 120, 121 and 187). It also has on the bust side what may be a deliberately made punch mark, a feature of many of the coins in cemetery sets (eg Scull 1990, fig 2).

At this point, the three heaviest coins can be considered. Number 155, at 4.75g, is just within a 0.2g tolerance range of a Byzantine *solidus* weighing a notional 4.55g, ie three eight-*siliquae tremisses*, but is not a weight that figures in the grave sets – nor is it close to any recorded late Saxon weight (one from York, at 4.95g, is the closest: Kruse 1992, 87). No 151, however, at 10.69g, is more likely to be significant: it is precisely the same weight as a coin, punched presumably to make it usable as a weight, in Canterbury Museum, and Smith pointed out that this is one-third of a troy ounce (1923, 127). The troy ounce system has close equivalence to the 'Kentish shilling' unit, since it divides into a grain weight of 0.065g (to three decimal places), and 20 grains of 0.065g equal 1.30g, which is close to the seven-*siliquae* 1.33g tremissis (Scull 1986, 122). At 10.69g, no 151 is very close to the point where the two weight systems coincide, at 10.64g (Table 2), so it probably really was being used as a weight, though it is not a unit known from later English sites (Kruse 1992, 87). Finally, no 152, at 19.36g, is a disappointment: there is nothing close to it either in the grave sets (Scull 1986) or in the towns (Kruse 1992, 87 or, for Winchester, Biddle 1990C, 912).

Scull's work was done on material from graves where the contexts make it likely that weight sets, or parts of sets, were present. Five of the Hamwic Roman coins (nos 155–9) were found together, in a pit, and could therefore be regarded as having been a set or part-set of some kind. There does not seem to be any reason to suppose that they could not have originated from a hoard, so it cannot be argued that they had been sought out over a period of time to make up a series. All the recorded sets from graves include several units which are much lighter than the lightest from the Southampton pit: this is no 158, already noted as very close at 3.10g to Smith's 'target' of 3.11g, or can be said to be 'acceptable' as a doubled eight-*siliquae tremissis* of 1.52g, ie 3.04g. Another in the group, no 155, at 4.75g, has also been noted as within range of the *solidus* of 4.55g. Three of the five appear to have been deliberately nicked, and no 158 may have been punched. Cumulatively, these points suggest that the group may indeed have been part of a set. No objects from the pit can be identified as non-coin weights, however. The combined total weight of the five coins is 19.11g – surprisingly close to no 152's 19.63g.

There is some reason to suppose from this discussion that a few of the Roman coins from Saxon Southampton might have been used as weights, but only a small minority even of those over 1g can be shown to have any possible significance, and the idea receives no support from Anglian York, as no Roman coins are reported from Fishergate (Rogers 1993). The paucity of other weighing equipment therefore may be explained by suggesting that weighing did not play a fundamental part in most of the transactions that took place in the town. One reason for this could be that gold was rarely seen – there are no finds of seventh-century gold coins, and the single gold ninth-century *solidus* (Pagan 1988B) may not have been valued as currency but as a 'primitive valuable'. Silver, in the form of sceattas, was widely used, but these coins were perhaps acceptable at face value: their weights vary far more than do those of the earlier gold *tremisses*, though leaching may have exaggerated the variation (Metcalf 1988, 37–51). Scull has pointed out (*in litt*) that the mid- to late seventh-century Barton-on-Humber assemblage did not fit any recognisable metrological pattern, so it may be that as the gold coins became increasingly scarce, weighing equipment was decreasingly used in England, until revived by Viking merchants, using weight systems different from the Merovingian and Byzantine of the earlier period (Kruse 1992). There is convincing evidence that the scales and weight sets in the sixth- and seventh-century cemeteries cannot necessarily be simply attributed to traders (Scull 1990, 207–8; and for a Viking leader's needs, see Wormald 1982, 132).

The paucity of scale-pans and balance-arms, and the limited and very uncertain evidence about the use of weights, suggests that Hamwic's merchants were dealing principally in commodities that did not require weighing; they were handling objects like glass vessels, selling slaves and bales of cloth, or buying wine, all of which were valued by eye and opinion, rather than by precise reckoning. This may have been the same in Anglian York: no weighing equipment is reported from the Fishergate site (Rogers 1993). Their successors in ninth-century and later York's Coppergate, Ipswich and London seem to have made much more use of weights (Kruse 1992, 87–9), which suggests different modes of trade. (Crude lead weights of no metrological significance are discussed as Identified Objects, below.)

TABLE 2
a) The heavier Roman coins from Hamwic

Metcalf number	Weight (g)	Site and item number
151	10.69	169/1865
152	19.36	125/101
153	1.14	24/794
154	2.93	20/27
155	4.75	11/117
156	3.75	11/118
157	3.66	11/119
158	3.10	11/120
159	3.85	11/121
160	1.66	169/317
161	1.02	15/370
162	1.52	169/1183
163	1.33	169/2823
164	1.22	169/3037
166	1.27	26/400
166 bis	1.97	85/7
167	1.21	169/1968
168	1.67	99/33
171	1.60	24/802
172	1.49	169/347
173	1.56	32/192
175	1.72	169/14
176	1.34	99/22
187	3.25	26/136
Later find	1.75	258/408

Note: Most weights have been checked against those in Metcalf 1988, 55–6. Coins or fragments weighing less than 1g have been omitted.

CATALOGUE

b) The Byzantine and Merovingian Systems compared

multiples	x1	x2	x3	x4
Byzantine system, c	1.52g	3.04g	4.56g	6.08g
possible 'tolerance' zone	1.3–1.7g	2.8–3.3g	4.3–4.8g	5.8–6.3g
Merovingian system, c	1.33g	2.66g	3.99g	5.32g
possible 'tolerance' zone	1.1–1.5g	2.4–2.9g	3.7–4.2g	5.1–5.5g
multiples	x7	x8	x13	x15
Byzantine system, c	10.64g		19.76g	
possible 'tolerance' zone	10.4–10.9g		19.5–19.9g	
Merovingian system, c		10.64g		19.95g
possible 'tolerance' zone		10.4–10.9g		19.7–20.2g

Table 2. Weights of Roman coins from Hamwic.

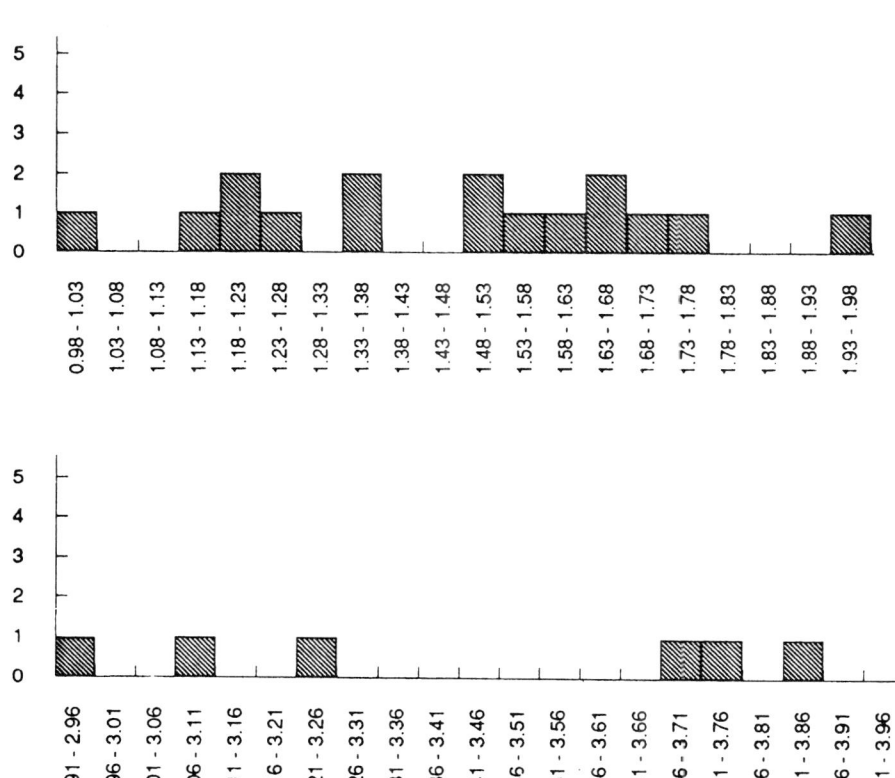

Table 3. Bar chart showing distributions of the weights of the Hamwic Roman coins.

OTHER IDENTIFIED OBJECTS (fig 26)

24 648 (not illus) ?Plug
Lead or pewter. Discoid, with ?stud on back.
Diam 21mm
Context 13624

26 585 (not illus) Clip
Copper or bronze, possibly tin-plated (AML).
Wire.
L 15mm
Context 1514

32 177 (fig 26) ?Ferrule
Copper alloy. Hollow, cast, tapering object.
L 45mm
Context F366, general clearance (not certainly an Anglo-Saxon context)
Published Addyman and Hill 1969, 70 and fig 27, 11

32 526 (fig 26) Weight
Lead alloy.
Diam 26mm
Context not known
Published Addyman and Hill 1969, 71 and fig 28, 3

36 117 (fig 26) ?Bell
Leaded bronze (XRF analysis, table 5) lining an iron outer case, much corroded. Sub-rectangular. Distorted suspension loop at the top. Broken at the bottom, but a small joining piece may include part of the lip. Inside, iron corrosion apparently partly preserving a straight, thin rod which may have been the clapper.
Ht 37mm, W 16mm
Context Pit 8

169 790 (fig 26) Weight
Lead alloy, with corroded iron attachment at top.
Diam 20mm
Context 8419

254 1305 (not illus) Tack
Copper alloy. Domed head.
Diam 11mm
Context 1305
Published Hinton 1993C, no 16. ?Post-medieval

254 1494 (not illus) Nail
Copper alloy. Flat-topped head.
L 19mm
Context 3976
Published Hinton 1993C, no 15

Although broken and corroded, the identification of 36/117 as a bell seems reasonably likely, although copper-alloy plating occurs on other objects such as padlocks. Iron bells with plated internal linings are known from a few graves of the sixth century or later (eg Tattershall Thorpe: Hinton 1993A, 160–1 and fig 10, a); two from women's graves at Kingston Down, Kent, are smaller than 36/117 (Bruce-Mitford 1983, 894–5). Cast copper-alloy bells are a little more common in England (*ibid*, 897–9). Although shrines in the shape of bells, and bells themselves, indicate ecclesiastical use in Ireland, there is nothing to suggest that they had exclusively religious associations in England, and may have had a range of entirely secular and prosaic functions.

None of the other three illustrated objects is indubitably Saxon. The presumed ferrule, 32/177, was described quarter of a century ago as having 'no exact parallel in the Anglo-Saxon period' (Addyman and Hill 1969, 70), which seems still to be true. Its solidity and its casting ridges make it seem out of place, and it is not from a proven Anglo-Saxon context. What are identified here as weights may have been used as net-sinkers, plumb bobs or for any similar purpose. 169/790 is not securely stratified, and may not be Saxon, but there is a lead object from Dorestad which has iron at the top, presumably for a loop (van Es and Verwers 1980, 189).

UNIDENTIFIED OBJECTS (fig 27)

5 70 (fig 27) Object
Copper alloy. Cast, broken object of uncertain use.
L (extant) 30mm
Context F14

11 91 (fig 27) Rod
Copper alloy.
L (extant) *c* 70mm
Context F15

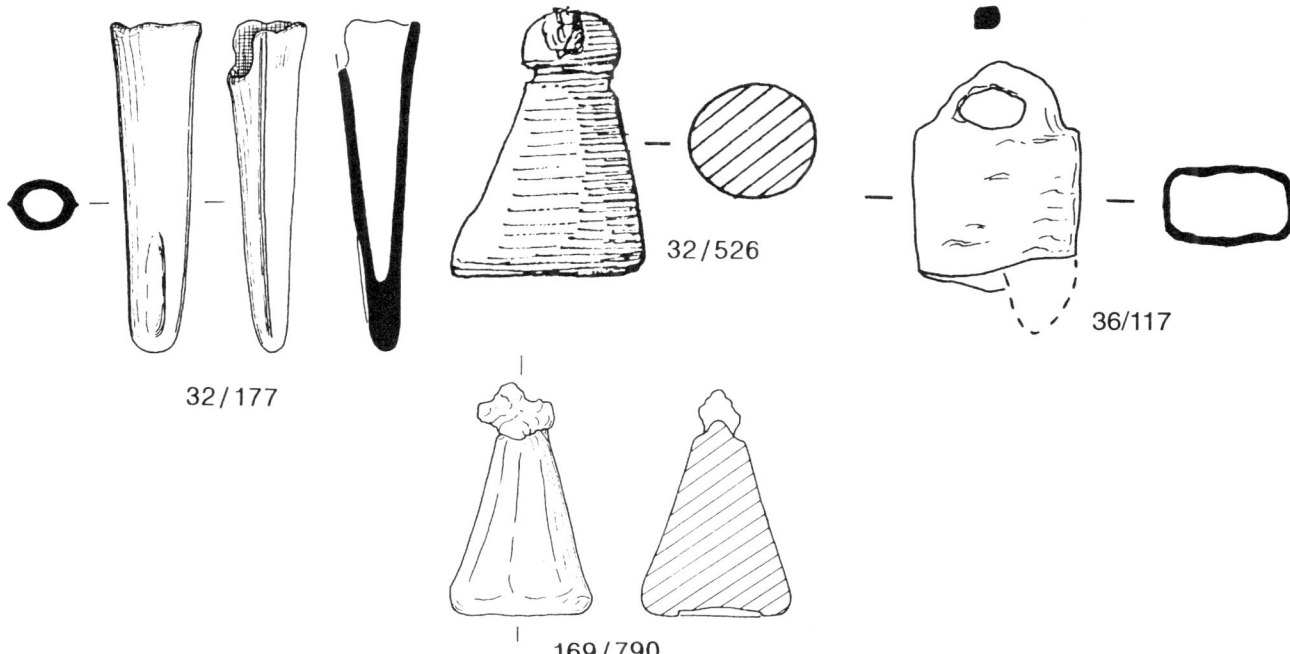

Figure 26. Other identified objects. Scale 1:1

18 16 (fig 27) ?Ring
Silver or silver-based metal. A length of ten tightly-twisted wires in herring-bone patterns, one end broken, the other a triangular terminal with a loop, into which the wires are fitted. The loop apparently drilled through an expanded end: a fragment of another wire passes through it.
L (extant) c 70mm
Context F24

20 6 (fig 27) Strip
Copper alloy. Flat sheet widening into lozenge-shaped field, with punched circles and dots. Both ends broken. Use uncertain.
L (extant) c 36mm
Context F70, 1
Published Hinton 1980, 73 and fig 13, 1 no 4

24 1 (fig 27) Block
Copper alloy. Cast, rectangular.
L 23mm
Context General clearance

24 26 (fig 27) Rod
Bronze (XRF analysis, table 5). Long rod with flattened end, broken.
Extant L 224mm
Context 9439

30 183 (fig 27) Strip
Copper alloy. One side punched with arrows and other lines. Broken.
L (extant) 45mm
Context 4410

31 2474 (fig 27) Rod
Copper alloy. Broken.
L (extant) 37mm
Context 6068

32 5 (fig 27) Object
Leaded bronze (XRF analysis, table 5). Semi-circular, hollow-sectioned cast object with transverse mouldings and four lugs, one broken and with iron corrosion in another.
L 33mm
Context F553
Published Addyman and Hill 1969, 70 and fig 27, 7

32 179 (fig 27) ?Ingot
Lead or lead alloy.
L 27mm
Context General clearance
Published Addyman and Hill 1969, fig 28, no 1

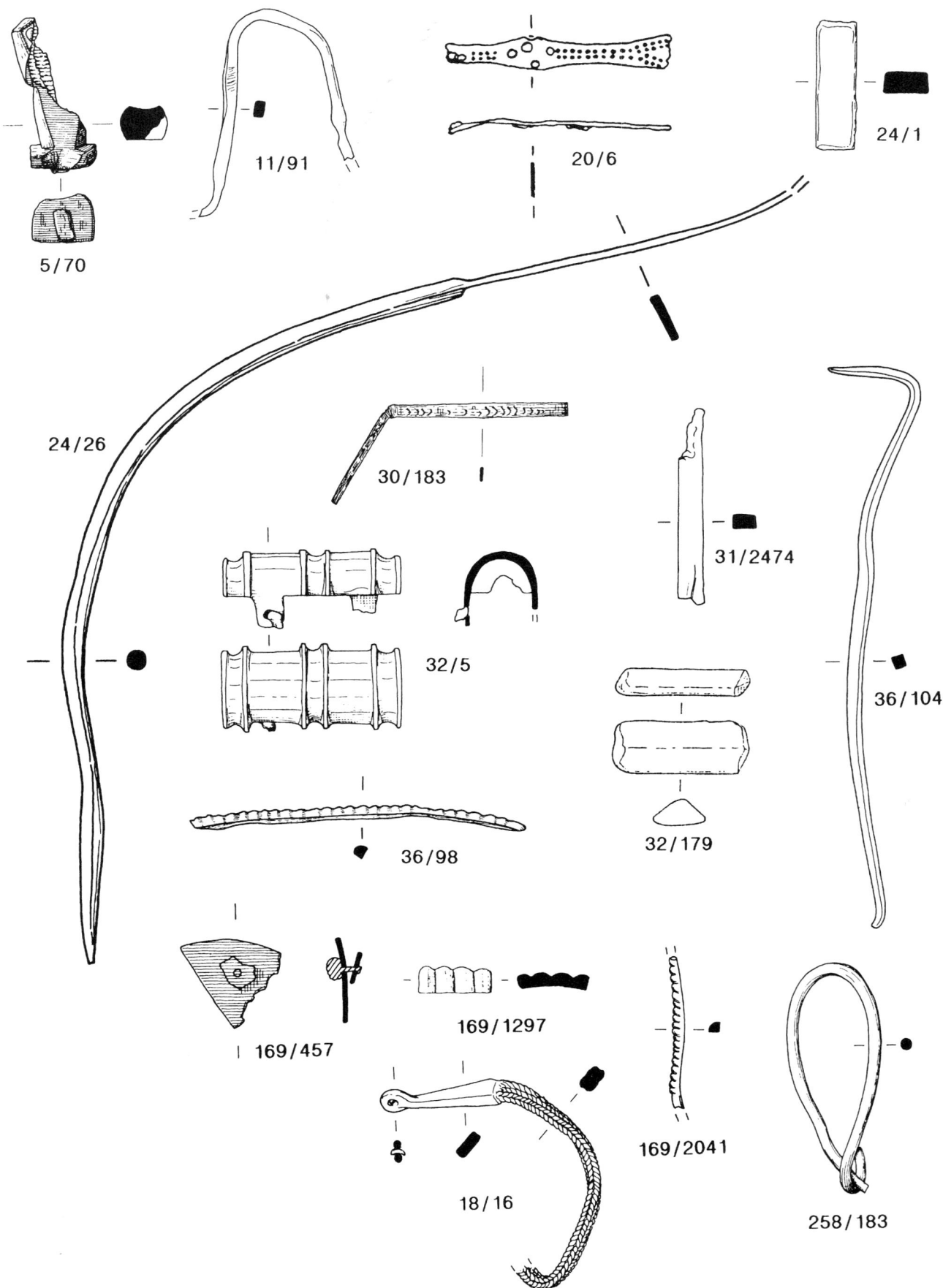

Figure 27.   Unidentified objects.   Scale 1:1

36 98 (fig 27) Bar
Copper alloy. Plano-convex section, with corrugated outer edge. Broken.
L (extant) 60mm
Context Pit 16, 4

36 104 (fig 27) Bar
Copper alloy. Square-sectioned bar, apparently cast. Possibly deliberately bent to present shape. Broken.
L (extant) c 130mm
Context Pit 6, 3

169 457 (fig 27) Sheet
Copper alloy. Fragment, pierced by rivet. X-ray photograph reveals two concentric lines with ring-and-dot ornament between them.
L (extant) 18mm
Context 8551

169 1297 (fig 27) Bar
Bronze (XRF analysis, table 5). Cast in ridges.
L (extant) 12mm
Context 12106

169 1821 (not illus) Object
Lead or lead alloy. Shafted, one end perforated, the other end with a semi-circular projection. Use uncertain.
L 38mm
Context 12339

169 2041 (fig 27) Bar
Copper alloy. Decorated edge.
L (extant) 28mm
Context 8419

258 183 (fig 27) Wire
Copper alloy. Looped and interleaving.
Present L 52mm
Context 908

A few items in this category are illustrated, despite uncertainty over their use and, in some cases, their date. 5/70 and 32/5 are both cast items; the latter in particular is doubtfully of Saxon origin, with its symmetrical mouldings. 258/183 may never have been meant for use. Several other pieces, such as 24/1, are illustrated because they may be ingots awaiting melting down, and should be considered with the metalworking residues described by Oddy, below.

There is considerable uncertainty about 18/16, which was originally thought to be of lead alloy, and relatively modern, despite its context, which was the fill of a post-hole which also contained two Anglo-Saxon pottery sherds, and is not thought to have been intrusive. Recent conservation has revealed that the object is in fact made of silver, or of a silver-based material, and it might therefore be part of an early medieval arm- or neck-ring. There are objections to this identification, however: the wires seem more evenly twisted than is usual with such rings, and they are more tightly pressed together; terminals on the early medieval rings are normally formed by hammering the ends of the wires together; if the rings are penannular, the terminals are usually left as knops, but if they are to be joined together to form a complete circle, they are usually knotted, not formed into loops; the few examples of loops at the terminals are usually open hooks, and the few which are closed are not usually slightly thickened; and when broken, the wire rings tend to separate into their different strands at the break. Furthermore, arm- and neck-rings tend to be tenth and eleventh century in England, as are the majority in the Scandinavian areas where they are most often found (eg Roesdahl and Wilson 1992, 200, 291, 303). None of these is a sufficient reason alone for 18/16 to be discarded from the list of Hamwic's Saxon objects, but cumulatively they seem to justify omitting it from further discussion until the metal can be analysed and its constituents compared to coins and other objects certainly of the period. It is too corroded for details of the way that it was worked to be clearly visible under a microscope.

METALLURGICAL ANALYSES OF PINS AND OTHER MID-SAXON COPPER-ALLOY OBJECTS FROM SAXON SOUTHAMPTON

(Adapted from Ancient Monuments Laboratory Report No 4344, submitted August 1984.)

BY PAUL WILTHEW

A large number of mid-Saxon copper-alloy small finds, about half of which were pins, from various sites in Southampton were analysed qualitatively by energy dispersive X-ray fluorescence (XRF). No surface preparation was carried out prior to analysis, and so, because X-ray fluorescence involves analysis of the surface, the results obtained will have been affected by alterations in the composition of the surface of the objects. Corrosion of base metal, the deposition of contaminants during burial and deliberate surface treatments such as tinning can all affect analytical results. For this reason each object or part of an object is described only in terms of an alloy type which can normally be assigned with confidence.

Apart from a few silver objects, the significant elements detected were copper, zinc, lead and tin, and the alloy name assigned to the copper-alloy objects depends on the proportions of zinc, lead and tin. The relationship between alloy name and composition is shown schematically in fig 28, in which the further an area within the triangle is away from the point labelled with an element's name, the less of that element is present. It can be seen that there are no sharp divisions between the different alloys, but general categories can nevertheless be usefully applied:

Bronze: an alloy containing copper and tin with, at most, a small amount of zinc

Brass: an alloy containing copper and zinc with, at most, a small amount of tin

Gunmetal: an alloy containing significant amounts of copper, zinc and tin.

In addition, if the results suggested that an alloy contained a few per cent or more of lead, it was

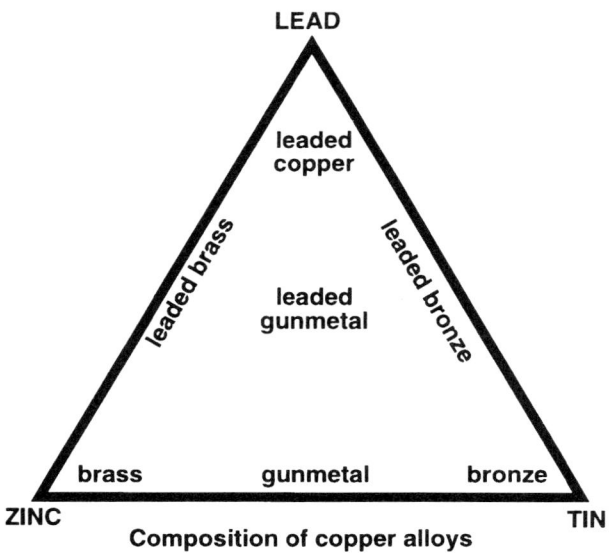

Figure 28. Ternary diagram to illustrate composition of copper alloys.

described as 'leaded'. Undoubtedly, some of the 'leaded' alloys contained much more lead than others, but it was not possible, with the method used, to estimate with any accuracy the amount of lead present.

PINS – TYPOLOGICAL GROUPS AND ANALYTICAL RESULTS
The results of XRF analysis of the objects identified as pins or parts of pins are given in Table 4. In each case the shaft was analysed. The head was also analysed if it appeared to be a separate piece of metal from the shaft. Although a large majority of the pins were either bronze or leaded bronze, there were significant variations in composition which it was hoped could be related to the typology of the pins. The pins were therefore assigned to various typological groups and the analytical results are discussed in terms of these groups.

Type A: Spherical-headed pins
There were few differences in the patterns of the analytical results between the pins with decorated heads of this type, the great majority being leaded bronze.

Type B: Polyhedral-headed pins
No correlation was observed between variations in composition and different head types, nor were those with decorated heads more likely to be in one alloy than another, in contrast to Type A pins. There was much greater variety among the twenty-eight pins with undecorated heads. The alloys found included leaded bronze, bronze, leaded gunmetal, brass and silver.

Type C: Bi-conical-headed pins
In this group, there was a difference between alloys used for different forms of the heads: all those with a simple bi-conical head, or with median bands, were either brass or leaded brass, but other variations were leaded gunmetal, leaded bronze or bronze.

Type D: Spiral-headed pins
All seven of the spiral-headed pins analysed were leaded bronze.

Type E: Disc-headed pins
Only two pins of this type were analysed and both consisted of a leaded bronze pin with a flat disc head (in the plane of the shaft) with a thin decorated bossed sheet attached (?soldered) to one side. The sheet on 169/634 was bronze with only a very low lead content, but the sheet on 169/568 was leaded bronze (although part of the high level of lead detected may have been due to contamination, from the pin (or the ?solder)).

Other pin types
These were too few for correlations to be apparent.

DISCUSSION
Overall, there appeared to be some correlation between the typology and composition of the pins, although too few examples of some types were analysed for any conclusions about those types to be drawn. Almost all the decorated spherical-headed pins were leaded bronze, and two of the exceptions were leaded gunmetal, a similar alloy but containing some zinc. The other Type A pin was, however, leaded brass. All the spiral-headed pins were also leaded bronze. Other types showed greater variation in composition, but two forms of bi-conical-headed pin were all either leaded gunmetals, bronzes, or leaded bronzes, in contrast to other forms which were made from brass or leaded brass – it is possible that the former would be better considered as subgroups of the spherical-headed pins (Type A) which were mainly leaded bronze.

The tendency of particular types of pin to have a specific composition could suggest that each type of pin was produced at a single site, or a limited range of sites, and that the alloy composition was deliberately controlled. If the pins had been produced at a large number of independent sites, or from arbitrarily selected scrap material, a wider range of composition would be expected. It is not possible to say whether different types were produced at different sites, or if several types were likely to have been produced at one site, nor, unfortunately, whether any types were produced for only limited periods. It is possible that the occasional pin of exceptional composition, such as the brass and leaded brass examples of Type B pins, were produced (perhaps locally) away from the main production site.

No archaeological information about the pins was available at the time that this report was prepared, so no attempt has been made to relate the analytical results to the archaeology of the various sites. It is possible that further conclusions could be drawn if the analytical results were considered in terms of the archaeology of the sites. It is also possible that the differences in composition between different types of pin relate to different methods of producing the pins. A more detailed metallurgical examination of at least some of the pins would be necessary to decide if this was the case. It would also now be possible to test any conclusions by analysing the more recent discoveries of pins of similar types.

OTHER OBJECTS – ANALYTICAL RESULTS

The analytical results for the objects other than pins are given in Table 5, together with an identification of each object. Several of the items analysed were fragments and could not be identified as forming part of a particular type of object. Some may have been scrap metal, and are described as fragments, others clearly formed part of an object, and are described as fragments of objects.

Numerous different types of object were analysed, but only a small number of any individual type was included. A wide range of alloys had been used but there was some correlation between object type and composition, notably amongst the tweezers, three of those analysed being bronze, and the fourth leaded bronze. Another pair of tweezers, however, 24/12, was formed from two bent strips of brass with the two strips apparently joined at one end with a lump of silver. The analysed brooches were all made from bronze or leaded bronze, whereas most of the buckles and strap-ends were brass or leaded brass.

The fragments, pieces of rod and pieces of channelled bar, which were largely from Site 8, were, in contrast, almost entirely bronze and leaded bronze although one leaded brass fragment was found. It is possible that much of this material was scrap or waste metal associated with metalworking (see Oddy in Morton, below), but traces of a much wider range of alloys have been found on crucibles from Saxon Southampton (see Bayley, below).

TABLE 4

Results of X-ray Fluorescence Spectrometry Analyses of Pins

Site	Item	Elements detected (see note)	Alloy Type
4	2	Cu Pb Sn Zn	Leaded bronze
4	4	Cu Zn (Pb Sn)	Brass
4	84	Cu Pb Sn Zn	Leaded bronze
4	89	Cu Pb Sn	Leaded bronze
5	1	Cu Sn Pb Zn	Leaded bronze
5	3	Cu Pb Sn Zn	Leaded bronze
5	6	Cu Pb Sn	Leaded bronze
5	74	Cu Zn Pb	Brass
8	19	Cu Pb Sn	Leaded bronze
8	33	Cu Pb Sn	Leaded bronze
8	44	Cu Pb Sn	Leaded bronze
11	1	Cu Pb Sn	Bronze
15	6	Cu Sn Pb	Leaded bronze
15	7	Cu Sn Pb Zn	Leaded bronze

CATALOGUE

Site	Item	Elements detected (see note)	Alloy Type
15	218	Cu Pb Sn	Leaded bronze
15	287	Cu Zn Pb Sn	Leaded gunmetal
20	1	Cu Sn Pb Zn	Leaded bronze
20	3	Cu Zn Pb	Brass
20	8	Cu Pb Sn Zn	Leaded bronze
23	2	Cu Zn (Pb)	Brass
23	4	Cu Pb Sn Zn	Leaded bronze
23	6	Cu Zn Sn (Pb)	Gunmetal
23	127	Cu Pb Sn	Leaded bronze
23	128	Cu Pb Sn (Zn)	Bronze
23	130	Cu Zn (Pb)	Brass
23	132	Cu Pb Sn	Leaded bronze
24	2	Cu Zn Pb	Brass
24	3	Cu Zn (Pb Ag)	Brass
24	10	Cu Sn Pb	Leaded bronze
24	13	Cu Zn Pb	Leaded brass
24	14	Cu Pb Sn	Leaded bronze
24	18	Cu Zn (Pb, Sn)	Brass
24	23	Cu Zn Pb Sn	Leaded gunmetal
24	24	Cu Pb Sn	Leaded bronze
24	819	Cu Zn Pb Sn	Leaded gunmetal
24	822	Cu Pb Sn Zn	Leaded bronze
24	826	Cu Zn (Pb)	Brass
24	30	Cu Pb Sn Zn	Leaded bronze
26	5	Cu Zn (Pb)	Brass
26	144	Cu Pb Sn	Leaded bronze
26	177	Cu Pb Sn	Leaded bronze
26	300	Cu Zn (Pb)	Brass
26	393	Cu Zn Pb Sn	Leaded brass
26	398	Cu Pb Sn Zn	Leaded bronze
26	624	Cu Ag	Silver, debased with copper
26	666	Cu Zn Pb Sn	Leaded gunmetal
26	674	Cu Zn (Pb)	Brass
26	679	Cu Pb Sn Zn	Leaded bronze
26	765	Cu Zn Pb	Brass
30	66	Cu Pb Sn	Leaded bronze
30	68	Cu Zn Pb Sn	Leaded gunmetal
30	72	Cu Pb Sn	Leaded bronze
30	73	Cu Sn (Pb)	Bronze
30	99	Cu Zn Pb	Brass
30	161	Cu Pb Sn	Leaded bronze
30	328 (Shaft)	Cu Ag Au Pb	Silver, debased with copper
"	" (Ring)	Cu Ag Au Pb	Silver, debased with copper
30	329	Cu Zn Pb	Brass
30	330	Cu Pb Sn	Leaded bronze
30	442	Cu Zn Pb Sn	Bronze
31	11	Cu Pb Sn Zn	Leaded bronze
31	157	Cu Pb Sn Zn	Leaded bronze
31	520	Cu Pb Sn	Leaded bronze
31	574	Cu Zn Pb	Leaded bronze
31	600	Cu Zn Pb Sn	Brass
31	672	Cu Pb Sn	Leaded bronze
31	677	Cu Pb Sn Zn	Leaded bronze
31	882 (Shaft)	Cu Zn Pb Sn	Leaded gunmetal

Site	Item	Elements detected (see note)	Alloy Type
31	882 (Ring)	Cu Zn (Pb)	Bronze
31	982	Cu Zn Pb Sn	Leaded gunmetal
31	1025	Cu Pb Sn Zn	Leaded bronze
31	1058	Cu Pb Sn	Bronze
31	1258	Cu Pb Sn	Leaded bronze
31	1428	Cu Pb Sn Zn	Leaded bronze
31	1434	Cu Pb Sn	Leaded bronze
31	1460	Cu Zn Pb Sn	Leaded gunmetal
31	1466	Cu Ag Zn Au Pb Sn	Silver, debased with copper
31	1487	Cu Pb Sn	Leaded bronze
31	1562	Cu Pb Sn (Zn)	Leaded bronze
31	1563	Cu Zn (Pb Sn)	Brass
31	1567	Cu Pb Sn	Leaded bronze
31	1644	Cu Pb Sn (Zn)	Leaded bronze
31	1645	Cu Pb Sn	Leaded bronze
31	1648	Cu Pb Sn	Leaded bronze
31	2102	Cu Zn Pb (Sn)	Leaded brass
32	157	Cu Pb Sn	Bronze
32	159	Cu Pb Sn	Leaded bronze
32	160	Cu Zn Pb Sn	Leaded gunmetal
32	161	Cu Zn (Pb)	Brass
32	162	Cu Zn Pb	Leaded brass
32	163	Cu Pb Sn	Leaded bronze
32	164	Cu Zn Pb (Sn)	Leaded brass
32	165	Cu Zn Pb Sn	Leaded gunmetal
32	167	Cu Pb Sn	Leaded bronze
32	168	Cu Pb Sn (Zn)	Leaded bronze
32	171	Cu Pb Sn Zn	Leaded bronze
32	420	Cu Pb Sn	Leaded bronze
34	88	Cu Zn Pb Sn	Leaded brass
35	5	Cu Pb Sn Zn	Leaded bronze
36	95	Cu Pb Sn Zn	Leaded bronze
36	97	Cu Pb Sn	Leaded bronze
38	42	Cu Pb Sn	Leaded bronze
39	41	Cu Pb Sn	Bronze
39	44	Cu Pb Sn	Bronze
39	45	Cu Pb Sn Zn	Leaded bronze
85	14	Cu Sn Au Hg (Pb, Zn)	Mercury-gilded bronze
99	25	Cu Zn Pb Sn	Brass
99	136	Cu Zn Pb	Leaded brass
169	1	Cu Pb Sn	Leaded bronze
169	21	Cu Pb Sn	Leaded bronze
168	180	Cu Zn Pb (Sn)	Leaded brass
169	213	Cu Pb Sn Zn	Leaded bronze
169	245	Cu Zn Pb Sn	Gunmetal
169	327	Cu Pb Sn	Leaded bronze
169	341	Cu Pb Sn Zn	Leaded bronze
169	442	Cu Zn Pb	Leaded brass
169	555	Cu Pb Sn	Leaded bronze
169	568	Cu Pb Sn Zn	Leaded bronze (both parts)
169	616	Cu Pb Sn	Leaded bronze
169	634	Cu Pb Sn Zn	Leaded bronze (sheet = bronze)
169	748	Cu Ag (Zn, Au, Pb, Sn)	Silver
169	817	Cu Pb Sn	Leaded bronze

CATALOGUE

Site	Item	Elements detected (see note)	Alloy Type
168	818	Cu Pb S̲n̲ Zn	Bronze
169	914	Cu P̲b̲ S̲n̲	Leaded bronze
169	915	Cu P̲b̲ S̲n̲	Leaded bronze
169	1163	Cu P̲b̲ S̲n̲	Leaded bronze
169	1286	Cu P̲b̲ S̲n̲	Leaded bronze
169	1408	Cu P̲b̲ S̲n̲	Leaded bronze
169	1409	Cu A̲g̲ Au Pb Sn	Silver
169	1447	Cu P̲b̲ Sn Zn	Leaded bronze
169	1503	Cu Zn P̲b̲ S̲n̲	Leaded bronze
169	1504 (both)	Cu Zn Pb	Leaded brass
169	1605	Cu Zn Pb	Leaded brass
169	1698	Cu Zn (Pb)	Brass
169	1747	Cu Zn P̲b̲ Sn	Leaded brass
169	1867	Cu Zn Pb Sn	Leaded gunmetal
169	1905	Cu P̲b̲ S̲n̲	Leaded bronze
169	1973	Cu Z̲n̲ Pb	Leaded brass
169	2140	Cu P̲b̲ S̲n̲	Leaded bronze
169	2244	Cu A̲g̲ (Zn Au Pb)	Silver
169	2376	Cu Pb Sn	Leaded bronze
169	2390	Cu Z̲n̲ Pb	Leaded brass
169	2418	Cu Pb S̲n̲ Zn	Leaded bronze
169	2469	Cu Z̲n̲ P̲b̲ S̲n̲	Leaded gunmetal
169	2499	Cu P̲b̲ S̲n̲	Leaded bronze
169	2568	Cu Pb S̲n̲ Zn	Bronze
169	2955	Cu P̲b̲ Sn	Leaded bronze
169	2998	Cu Z̲n̲ P̲b̲ S̲n̲	Leaded gunmetal

Note: Elements present at particularly high levels (except copper in copper alloys) are underlined. Minor elements in brackets.

Table 4. Results of X-ray fluorescence spectrometry analyses of pins.

TABLE 5
Results of X-ray Fluorescence Spectrometry Analyses of Objects other than Pins

Site	Item	Object Type		Elements detected (see note)	Alloy Type
2	4	Decorated strip		Cu Pb S̲n̲	Bronze
4	5	Tweezers, curved edge		Cu S̲n̲ (Pb)	Bronze
4	7	Strip with square perforated ends		Cu Zn Sn (Pb)	Gunmetal
5	2	Decorated plate	Front	Cu Z̲n̲ Pb	Brass
5	67	Rod		Cu P̲b̲ S̲n̲ (Zn)	Leaded bronze
5	71	Strap-end		Cu A̲g̲ Pb	Silver
6	1	Rod, partially flattened		Cu S̲n̲ Pb	Bronze
7	1	Brooch – square-head		Cu S̲n̲ Pb	Leaded bronze
8	1	Strip		Cu Pb Sn	Bronze
8	2	Fragments (? of brooch)	Rod, lumps	Cu P̲b̲ S̲n̲	Leaded bronze
			Lumps	Cu Sn (Pb)	Bronze
8	3	Fragment		Cu Pb Sn	Bronze
8	4	Fragments		Cu Pb Sn	Bronze
8	5	Fragments	Rod	Cu Z̲n̲ Pb Sn	Leaded brass
			Plate and lumps	Cu S̲n̲ Pb	Leaded bronze
8	6	Fragments	Sheet	Cu Sn (Pb)	Bronze

Site	Item	Object Type		Elements detected (see note)	Alloy Type
			Lump	Cu <u>Sn</u> Pb	Bronze
8	20	Rod		Cu <u>Pb Sn</u>	Leaded bronze
8	21	Channelled bar		Cu <u>Pb Sn</u>	Bronze
8	22	Rod		Cu <u>Sn</u> Pb	Bronze
8	23	Fragments	Sheet	Cu <u>Pb Sn</u>	Leaded bronze
			Rod and lump	Cu Sn Pb	Bronze
8	24	Channelled bar		Cu <u>Sn</u> Pb	Bronze
8	25	Plate fragment		Cu <u>Sn</u> Pb	Bronze
8	26	Chain links		Cu <u>Sn</u> Pb	Bronze
8	27	Fragments	Rod and lump	Cu Sn Pb	Bronze
				Cu <u>Sn</u> Zn	Bronze
8	28	Fragment		Cu <u>Sn</u> Pb	Bronze
8	29	Channelled bar		Cu <u>Sn</u> Pb	Bronze
8	30	Rod		Cu Sn Pb	Bronze
8	31	Strip		Cu <u>Sn</u> Pb	Bronze
8	32	Fragments		Cu <u>Sn</u> Pb	Bronze
8	34	Bar		Cu <u>Sn</u> Pb	Bronze
8	35	Fragments (? of chain link)		Cu <u>Sn</u> Pb	Bronze
8	36	Fragment		Cu <u>Sn</u> Pb	Bronze
8	37	Rod fragments		Cu Sn Pb	Bronze
8	38	Fragment		Cu <u>Sn</u> Pb	Bronze
8	40	Fragment		Cu <u>Sn</u> Pb Zn	Bronze
8	41	Rod fragment		Cu <u>Pb Sn</u> (Zn)	Leaded bronze
8	42	Rod fragment		Cu <u>Sn</u> Pb	Bronze
8	43	Channelled rod		Cu <u>Sn</u> Pb	Bronze
11	3	Strap-end		Cu Zn Pb Sn	Leaded gunmetal
13	1	Decorated (? ornamental) object	Bars	Cu <u>Pb Sn</u> Zn	Leaded bronze
			Plate and lumps	Cu <u>Pb Sn</u>	Leaded bronze
13	2	Buckle	Ring	Cu Zn Pb Sn	Gunmetal
			Bar	Cu <u>Zn Pb Sn</u>	Leaded gunmetal
13	49	Twisted strip		Cu (Pb)	Copper
13	58	Ingot		Cu <u>Pb Sn</u>	Leaded bronze
15	1	Brooch		Cu <u>Pb Sn</u>	Leaded bronze
15	2	Fragment of object		Cu <u>Zn Pb Sn</u>	Leaded gunmetal
15	4	Strap-end		Cu Ag (Pb, Zn, Sn)	?
15	282	Bar		Cu Zn Pb Sn	Gunmetal
20	9	Small buckle	All parts	Cu <u>Zn</u> (Pb)	Brass
23	10	Buckle plate		Cu <u>Zn</u> Pb Sn	Leaded brass
23	129	Strap-end		Cu <u>Zn</u> (Pb, As)	Brass
23	134	Equal-arm bow-brooch		Cu <u>Sn</u> Pb	Leaded bronze
24	7	Flat 'spoon-shaped' strip		Cu Sn Pb	Leaded bronze
24	12	Tweezers	Strips	Cu <u>Zn</u> (Pb)	Brass
			Join	<u>Cu</u> Ag Zn Pb Sn	Silver
24	26	Rod with flattened end		Cu <u>Sn</u> Pb Zn	Bronze
24	83	Strap-end		Cu <u>Zn Pb</u> Sn Ag	Leaded gunmetal
24	83	Buckle loop (?)		Cu <u>Zn</u> Pb Sn	Brass
25	63	Brooch		Cu Zn <u>Pb</u> Sn	Leaded bronze
26	145	Decorated plate		Cu Zn Pb Sn	Leaded gunmetal
26	181	Strap-end. Traces of silver on front may be remains of coatings or niello		Cu <u>Zn</u> Ag Pb	Leaded brass
26	193	Decorated plate		<u>Cu</u> Ag Au Pb Sn	Silver debased with copper or silver plated
26	593	Rod and plate	Plate and rod	Cu Pb <u>Sn</u>	Leaded bronze

CATALOGUE

Site	Item	Object Type		Elements detected (see note)	Alloy Type
			Small fragment	Cu Pb	Copper
30	177	Strap-end		Cu P̲b̲ S̲n̲ Zn	Leaded bronze
30	178	Double-ended hook		Cu (Pb Sn)	Copper
30	266	Rod and chain	Both parts	Cu S̲n̲ Pb	Bronze
30	356	Decorated plate		Cu S̲n̲ (Pb)	Bronze
31	101	Strip		Cu S̲n̲ Pb	Leaded bronze
31	547	Strip with wide, grooved end		Cu Z̲n̲ Pb	Brass
31	653	Finger-ring		–	Mercury-gilded bronze
31	1391	Hook or mount		Cu Sn Pb	Leaded bronze
31	1647	Hook or mount		Cu S̲n̲ Pb	Bronze
32	5	Half cylinder with lugs		Cu P̲b̲ S̲n̲	Leaded bronze
32	170	Hooked tag		Cu Zn Pb Sn	Leaded gunmetal
32	172	Strap-end		Cu Z̲n̲ Pb (Sn)	Leaded brass
33	86	Ring – flat band		Cu Z̲n̲ (Pb)	Brass
34	6	Brooch		Cu S̲n̲ (Pb)	Bronze
34	8	Double-ended hook		Cu Zn (Pb)	Brass
34	84	Tack		Cu (Pb Sn)	Copper
36	96	Object (cast)		Cu P̲b̲ S̲n̲	Leaded bronze
36	99	Strap-end		A̲g̲ (Cu Au Pb)	Silver
36	103	Finger-ring – mount missing		Cu Z̲n̲ Pb Sn	Brass
36	117	?Bell		Cu P̲b̲ S̲n̲ Fe	Leaded bronze (+ iron)
36	120	Lump		Cu Sn (Pb)	Bronze
38	40	Tweezers		Cu S̲n̲ (Pb)	Bronze
38	41	Bar		Cu P̲b̲ S̲n̲ Zn	Leaded bronze
39	43	Decorated rod		Cu P̲b̲ S̲n̲ (Zn)	Leaded bronze
99	75	Tweezers		Cu Pb Sn	Bronze
99	91	Mount (?)		Cu S̲n̲ Pb	Bronze
169	238	Twisted wire		Cu P̲b̲ Sn Zn	Leaded bronze
169	318	Buckle	Ring	Cu Zn Pb (Sn)	Leaded brass
			Bar	Cu Zn Pb (Sn)	Leaded brass
169	397	Strap-end. Silver may be remains of inlay or coating		C̲u̲ Z̲n̲ P̲b̲ Ag Sn	Leaded brass
169	48	Hooked tag		Cu Z̲n̲ P̲b̲ Sn	Leaded brass
169	66	Strip		Cu P̲b̲ S̲n̲	Leaded bronze
169	1270	Strap-end with niello (or possibly silver) inlay on front	Front	Cu Zn Ag Pb	Brass
			Back	Cu Zn Pb	Brass
169	1297	Shaped lump		Cu S̲n̲ (Pb)	Bronze
169	1515	Hook or mount		Cu P̲b̲ S̲n̲	Leaded bronze
169	2037	Strap-end		Cu Z̲n̲ P̲b̲ Sn	Leaded gunmetal
169	2169	Strap-end with niello or (possibly) silver on the front	Front	Cu Zn Ag (Pb)	Brass
			Back	Cu Zn (Pb)	
169	2548	Tweezers with ring	Tweezer	Cu P̲b̲ S̲n̲ Zn	Leaded bronze
			Ring	Cu S̲n̲ Pb	Bronze
169	2622	Decorated hook		Cu Z̲n̲ Pb	Leaded brass
169	2700	Wire ring		Cu Zn (Pb Sn)	Brass
169	2831	Disc		Cu Z̲n̲ P̲b̲ S̲n̲	Leaded gunmetal

Note: Elements present at particularly high levels (except copper in copper alloys) are underlined. Minor elements in brackets.

Table 5. Results of X-ray fluorescence spectrometry analyses of objects other than pins.

NON-FERROUS METALWORKING EVIDENCE

THE EVIDENCE OF METALWORKING FROM SAXON SOUTHAMPTON, SITE SOU 8

By A D MORTON

INTRODUCTION

The report on this site has already been published (Morton 1992, 87–95), but sections are repeated here because of the importance of the metalworking evidence that was located. The site was just to the north of the modern Standford Street (frontispiece), and was excavated in January 1973 by mechanical removal of topsoil, followed by hand-cleaning of the top of the surviving natural soil, usually referred to as brickearth, which here overlies gravel.

Occupation of this area of Hamwic seems to have commenced in the eighth century, probably early in that century, and to have ended at some point in the ninth century. A feature of this occupation was the industrial use of copper alloy, an activity seemingly confined to the easternmost part of the site. Direct evidence of this industry is provided by the objects recovered mainly from two pits, F41 and F48.

THE PITS (fig 29)

F 41 (fig 29) was sub-rectangular in plan and section, and survived to a maximum depth of 2.5m. Its relationship with the post-holes, F33 and F34, is discussed below. Ploughing across the top of this pit was probably partly responsible for the creation of F32e.

The bottom layers were 'fine greensand' (layer 7), containing charcoal and small pieces of burnt clay, and a thin, intermittent layer of charcoal (layer 6). Layer 7 was a small patch in the southern half of the pit and contained no diagnostic finds. Its colour may have derived from staining from the cuprous objects present in this pit in large quantity. Layer 6 was generally confined to the centre of the pit. It contained a small amount of burnt clay and twenty fragments of animal bone. It may represent the bottom of a burning layer, but there is no record that the natural soil into which F41 was cut was heat-discoloured. In view of its inclusion, the layer is perhaps best interpreted as a secondary, mixed deposit. Immediately over layer 6 was layer 5, 'orange clay' or 'light brown/yellow clay with charcoal'. This was also confined to the centre, with some slag, a small amount of burnt clay, and about seventy fragments of animal bone. Its origins appear to have been threefold: as redeposited brickearth, as domestic refuse, and as industrial waste.

Layer 2, which covered all these, appears to have been two layers separated from each other by a 'charcoal lens with some bone' (layer 3). The finds records indicate that more than seventy bone fragments were recovered from layer 3, a few of which had been stained green through contact with cuprous objects. Also found was fuel-ash slag with traces of copper. It seems, therefore, that layers 3 and 6 represent repeated actions, perhaps the dumping of mixed deposits, and that the two parts of layer 2 were also connected with the charcoal layers. Layer 2 was described as 'black [or grey] clay with much

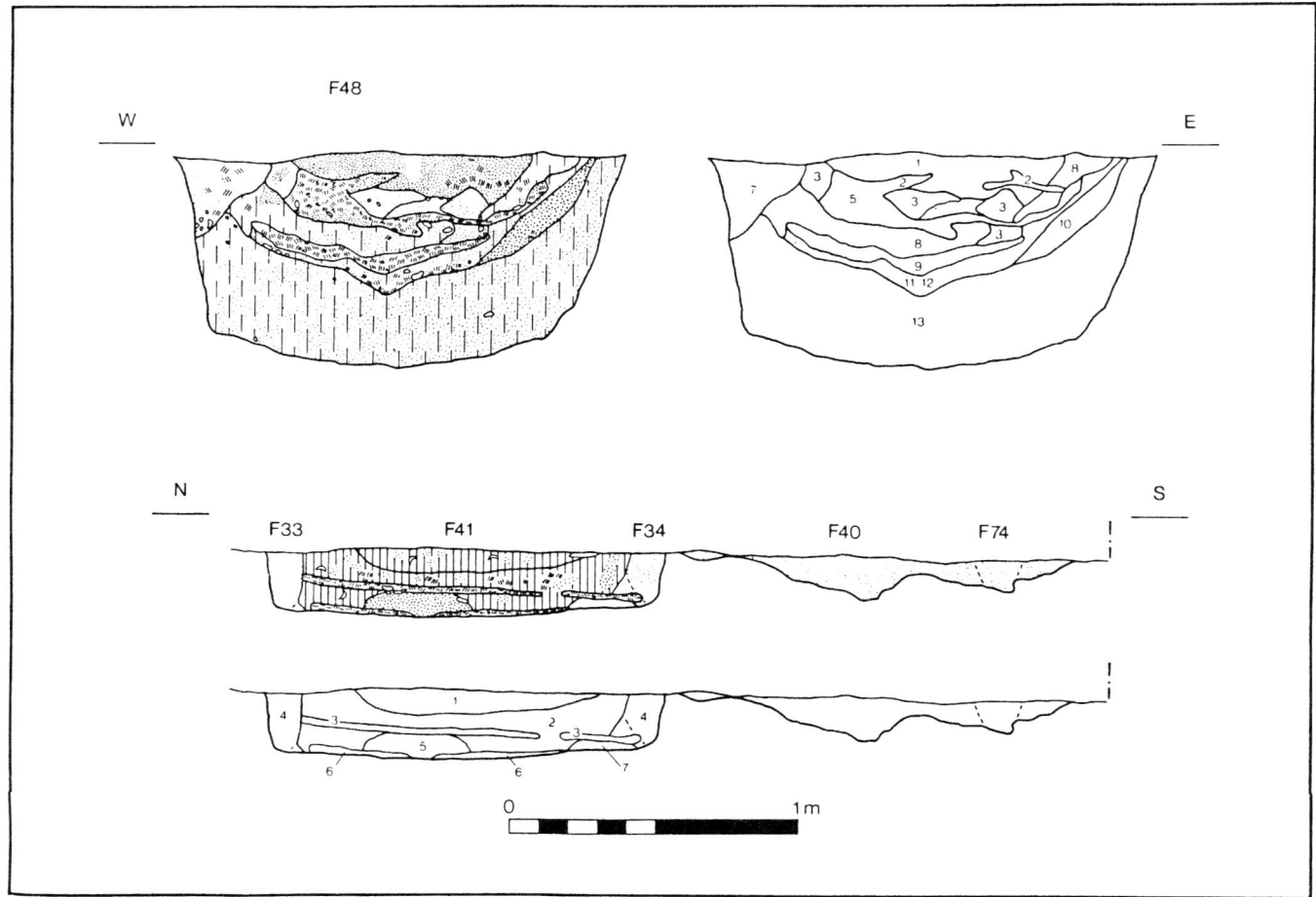

Figure 29. Site SOU 8, pits F41 and F48. Originally published Morton 1992, fig 20.

charcoal'. The charcoal seems generally to have been connected in the upper half, where small inclusions of 'clean orange clay' or 'yellow clay' were also found. These inclusions, scattered throughout the layer, were probably comparable with layer 5. In its entirety, the layer contained 'several small bronze fragments' and the shaft of a pin, the rim sherd of a copper-alloy-working crucible, and three tile fragments, all of which are considered below; about sixty fragments of animal bone, some of which had been stained green; and a small amount of burnt clay and oyster shell. Like layers 3 and 6, layer 2 appears to have been a mixture of domestic rubbish and industrial waste.

Layer 1, 'black clay with much charcoal' or 'with some dirty brown clay and a few oyster shells', was similar to layer 2, though it was perceived to be darker. It (or perhaps layer 2) contained a complete copper-alloy-working crucible, discussed below, a small amount of burnt clay, and animal bone, some of which was stained green.

Layers 1–3 and 5–7 can be interpreted as a series of dumps of domestic and industrial waste. Layer 4 is less easy to interpret. It is shown on plans as a continuous deposit of yellow 'brickearth'. But on the section drawing it is divided into the parts shown in fig 29 and is described as 'silty brown clay (post-holes?)', which scarcely touches the bottom of the pit. Drawn on the overall site plan are several stains within F32e, two of which have been interpreted by this writer as post-holes and numbered F33 and F34. These putative post-holes are not shown on the layer plans of F41, which, however, do not show the entire length of the excavated feature. 'Two large stake-holes on either (north–south) edge of the pit' are mentioned in the site notebook. All this contradictory evidence might be taken as showing firstly that the

METALWORKING EVIDENCE

pit was lined along its sides with redeposited brickearth, and secondly that it was later cut by two post-holes, or perhaps combined a lining with post-holes. Against this interpretation must be set the fact that a great many finds are provenanced to layer 4; some stone, including a piece of sandy limestone (perhaps comparable with that found in layer 5), a complete copper-alloy-working crucible, three grooved tile fragments, and about 115 fragments of animal bone. It is possible that the crucible, stones, and tiles were all redeposited into the fill of F33 and F34, but at least the majority of animal bone must have been recovered from layer 4. This seems a strange inclusion to find in a deliberate lining, and it is probable that layer 4, like layer 6, was a dump of brickearth, domestic rubbish, and industrial waste. It is likely that, shown on the section drawing, are two post-holes and a small remnant of layer 4. The relationships of these post-holes are considered below.

F48 (fig 29) was oval in plan and sub-rectangular in section, though with an eastern side that deviated from the vertical by some 23°. It survived to a depth of 0.78m.

The depositional history of the pit is not easy to unravel, especially since the original records contradict one another or are otherwise incomplete. Thirteen layers were numbered in the site notebook; fourteen in the finds cards; and in the quadrant plans the highest-numbered was layer 13. The layers were not numbered on the section drawing. Descriptions of the layers in the site notebooks, the section drawing, and the plans are all at variance. With two minor exceptions there is no strong guide to the order of the layers. That they were not necessarily numbered in stratigraphic order is proved by the statement in the site notebook that 'under layer 5 was layer 3'. It is likely that separate, but similar, layers were given one number. The confusion may have been compounded by the method of excavation, which consisted of the serial removal of adjacent quadrants.

The writer has sorted out this muddle to his own satisfaction only insofar as he can certainly identify layers 1, 7, and 13. The location of layers 2–6 and 8–12 are perhaps as shown on the published version of the section. The existence of a fourteenth layer cannot be proved: it was probably listed on the finds cards after an error in transcription. (Note that these given numbers are an attempt to reconstruct the excavator's view of the infilling: they do not exactly represent the writer's view.) Because of all these doubts, and despite the importance of understanding the depositional history of this pit, there is little point in describing each layer in its variously described detail.

There seem to have been three main phases in the infilling of this pit. In the first phase, it was filled with 'darkish green-brown clay with much bone, charcoal, and small gravels' (layer 13). This was thought to have been a rubbish fill. Later, perhaps after the layer had subsided, a complex series of layers had been thrown into the pit. These, which comprise the second phase of filling, are interpreted below. Finally, after they in turn had subsided away from the edge of the pit, there was a final fill of 'very dirty brown clay' which contained some charcoal, a piece of burnt daub, and one piece of animal bone. This layer probably resulted in part from a natural weathering of the earlier layers.

It is the second phase of infilling that is of most importance here; a phase where, unfortunately, only one of the ten numbered layers can be identified with any great confidence.

There were three or four layers of charcoal. The lowermost one was an intermittent spread that may not have been numbered, or been numbered layer 12 ('medium brown clay with many charcoal flecks – flint pebbles'). Higher in the pit was a thick charcoal layer, underlying and in part containing a spread of burnt clay. This was perhaps layer 9 ('very black clay with charcoal'). Even higher was a thick bifurcated dump of charcoal, intermixed with 'yellow clay'. The lower branch may have been layer 5 ('charcoal, dense to the bottom') and layer 6 ('deep brown silty clay with charcoal – within layer 5'); and the upper branch may have been layer 2 ('charcoal with patches of yellow clay').

Over the intermittent spread of charcoal (layer 12) were layers described on the section drawing as 'clean, light brown clay' (brickearth?) and 'grey brown clay with compact round pebbles'. The first of these was probably layer 10 ('light brown clay mixed with charcoal') which was 'clean' in that it contained no finds. The second may have been layer 11 ('dark brown clay with many charcoal flecks – flint pebbles').

Over the charcoal layer supposed to have been layer 9 was a small patch of 'charcoal staining', perhaps taken by the excavator as part of layer 3 (described in the following paragraph), and a 'dark brown clay' layer. This was probably layer 8, which was similarly described in the site book; the main difference being the addition of the epithet 'dirty' – a word probably explained by the inclusions of charcoal within the layer, shown on the section drawing. Other inclusions, as shown on the drawing, were burnt clay, 'yellow clay', and green-stained bones. None of these is mentioned elsewhere. The 'clays' may have been removed as part of the higher layers, and the green-stained bones, none of which is listed in the finds records for layer 9, may similarly have been included with material from layers 4 or 5.

The depositional history of the upper 0.3m of the layers in the pit is most difficult to unravel. Over, under, and among the forked layer of charcoal are shown patches of 'yellow clay'. (Some of these, it is suggested above, were numbered as layer 5, and others mentioned only as 'patches of yellow clay'.) An intermittent spread of 'charcoal staining' appears between the bifurcations, below the lower branch of charcoal, and apparently as a western continuation of the charcoal layer. (It was perhaps all numbered as layer 3, 'green-brown clay with charcoal flecks'.) Interspersed with the 'charcoal staining' appear patches of 'dark brown clay' and 'medium brown clay with fine gravel'. The former was removed perhaps as layer 8 (described in the previous paragraph), and the latter perhaps as layer 4 ('light brown clay').

It may be argued with hindsight that the excavator, faced with this hotchpotch of soils, effected an expedient but unfortunate compromise: he should have described it either as far more than four layers (layers 2–5) or as a single, very mixed layer. This mixture seems to have extended into the top layer, layer 1 (described in the site notebook as 'orangey brown clay' and on the section drawing as 'hard dry brickearth'), for the upper branch of charcoal as well as charcoal lenses intrude into this layer and into lower layers. Some of this may have resulted from later, natural disturbance: even so, at least the final part of the second phase of infilling appears to have been a mixture that accumulated within a short space of time. The layers comprising the earlier part of the phase may have been layers of *in situ* burning, but those comprising the final part were probably secondary deposits, deriving perhaps from the stratified layers in another pit, and confused in the process of clearing them out. If such an interpretation is allowed, these layers may be compared with those in F41, especially layer 5, supposed to have been of threefold origin (see above).

A domestic origin for much of the material dumped during the second phase of infilling may be inferred from the comparatively large amounts of animal bone recovered. Some 240 fragments are recorded in the finds cards, a third of which (79) came from layer 3, a quarter of which (58) from layer 4, and large fractions of which came from layers 1 (20), 2 (39), and 11 (35). Two points are apparent. In the first place, the majority of the fragments came from what has been interpreted as the layer part of the infilling: 81.7% or 195 fragments from layers 1–4. The contrary fact, that few bones were recovered from the lower layers, may support the argument that the earlier part comprised *in situ* burnt layers. The small amount of animal bone from layer 5 (six fragments) may be an indication that at least part of this layer was itself part of the burning. Secondly, the animal bone from the upper layers (layers 1–4) was found in a large variety of deposits; brickearth, charcoal, and brown clays. This fact may be further evidence that the later part of the infilling comprised mixed, secondary deposits.

Much of the bone found in layers 1, 2, 4 and 5 (or 8, according to the section drawing) had been stained green through its nearness to cuprous objects. Evidence for copper-alloy working, which is considered in greater detail below, principally comprised the rim sherds from two crucibles (item 15), found in layer 1; a 'heating tray' (item 13), found in an unknown layer; an ingot mould of lias limestone (item 94), found in layer 8; and two fragments of tile in layer 3. These latter fragments may have no more significance than the pieces of Roman brick found in the western half of the trench (in F7, F25, and F28), but it seems more likely that too had been parts of a mould such as were recovered from F41. Found almost exclusively in layers 2–5 (the exception is item 26 from layer 11), and especially in layer 2, were thirty-two copper-alloy items that might have been directly connected with the nearby copper-alloy working.

The heating of copper alloy in crucibles may have been done in this pit, early in its second phase of use. The 'compact round pebbles' (layer 11?) may have been used to form a hard base to a hearth, and the burnt clay overlying the supposed layer 9 may have been the remains of another lining. However, there were no

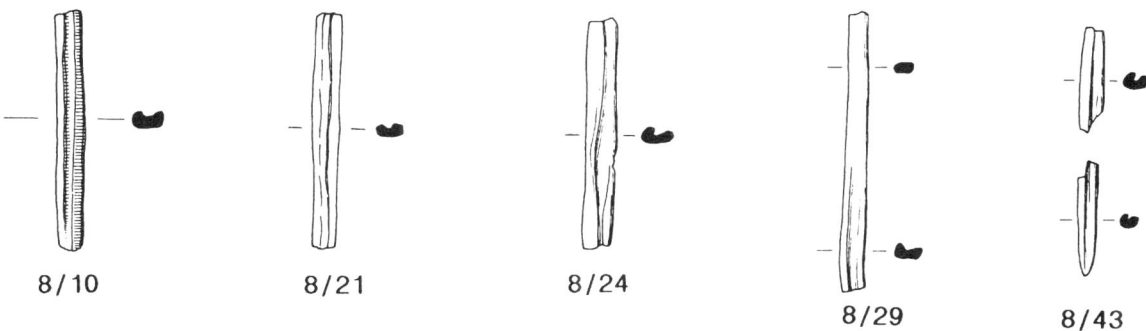

Figure 30. Debris perhaps from the manufacture of copper-alloy wire by folding.   Scale 1:1

indisputable signs of *in situ* burning – most notably no sign of heat-discoloration of the underlying layers. One might conclude therefore that the heating of copper alloy occurred close to F48, but probably not inside it.

Of the thirty-six copper-alloy objects, or groups of small fragments, the vast majority was recovered from F48: thirty (83.3%) from layers 2–5, one (2.8%) from layer 11, and one from an unspecified layer. Twenty-three of these items can be recognised as finished objects, mainly pins. Again, the majority was found in F48: nineteen objects (82.6%), all recovered from layers 2–5. However roughly, this preponderance of copper-alloy objects in the upper layers of F48 points to a connection with the copper-alloy-working evidence largely recovered from the same contexts. It is curious, therefore, that no more than 'several, small bronze fragments' were recovered from F41. Although admittedly it was considerably smaller than F48, F41 may have been filled at the same time as F48 and otherwise seems to have been filled in a similar manner. It is possible that some distinction was preserved in the use of these two pits – a distinction perhaps indicated by the fact that all the grooved tiles were found in F41 (see below) and all the grooved stone either in or near to F48 (see below), which also contained all the objects thought to have been evidence of the manufacture of wire, described by Oddy below. However, the narrowness of the site precludes any spatial analysis; and it is scarcely possible to argue for instance that, of the two pits, one approaches a norm and one deviates from it.

SCRAP-METAL FRAGMENTS (fig 30)
BY AD MORTON AND WA ODDY

Scrap metal seems to be represented by at least two fragments from pit F48, 8/79 and 8/80, and by objects described below by Oddy. The site also yielded the usual range of objects and broken fragments, some of which may of course have been manufactured there. Three objects, 8/21, 8/24 and 8/29, were submitted for comment; a fourth is illustrated as it is clearly another example (fig 30).

WA Oddy comments: these pieces might have been debris from the manufacture of wire by the process known as folding. The technique dates back to the Bronze Age in the Middle East, but there is some evidence that it was used much later in Sweden. The scarcity of evidence reflects the lack of work on the metallurgical study of fragments of wire from the medieval period rather than any implication that the technique was unusual at a later period.

MOULDS, CRUCIBLES AND CUPEL
BY AD MORTON

These are described below by Morton and Bayley. Fragments of ten crucibles were found on Site 8, four from the upper layers of pit F41 (8/14, 8/17, 8/18 and 8/70), others from the upper layers of pit F48 (8/15, 8/69, 8/81, 8/82 and 8/83). A piece of a cupel was found in pit F48. Four tiles and two stones grooved for use as moulds were found in F41 (details below).

A MORTAR FOR GRINDING GOLD AND MERCURY FOUND IN SAXON SOUTHAMPTON, SITE SOU 169 (fig 31)

DESCRIPTION

During the excavation of one of the Six Dials sites in the northern part of the Saxon town, a nearly square, flat stone with a hemispherical depression in the centre (SOU 169/752, fig 31) was found in a shallow pit (F10272), and it was observed that flecks of a gold-like yellow substance and traces of black and reddish powder were visible on its surface. The stone has subsequently been identified as having been used for grinding together gold and mercury, and was therefore used in preparing materials for fire-gilding artefacts, a few of which have been found in Hamwic, such as the two finger-rings and a few pins, eg 85/14 and 169/2959. There was no other evidence of the craft in pit F10272, but there was a small hearth (F10081) nearby; there were also three lead 'runners' deposited just to the west (Andrews 1995, forthcoming). The pit and hearth were contained within a building, Structure 61, which may eventually have been destroyed by fire. There is no substantial dating evidence associated with these features, but their phasing is assigned to the first half of the ninth century (*ibid*).

169 752 (fig 31)
Stone, Pennant Sandstone, from the top of the Carboniferous, Mendip/Bristol area outcrops (identification by DPS Peacock). Sub-rectangular, having hemispherical depression on one side, and flecks of gold and mercury amalgam embedded in it.
L (max) 380mm, W 140mm
Context 10272

REPORT ON THREE SAMPLES TAKEN FROM THE GRINDING MORTAR BY DR HOOK AND MS TITE, BRITISH MUSEUM RESEARCH LABORATORY
(Adapted from British Museum RL File 4964, submitted November 1983.)

Samples were sent for examination and possible identification of any metallic elements present in order to try to determine the function of the stone. The largest sample (20672W), from a 'flaw hole' in the

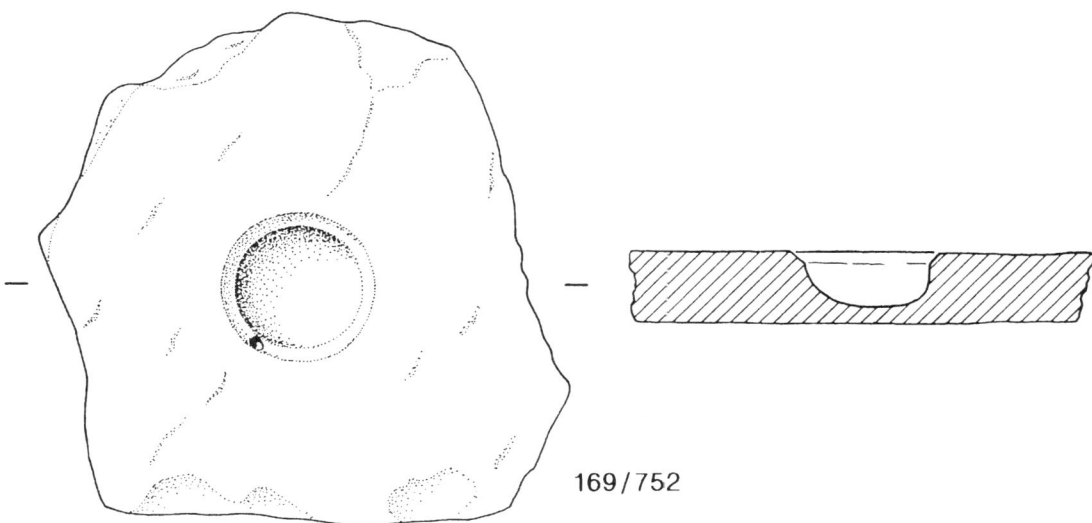

Figure 31. Stone grinding mortar. Scale 1:2

depression in the centre of the stone, was examined with a Link System energy dispersive X-ray fluorescence spectrometer (XRF), and part of it was also examined by the more sensitive emission spectroscopy method. The latter was used also on sample 20673U, taken from the surface of the depression. Neither method yields quantifiable data under these conditions of sample preparation.

Sample 20672W (yellow metal and black powder): i) XRF detected Au, Ag and Pb, with traces of Cu and Fe. Yellow specks visible on the sample were probably a gold alloy containing silver, lead and copper. The iron was likely to have been a component of the stone, or to have derived from deposition circumstances.

ii) Emission spectroscopy detected Au, Ag, Cu, Pb, Hg and Si, with traces of Zn, Fe, Mn and ?Co.

Sample 20673U (yellow metal and reddish powder): Emission spectroscopy detected Au, Ag, and Cu, with traces of Pb and Hg.

The detection of mercury (Hg) in both samples examined by emission spectroscopy suggests that the depression in the stone was used as a mortar for preparing an amalgam for use in mercury-gilding. As a relatively low temperature is required to drive off the mercury during the actual gilding process, it is likely that a hearth rather than a furnace would have been used and therefore the remains of an adjacent hearth may be significant. The reddish powder in 20673U is likely to be a mercury salt, probably the oxide or sulphide.

The stone is an important find as representing the first identified remains of Dark-Age gilding equipment. It also adds mercury-gilding to the crafts practised at Hamwic.

FIRE-GILDING IN EARLY MEDIEVAL EUROPE
BY WA ODDY, BRITISH MUSEUM DEPARTMENT OF CONSERVATION

(This note was written by Dr Oddy in 1985 and is printed with his permission; it has not been amended to take account of subsequent discoveries.)

Until recently, the only evidence for the technique used in the gilding of silver, copper, bronze and brass in the Roman and medieval periods has resulted from the scientific examination of numerous relevant objects (Lins and Oddy 1975; Oddy 1985; Oddy 1988), combined with the evaluation of the meagre contemporary texts. Of the latter, by far the most important is the book written under the pseudonym of Theophilus (Hawthorne and Smith 1963) in the early twelfth century, and this clearly describes the fire-gilding process as it is understood today. Before the twelfth century there are two seventh- or eighth-century compilations of recipes (Smith and Hawthorne 1974; Burnam 1920) and a fourth-century one (Halleux 1981), but these either give little detail or have become corrupt with repeated copying.

Nevertheless, the general picture is now clear, with fire-gilding having become the standard process for the gilding of silver and copper from about the third century AD, having been rather rare before that in the Classical world, although it was known in China in about the fourth or third century BC. How it reached the Mediterranean from China, if indeed that is what happened, is unknown, but fire-gilding appears to have been unknown to the Parthians in Iran (Oddy and Meeks 1978) while commonplace in the succeeding Sasanian era (Lins and Oddy 1975; Harper and Meyers 1981).

The technique of fire-gilding is relatively simple. First the surface of the silver or copper alloy must be scrupulously cleaned by a mixture of abrasion and chemical cleaning and then mercury is rubbed on. In modern traditional practice the mercury is first mixed with powdered charcoal (Oddy, Bimson and La Niece 1981). Once the surface has been amalgamated in this way, the gold is applied either by laying pieces of gold leaf on to the surface or by rubbing on a mixture of gold and mercury. This mixture was usually made by dissolving gold leaf or powder in hot mercury and then squeezing through a chamois leather when cool to remove excess mercury.

When the gold has been applied evenly all over the surface by either method, the object is heated over hot embers to boil off the mercury and leave behind a firmly bonded layer of gold. This technique of gilding often leaves several characteristic features on the surface (Oddy 1988), but the unequivocal evidence that this method of gilding has been used is the detection of residual traces of mercury in the gilded layer by means of a suitable technique of analysis (usually X-ray fluorescence or emission spectrography).

Clearly one other source of evidence for the use of fire-gilding is the finding of traces of the actual process. At Hérouvillette in Normandy, a Merovingian-period grave was found which contained metalworking tools along with some metallic mercury (Decaens *et al* 1971, grave 10). Mercury was also found in the Viking-period town of Haithabu in four separate places, but unfortunately this cannot be associated with other metalwork debris with any certainty (Ulbricht, I, pers comm; Drescher 1984). A third find of mercury from the early medieval period was in a jewellery workshop in Lund, southern Sweden, dating from about AD 1100 (Bergman and Billberg 1976). Here, however, the mercury was associated with moulds and evidence for casting and there is a high probability that the presence of mercury is an indication that fire-gilding was in use.

Apart from the presence of mercury providing direct evidence for the use of fire-gilding, evidence for the working of gold might provide indirect evidence of the process on some sites. At Faccombe-Netherton in Hampshire, for instance, metalworking was clearly being practised in a ninth- or tenth-century context and scraps of gold were found on the site, together with at least one fire-gilded object and a crucible with globules of gold embedded in the fabric (Fairbrother 1990, 263–4). Similarly, three fragments of crucibles from the Saxon palaces at Cheddar were shown to contain traces of gold (Rahtz 1979, 258) as did some crucible fragments from the tenth-century Viking site of Coppergate, York (Bayley, J, pers comm, and, now, Bayley 1992A, 794–8). Unfortunately none of these sites provided direct evidence for fire-gilding, but the rarity of solid gold objects in the late Saxon/Viking period compared with the widespread occurrence of fire-gilded ones may indicate that evidence for gold working is to be associated with the gilding process.

From the Six Dials site in Hamwic, however, there seems to be irrefutable evidence of fire-gilding in the form of the stone with a hemispherical depression containing traces of gold which itself contains some mercury, along with numerous other elements. This object must be interpreted as a mortar for grinding together the gold and mercury to form an amalgam. This technique is a variant on the method of making the amalgam by adding gold to hot mercury in a crucible, but grinding in a mortar would produce a perfectly good amalgam, albeit rather more slowly.

In the context of fire-gilding in the Dark Ages there is one more facet of the gilding process which is of interest, and that is the composition of the substrate copper alloys. Fire-gilding does not work well on copper alloys containing large amounts of lead or zinc, and in the Romanesque period most gilt 'bronzes' are not actually bronze at all, but copper containing few or no additional elements, other than tin (Oddy, La Niece and Stratford 1986, 9–11). Even true bronze (copper and tin) does not appear to have been as easy to gild as pure copper, but whether the importance of composition was known in the Dark Ages, is, as yet, impossible to say.

Very few analyses of related types of gilded and ungilded objects of early medieval date have been analysed and those that have suggest that the smiths were not aware of the importance of removing zinc and lead from the alloy (see appendix 1 in Oddy, La Niece and Stratford 1986). This general picture is confirmed by the qualitative analyses of the gilded objects from Hamwic (Wilthew, above) which are mostly made of leaded bronze etc, only one piece of wire being apparently made of fairly pure copper which was then fire-gilded (24/419).

CLAY PIECE-MOULDS (fig 32)

By JUSTINE BAYLEY

Thirteen clay piece-moulds were found in the excavation of Cook Street, in the south part of Saxon Southampton, site SOU 254. They have been published previously in Bayley 1993B, but are republished here to complete the Southampton corpus.

254 2293 (fig 32, 1–3)
Three clay piece-mould fragments, being the edge of one lower and one upper valve and a fragment from an upper valve. XRF analysis of the lower valve revealed the presence of traces of zinc and lead.
L (extant) 54mm, 32mm and 23mm
Context 4432

254 2294 (not illus)
One clay piece-mould fragment, from upper valve.
L (extant) 19mm
Context 4403

254 2315 (fig 32, 4–7)
Four clay piece-mould fragments, being two edges and two corners of lower valves.
L (extant) 42mm, 18mm, 21mm and 26mm
Context 4432

254 2321 (fig 32, 8)
One clay piece-mould fragment, being the corner of a lower valve, with ?in-gate.
L (extant) 23mm
Context 4443

254 2322 (fig 32, 9)
Three clay piece-mould fragments, two joining, being from upper valves, one with in-gate.
L (extant) 32mm, and 25mm
Context 4443

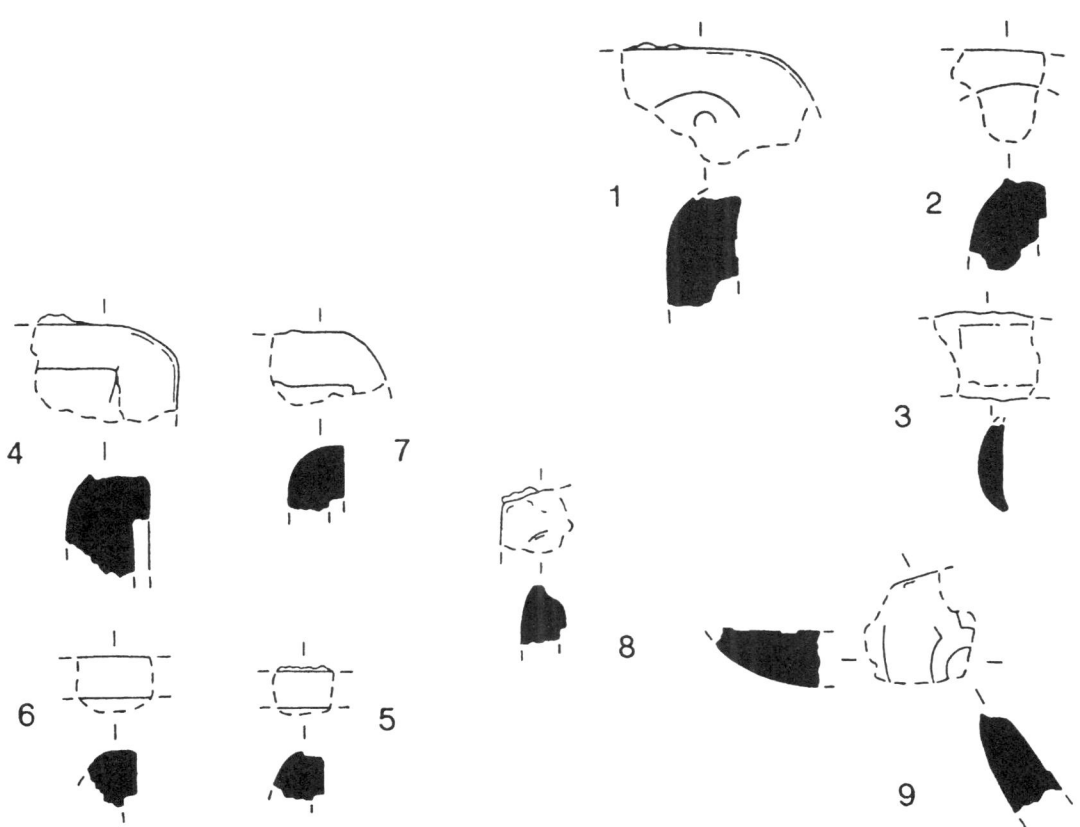

Figure 32.   Clay piece-moulds. Originally published Garner 1993, fig 33.   Scale 1:2

254   2350 (not illus)
One clay piece-mould in-gate fragment, with massive traces of metal adhering. XRF analysis revealed the presence of traces of zinc, lead and copper.
L (extant) 28mm
Context 4174

These moulds are the first clay piece-moulds that have been recognised from Saxon Southampton and are one of only a small number of groups of clay moulds of this period known from England (Bayley 1991). Some of the fragments definitely come from the lower valve of a two-piece mould while others which are less massive and have a convex rather than flat outer surface come from the upper valve. Several pieces are from the in-gate (sprue cup), one of which (in 254/2321) is definitely part of a mould valve; the others may also be parts of valves or may have been added to the two-piece mould assembly together with the luting clay which sealed the valves together. Massive traces of the metal poured into the mould survive on the in-gate fragment 254/2350.

As is normal with piece-moulds, the pattern in the lower valve is deep, with a less substantial impression in the upper valve. No complete impression of the object being cast survived; all that could be seen with any certainty were impressions of perforated circular discs on two of the 254/2293 fragments and one from 254/2322 (see fig 32). All the mould fragments are reduced-fired all through.

XRF analysis of clay moulds is usually uninformative. The slight traces of zinc and lead detected on the modelled area of the lower valve in 254/2293 show that it had been used, but provide no information on the composition of the metal being cast. The metal-rich deposit on in-gate 254/2350 indicates a copper alloy, though the presence of zinc and absence of tin in detectable quantities is probably not significant (see discussion of interpretation of XRF results in Bayley, below).

The context of these moulds is considered in the discussion of the crucibles and cupels that accompanied them (below).

STONE MOULDS (fig 33)

BY A D MORTON AND JUSTINE BAYLEY

Two stone moulds were recognised from site 8, but unfortunately both are now missing. The record cards state that both were blocks of lias limestone, but do not say who made the identification.

8   94 (fig 33)
Stone mould. ?Lias limestone. Sub-rectangular, with two grooves cut into one face: one 115mm long, 15mm wide, 11mm deep; one *c* 20mm wide, otherwise unrecorded. Charcoal adhered to at least one of the grooves. (Object now mislaid, description derived from record card and published illustration.)
L *c* 62mm, W *c* 34mm
Context F48
Published Keen 1975 and fig 15, 1

8   95 (fig 33)
Stone mould. ?Lias limestone. Approximately hexagonal, with a groove 125mm long, 15mm wide and 12mm deep cut into one face. (Object now mislaid, description derived from record card and published illustration.)
L *c* 52mm, W *c* 22mm
Context F46 (a post-hole 0.8m from F48, 2m from F41)
Published Keen 1975, and fig 15, 2

32   194 (fig 33)
Stone mould. Hard chalk (identified by DPS Peacock). Approximately square. In-gate at top. For casting a small ring.
L 52mm, W 54mm
Context General clearance (not definitely Saxon)
Published Addyman and Hill 1969, 68 and fig 25, no 5

169   1461 (not illus)
Stone mould. ?Limestone (identification uncertain). Described as 'a mould which would have produced several smaller rings'. Now mislaid.
Dimensions not recorded
Context 11961 (not definitely Saxon)

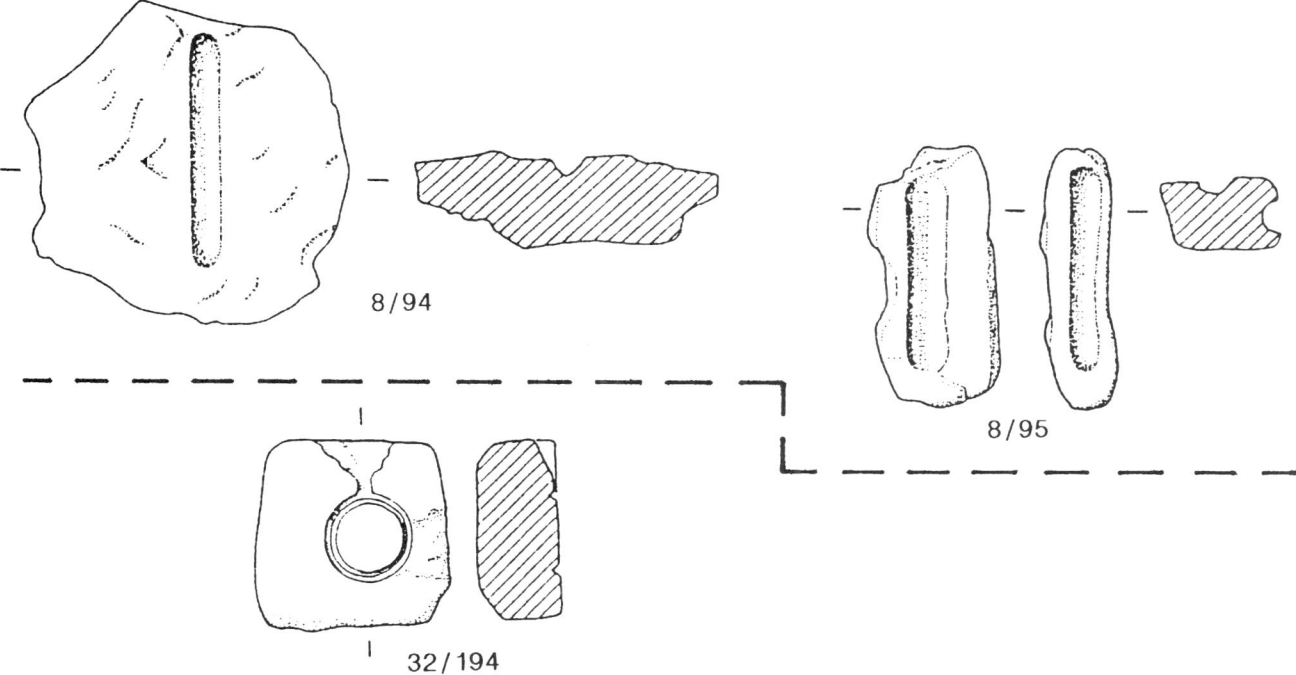

Figure 33. Stone ingot moulds. 8/94 and 8/95 originally published Keen 1975, fig 15, nos 1 and 2. Scales 1:2, 32/194; 1:4 8/94 and 8/95

TILE MOULDS (fig 34)

BY A D MORTON

Four fragments of tile, thought to be Roman, were found in site 8, pit F41, each with a shallow groove cut into one face:

8 89 (not illus)
Tile. Groove on one face originally longer than 17mm, 6mm wide, 4mm deep. Charcoal smears and signs of burning around the groove. Mortar adhering to underside.
Temporarily mislaid, measurements not recorded
Context F41, 2

8 91 (fig 34)
Tile. Groove originally longer than 75mm, 11mm wide, 4mm deep. Charcoal smears and signs of burning around the groove. Mortar adhering to the underside. (Object now mislaid, description derived from record card and published illustration.)
L c 120mm, W 100m
Context F41, 4
Published Keen 1975, 179 and fig 15, 4 (numbering of 90 and 91 is thought to have been transposed on the record cards)

8 92 (fig 34)
Tile. Groove originally longer than 51mm, 3mm wide, 4mm deep. Charcoal smears and signs of burning around the groove.
Extant L 130mm, W 90mm
Context F41, 4

Ceramic building material was also found in features 7, 25, 28 and 48, probably plundered from a Roman building. A tile in F48, 8/93, had been scored for keying, but had no groove cut into it and had no traces of burning. If used as a mould, all traces had been obliterated.

Simple ingot moulds occur at various early medieval sites, including now Anglian York (Rogers 1993, 1236–7). Those from Southampton may have been used for either precious or base metals; they have not been analysed for surviving traces of silver or copper alloys, but such analyses are not always successful.

A broken mould reusing a Roman tile was found in a pit containing late eleventh-century rubbish in London, and tile was similarly used in York and Haithabu, presumably because it provided a surface that could be more easily channelled than many stones, and had a reasonably smooth texture (Pritchard 1991, 166–7).

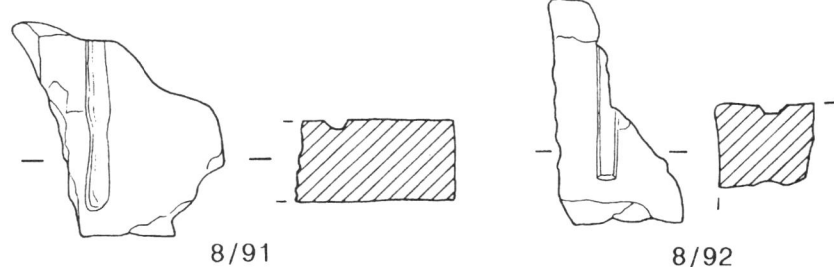

Figure 34. Tile ingot moulds. Originally published Keen 1975, fig 15, nos 4 and 5.   Scale 1:4

CRUCIBLES AND CUPELS (fig 35)

By JUSTINE BAYLEY

Fragments of crucibles have been found at ten sites in Saxon Southampton (Tables 6–16), two being sites where other metalworking evidence has been recognised, sites SOU 8 (Morton 1992, 87–95 and above) and SOU 254: the latter material has already been published, but is repeated here for completeness. Some non-crucible material was also examined. This included vitrified clay hearth lining from sites 23, 24, 34 and 169, and a tuyere from site 169. Crucibles are recorded from all but site 23 so these finds provide further evidence of metalworking. From site 8 came two groups of copper-alloy spillages and sheet fragments, 8/79 and 8/80. The spillages were analysed by X-ray fluorescence (XRF) and shown to be bronze (see Table 6).

CRUCIBLE FORM AND FABRIC

Most of the crucible fragments seem to come from vessels of the same form as the complete crucibles, that is, small, hand-made thumb pots with rounded bases. Several were illustrated by Addyman and Hill (1969, fig 25). They are of variable wall thickness, being thinnest at the rim and gradually thickening towards the base. This means that the thickness of individual body sherds cannot be related to the size of the vessels from which they came. The complete vessels show that the rim is not usually circular as pinched-out pouring lips and distortion during use both contribute to their irregularity. For this reason no attempt has been made to estimate the diameters of the vessels represented by the rim sherds. Most of the complete and nearly complete vessels range from 20–40mm external diameter and their brimful volumes are about 10–15ml. One sherd, 31/2204, indicates a diameter in excess of 60mm.

The exceptions to the standard form include similar hand-made vessels with walls that are far more uniform and only a few mm thick (eg 31/2668), and a globular vessel, 254/1303 (fig 35), which had a maximum diameter of 60–70mm, and was c 60mm high, with walls 6–8mm thick. Two sherds, 30/164 and 30/558, are quite different from the rest in both form and fabric. They come from rather larger, wheel-thrown vessels whose form is reminiscent of many Roman crucibles (eg Bayley 1984). Their coarse fabric is shared by two further rim sherds from sites SOU 17 and 31 which are similar in profile to 30/558 and so may come from similar vessels. The sherd from site SOU 17 has an external rim diameter of about 100mm while that of 30/558 is about 70mm.

Twenty-four contexts at site SOU 254, mostly of mid-Saxon date, produced sherds from crucibles, as well as clay piece-moulds (above). The fragments from post-Conquest contexts are indistinguishable from the earlier finds and are most likely to be residual. Many of the crucible fragments were very small (under 5mm, marked * in Tables 6–16) and were collected from samples that were wet sieved; their coloured and

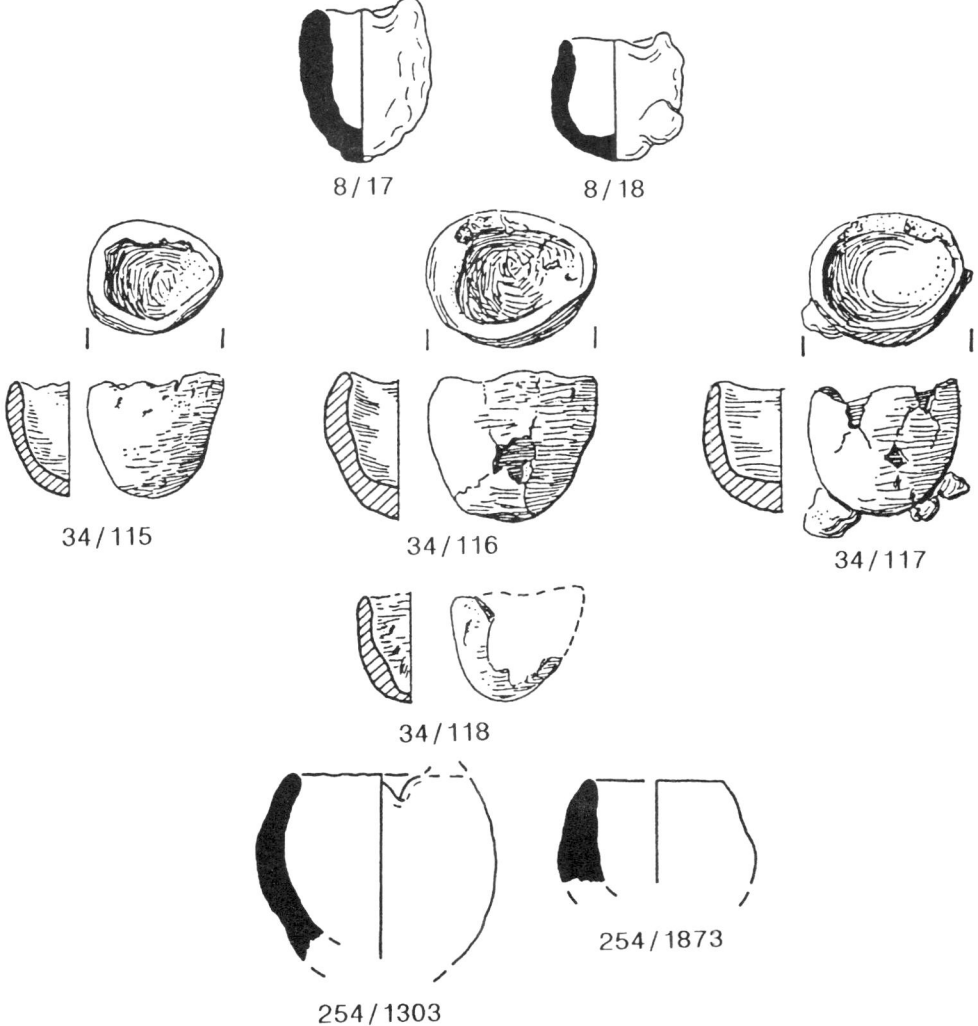

Figure 35. Crucibles from three Southampton sites. Scale 1:2

vitrified surfaces were easily recognised by those sorting the residues. (There are no corresponding small mould fragments, probably because small lumps of fired clay were not picked out.)

A single sherd, 31/2224, deserves some further comment. It appears to be a knob or lug from a crucible which could have acted as a handle. Crucibles of this type are rare in Britain, except in the Highland Zone (eg Youngs 1989). Other examples are now known from mid-Saxon contexts at Church Close, Hartlepool (Bayley 1988B) and Fishergate, York (Bayley 1993A).

In addition to these metal-melting crucibles a number of sherds from cupels were noted. Before their function was properly understood, they were identified as 'heating trays', a term coined by Roesdahl (1977) to describe these small, shallow dish- or disc-shaped vessels. They are now known to have been used for assaying or purifying small amounts of precious metals (Bayley 1988A). Tables 6–16 have three columns describing the individual sherds. The first describes the part of the vessel represented (eg rim or body sherd) or identifies it as part of a cupel. The second column records the thickness of the sherd in mm and the third one assigns it to a fabric group. There is some variation within these groups but it is difficult to make consistent sub-divisions as the variable degree of vitrification affects the appearance of the fabrics.

The main fabric represented among the sherds (Fabric A) is fairly soft and fires to a mid or dark grey colour. It contains some quartz temper, much of it quite fine. The noticeable degree of vitrification and distortion visible in many of these sherds demonstrates that this fabric is not very refractory. The other fabrics, B and C, are generally paler in colour and have a hackly fracture; both are quite refractory. The quartz temper in Fabric B is well graded with an average size of around 0.3mm while that in Fabric C has a wider range and grains over 1mm in diameter are not uncommon.

ANALYTICAL RESULTS AND THEIR INTERPRETATION

The metals detected by qualitative X-ray fluorescence analysis are noted in Tables 6–16 (where Cu = copper, Zn = zinc, Pb = lead, Sn = tin, Ag = silver, Au = gold). The relative amounts on each sherd are indicated by + symbols; major, minor and trace amounts are represented by +++, ++ and + respectively. In two cases gold droplets were visible though not detected analytically – here the +s appear in brackets. Some sherds (marked xx in the right-hand column) gave only very weak XRF signals and in these cases it is not possible to suggest what alloy was being melted, although the detection of traces of metals confirms that they were parts of crucibles that had been used. No weight should be placed on the universal detection of zinc as this is due to the metal's chemical nature which preferentially enhances its survival. Similarly, it is frequently detected on sherds where it is not a significant component of the alloy being melted, so allowance has been made for this in the interpretations presented below.

The crucibles from sites SOU 8, 31 and 34, and all but one of those from SOU 254, were used to melt tin-containing copper alloys, bronzes and/or gunmetals. The difference between the two groups of alloys is that bronzes contain mainly tin and copper while gunmetals additionally contain a significant amount of zinc. The XRF analyses are of relatively large areas which include not only the crucible slag but in some cases corroded metal droplets trapped in the slag too. The information that is sought is the composition of the uncorroded metal while that obtained is the average composition of slag and corroded metal. Extrapolating from one to the other is not an exact science and it is this uncertainty which is reflected in the range of alloys suggested. It should be noted that two spillages, metal 8/79 and 8/80, were bronze. The crucible from site SOU 99 was used to melt bronze as was one from site SOU 24 (24/927) while those from SOU 169 were used for brass (169/828 and 169/852) and bronze or gunmetal (169/3749). Although lead was detected on many of the crucibles it was never a major component of the alloy being melted which suggests that many of the products of these metalworkers were likely to have been wrought rather than cast objects. The range of copper alloys indicated by the deposits on the crucibles is consistent with the range of alloys used for metal objects from the same sites (Wilthew, above), suggesting at least some of them may be local products.

Somewhat more surprising perhaps than the evidence for working copper alloys was that for silver melting. No fewer than five sites (SOU 14, 17, 24, 30 and 254) produced crucible sherds with silver on them. In some cases traces of gold were detected too, almost certainly present as an impurity in the silver. The crucibles containing silver are of two distinct types, the ordinary, hand-made thumb pots and wheel-thrown pots of larger size made of a coarser and more refractory fabric. Although large numbers of silver objects were not found in the excavations it is possible that the silver workers were producing jewellery. An alternative end-product might, however, have been coins, as Southampton was almost certainly a mint in mid-Saxon times (Metcalf 1988). Indeed, here is the concrete evidence to support Addyman and Hill's supposition (1969, 63) that silver working was carried on.

The final group of sherds to be considered is the cupels. Until recently these forms had not been widely recognised on metalworking sites but they are not uncommon, particularly during the early medieval period (Bayley 1991). They were used for refining or assaying precious metals. The process involved the melting of the precious metal together with a relatively large amount of lead. An air blast then converted the lead to lead oxide which dissolved any base metals (eg copper or tin) mixed with the silver or gold, leaving a globule of pure metal sitting on the cupel. The lead oxide meanwhile reacted with the clay fabric of the cupel, producing the thick, vitreous, slag layers seen. Sometimes droplets of the precious metal failed to coalesce and were trapped in the vitreous surface, providing evidence of the metal being refined. Where only base metals are detected on the cupels it is not possible to determine the nature of the metal being refined as the craftsman had done a good job and not lost any of the precious metal.

Five of the six cupel fragments from Southampton are typical of the general class of object; they have a vitrified upper surface that is rich in lead. Silver was detected on two of them (15/P935 and 31/696) and gold on one (31/2669B). It is interesting to note that while they all come from sites that have produced crucibles, none of these had been used to melt precious metals; the sites that have crucibles with silver on them have no cupels. This suggests the cupels were not used by the craftsmen who worked silver; it seems the refining or testing of metal quality was not their responsibility.

The final cupel, 169/2203, was used in a quite different way. All that survives is a small area of vitrification and a circular outline a few millimetres across with traces of gold round its edge. This circle probably marks the position of a gold globule which slightly 'wetted' the ceramic, leaving traces of the metal behind. The most likely process to have produced this type of evidence is the melting of gold filings and scrapings to produce a coherent, re-usable piece of metal. Heat would have been applied from above by a blow-pipe which would also have produced the localised vitrification. It should be noted that site 169 also produced the stone mortar which was used for preparing amalgam for gilding (fig 31). It may be relevant that this site was the only one where crucibles that were used to melt brass were positively identified. Brass was a relatively uncommon copper alloy at this period – possibly new metal imported from Germany (Bayley 1988A and 1992C) – so craftsmen who worked it may have been supplying higher status customers for whom gold or gilded objects may also have been made.

TABLE 6
Crucibles from Site SOU 8

Finds No	Sherd description			Elements detected by XRF					
	type	(mm)	fabric	Cu	Zn	Pb	Sn	Ag	Au
8/69	body	5–6	B	+++	+	+	+		
8/70	body	7–9	A	+++	+	+	++		
8/81	rim	5	B	+++	++	+	++		
8/82	rim	6–7	A	+++	++	+	++		
8/83	rim	4–7	B	+++	+	+	++		
P 106 (8/100)	rim	c 6	A?	+++	++	+	++		
CR 1 (8/18)	complete			+++		+	++		
CR 2 (8/17)	complete			+++	+	+	++		
P 18 A (8/15A)	rim			+++	++	+			
P 18 B (8/15B)	rim			+++	++	+	+		
P 66 (8/14)	rim			+++	+	+	++		
P 94 (8/13)	cupel			+++	+	+++	++		

Table 6.   Crucibles from Site SOU 8.

TABLE 7
Crucibles from Site SOU 14

Finds No	Sherd description			Elements detected by XRF					
	type	(mm)	fabric	Cu	Zn	Pb	Sn	Ag	Au
14/1	body	6–9	A	++	+			++	

Table 7.   Crucibles from Site SOU 14.

TABLE 8
Crucibles from Site SOU 15

Finds No	Sherd description			Elements detected by XRF					
	type	(mm)	fabric	Cu	Zn	Pb	Sn	Ag	Au
P 936 (15/474)	cupel	8	A	++	++	+++		++	
P 1348 (15/475)	rim	4	A	+	+++				xx
P 1978 (15/476)	body	>13	A	+	++				xx

Table 8. Crucibles from Site SOU 15.

TABLE 9
Crucibles from Site SOU 17

Finds No	Sherd description			Elements detected by XRF					
	type	(mm)	fabric	Cu	Zn	Pb	Sn	Ag	Au
17/28	rim	6–8	C	++	+			++	

Table 9. Crucibles from Site SOU 17.

TABLE 10
Crucibles from Site SOU 24

Finds No	Sherd description			Elements detected by XRF					
	type	(mm)	fabric	Cu	Zn	Pb	Sn	Ag	Au
P 758 (24/1073)	body	7	B	+++	+	+		++	
P 1424 (24/1074)	rim	4–7	A	+	+	+		+++	+
24/927	rim	6	A	+++	+	+	++		
24/990	rim	5–6	A	+	++	+		+++	
24/991	body	>9	?	+	+				xx
24/992	rim	4	A	+	+				xx

Table 10. Crucibles from Site SOU 24.

TABLE 11
Crucibles from Site SOU 30

Finds No	Sherd description			Elements detected by XRF					
	type	(mm)	fabric	Cu	Zn	Pb	Sn	Ag	Au
30/164	base	7–10	C	+++	+++	+		+++	+
30/196A	body	c 10	A	+++	++	+		++	
30/196B	body	9–12	A	+	++				xx
30/558	rim	8		++	++	+		++	+

Table 11. Crucibles from Site SOU 30.

TABLE 12
Crucibles from Site SOU 31

Finds No	Sherd description			Elements detected by XRF					
	type	(mm)	fabric	Cu	Zn	Pb	Sn	Ag	Au
31/696*	cupel	5–6	A+	++	+	+++		++	
31/698	body	8–9	A	++	+	++	++		
31/1525	body	5–7	A	+	++	+	+		
31/1612	rim	4–6	C	+++	+	+	++		
31/2204	?base	7–8	A	+	+	+			xx
31/2219	body	3–6	A	+++	++	++	++		
31/2224	?knob		A	+	+				xx
31/2225	body	3–5	B	+	++				xx
31/2668	rim	3	A	+	++	+			xx
31/2669A	cupel	8	A	++	+	+++	++		
31/2669B	cupel	7	A	++		+++		(++)	

Table 12. Crucibles from Site SOU 31.

TABLE 13
Crucibles from Site SOU 34

Finds No	Sherd description			Elements detected by XRF					
	type	(mm)	fabric	Cu	Zn	Pb	Sn	Ag	Au
34/115	complete	3–4	?	+++	+		++		
34/116	complete	4–6	A?	+++	++	++	++		
34/117	half	4–6	A	+++	+	+	++		
34/118	rim	2–3	A	+++	+	+	++		

Table 13. Crucibles from Site SOU 34.

TABLE 14
Crucibles from Site SOU 99

Finds No	Sherd description			Elements detected by XRF					
	type	(mm)	fabric	Cu	Zn	Pb	Sn	Ag	Au
99/256	rim	6–8	A?	++	+	++	++		

Table 14. Crucibles from Site SOU 99.

TABLE 15
Crucibles from Site SOU 169

Finds No	Sherd description			Elements detected by XRF					
	type	(mm)	fabric	Cu	Zn	Pb	Sn	Ag	Au
169/828	body	4–5	A	+++	+++	+			
169/852	rim	5–6	A	+++	+++	++			
169/1229	rim	4–5	B	+	+				xx
169/2203	cupel	6–9	cf B	+	+	+		(++)	
169/2893	rim	3–5	A	+	++	+			xx
169/3120	body	4–6	?A	+	+	++			xx

Finds No	Sherd description			Elements detected by XRF					
	type	(mm)	fabric	Cu	Zn	Pb	Sn	Ag	Au
169/3748	body	5–10	A	+	+	+			xx
169/3749	rim	5	B	++	++	+	++		
169/3751	body	5	A	+	+				xx
169/3923	body	7	cf A	+		++			

Table 15. Crucibles from Site SOU 169.

TABLE 16
Crucibles from Site SOU 254

Finds No	Sherd description			Elements detected by XRF					
	type	(mm)	fabric	Cu	Zn	Pb	Sn	Ag	Au

Pre Mid-Saxon

254/1303	half	6–8		++	++	++		+++	

Mid-Saxon

254/2378	body *			+++	+	+	++		
254/3057	body *								
254/1870	rim			+	++	+			xx
254/2548	body *								
254/1873	rim	5–13		+	+	+			xx
254/2484	rim and body	11							
254/2390	rim			++	++	++	++		
254/2465	body (2)								
254/2485	body (4) *								
254/2963	body *								
254/2191	body			+++	+	+	++		
254/2293	rim and body (2)								
254/2698	body (2) *								
254/2315	rim and body								
254/2699	body (12) *								
254/2964	body *								

Post Conquest

254/2962	body (4) *								
254/1910	body *								
254/2777	body *								
254/2464	body *								
254/2778	body *								
254/1290	body (2) *			+	++	+			
254/2389	body (2)								
254/2697	body			+++		++	++		

* = very small fragments (under 5mm)
xx = sherds giving very weak XRF signals

Those sherds with no XRF results were not analysed
Numbers in brackets denote the number of non-joining sherds

Table 16. Crucibles from Site SOU 254.

DISCUSSION

THE NON-FERROUS METAL COLLECTION FROM SAXON SOUTHAMPTON

Any consideration of Hamwic's metalwork must begin with the qualification that the ironwork, including objects plated, inlaid or overlaid with non-ferrous metals, has not yet been studied in detail. There are also other types of artefact, notably in glass, bone and stone, which should be considered in any overall assessment of the town and its function. A review of the non-ferrous collection must necessarily therefore be only a preliminary to a wider study.

Non-ferrous metalwork also includes coins, and Southampton has been fortunate in the studies made of them (Metcalf 1988; Pagan 1988A, B). The only gold object so far found is a coin, a ninth-century *solidus* (Pagan 1988B). There is one brooch, 258/331, with sufficient gold in some parts for those to be described as electrum. Silver, like gold, is much better represented by coins, the numerous sceattas and pennies, than by a handful of pins and other objects (see table 17). The copper-alloy objects were sometimes gilded, to sparkle if not to deceive, and the grinding mortar, 169/752 (fig 31), is evidence that gold was available in Hamwic, albeit in very small quantities. The coins, of course, provide evidence that valuable objects were used, and buried or lost, in the town, but the other non-ferrous metalwork is not likely to be completely unrepresentative of what was generally available.

The sources of the metals used are not established. The gold could have come from melted-down objects, either heirlooms or new imports such as coins; by the time Hamwic was founded, gold was difficult to obtain in any form, let alone as bullion. The small amounts of mercury used in gilding would have had to be imported, from Italy, the Balkans or Spain (Arnold 1988, 63). Silver was needed in larger quantities, to sustain a coinage: recycling is unlikely to have been sufficient, and importing is likely, be it as coin, in rings or in ingots; the Poitiers area provided an alternative to Islamic-controlled supplies (Spufford 1988, 32–3). The copper, and the lead, tin and zinc mixed with it, could all in theory be from recycled scrap, even though in some cases the alloying metals may have been carefully selected for particular uses, as Wilthew argues for some of the pin types (cf Mortimer 1988); Bayley suggests that the presence of brass may indicate the import of new metal from Germany. The Roman coins and the Roman brooch are evidence of the collection of scrap, although it cannot be assumed that everything was intended for recycling.

The Hamwic copper-alloy objects may not therefore signal the import of new metal, from overseas or from elsewhere in England, but the quantities may seem too great for recycling alone to have provided a sufficient supply, if survivals of objects represent only a small sample of the original number. Because of recycling opportunities, the metal sample may be considerably less representative than pottery, yet few complete or even partly reconstructible vessels are found (Timby 1988, 75). The number of objects recovered is more impressive when viewed against a sherd recovery rate representing only 10% or less of nearly all the individual pots from which the sherds came.

The extent to which Hamwic's metalwork collection is in any way a valid sample of what entered the ground is very difficult to assess. Perhaps as much as 3% of the town has been excavated (Morton 1992, 16), but many features within that 3% were not fully emptied, and some objects will certainly have escaped the excavators' eyes. To assume that what is catalogued represents even a 1% sample would be hazardous, but the 156 pins of Types A, B and C (figs 8–10) would stand for 15,600 discards and losses if it were acceptable. Production over a 200-year period would thus create an annual loss-rate of seventy-eight . . . which seems a lot when allowing for the recycling opportunity in addition to a natural reluctance to lose such an object in the first place.

The Hamwic collection of survivals is a large one, though since the discovery of Flixborough, on Humberside (Whitwell 1991), it can no longer be assumed that sheer quantity of casually lost objects like pins is proof of a large, urban population. 'Prolific' sites have become a phenomenon of the mid-Saxon period, their role or roles often being obscure, one outstanding example being the Anglian site on the Yorkshire Wolds which has yielded more strap-ends and other artefact types than Whitby or York (Haldenby 1990, 1992). Because the nature of the excavations within Hamwic has varied so much, and there have been some post-excavation losses (see catalogue entries, and Morton 1992, 16–19), it is not usually meaningful to compare site with site in detail. It is, however, worth noting a comparison between Hamwic, with c 15,000 square metres excavated (Morton 1992, 17; Sites 254 etc add a little more to his estimates) which have yielded c 180 surviving copper-alloy pins with recognisable heads, and Anglian York, with c 2,500 square metres yielding 36 such pins (Rogers 1993, 1361). The proportions are not very different, which suggests that at least town may be compared with town.

The range of non-ferrous objects excavated at Anglian York is not greatly different from that at Hamwic, although there are some types of object, such as finger-rings with twisted-wire bezels (Rogers 1993, 1370–3), which are not represented at Hamwic. York's Anglian area has also produced a gold finger-ring, and rings with unjoined ends (*ibid*, 1371, 1373–4). Apart from the gold *solidus*, gold objects are conspicuously absent from Hamwic, although both its finger-rings were gilded, as were some other objects. Full comparisons with other *wic* sites in England cannot yet be made, but reports from Ipswich and London do not indicate spectacular differences from the occupation deposits (graves are discussed below). England's continental trading-partners are also difficult to consider in detail. As Hodges has recently pointed out, an emporium trading with Hamwic that was located at or near Rouen might be expected, but has yet to be discovered (1991, 85–6). Indeed, St Willibald and his party 'encamped near the city called Rouen. A mart was there (*Ibi fuit mercimonia*)' (Morton 1992, 60). The site of the well-documented Quentovic has been found, but its metalwork is said to be too heavily corroded to be identifiable (Hill *et al* 1990, 57; Leman 1990). Further north, Domburg, Schouwen and other sites have produced large quantities of data, but not from stratified levels: there does not seem to be a marked qualitative distinction between such places and Hamwic (Capelle 1976; Capelle 1978). Dorestad does have a small distinctive element, notably a gold cloisonné brooch set with garnets, glass and other stones, from an ordinary rubbish-pit, not a grave (van Es 1976), and the small selection reported from the Hoogstraat I site includes a pseudo-cameo brooch, but in base metal set with glass pearls (van Es and Verwers 1980, 173–4), and a gold ring (Maaskant-Kleibrink 1980); Hamwic has nothing to match those.

TABLE 17
Objects predominantly of silver

5/71	Strap-end, Type B*	5/72	Strap-end, Type B	24/12	Tweezers (loop only)*
26/193	Mount*	26/624	Pin, Type Aa 2ii*	30/328	Pin, Type Ga 1ii*
31/1464	Pin, Type Ad 2iii	31/1466	Pin, Type Aa 2iii*	33/89	Strap-end, Type A
36/99	Strap-end, Type A*	169/748	Pin, Type Aa 2ii*	169/1409	Pin, Type Aa 2iii*
169/2244	Pin, Type Aa 2iii*	169/2959	Pin, Type Ed 1; (washer only)	169/2960	Mount
254/115	Pin, Type Ad 2ii	254/1370	Pin, Type Ia 1ii	254/1613	Pin, Type Ad 2iii
258/27	Pin, Type Aa 2iii	258/181	Pin, Type Aa 1ii	258/331	Brooch, Type B (part electrum)

* Analysed by X-ray fluorescence spectrometry, see tables 4 and 5.

Object 18/16 (fig 27) has been excluded from this table.

Table 17. Objects predominantly of silver.

DATING

The expansion of the Wessex dynasty's area of control into Dumnonia, the Isle of Wight and Sussex is usually seen as the main catalyst for the foundation of Hamwic, although Morton (1992, 26) has pointed out that King Ine is often taken as its founder only because his long reign, 688–726, neatly encompasses the likely dates. The metal objects do not give more information about the precise years involved, but there are noticeably few which have close parallels in seventh-century cemeteries. Allowing for one or two heirlooms or scrap items, such as the sixth-century brooch 7/1 (fig 1), there is nothing that necessarily pre-dates the eighth century, although many things, such as some of the pins, might do so. This is less precise than the coin evidence, though the dates of the sceattas are themselves far from firmly established; nevertheless, the near-absence of any of the primary series continues to suggest that, at Hamwic, 'use of coinage was on a very small scale until almost the end of the seventh century' (Metcalf 1993A, 156). The other non-ferrous metalwork is entirely consistent with this, and does not suggest that there was substantial activity or a population nucleus of any size before c 700, a view shared by Morton (1992, 28), Garner (1993, 91, 124) and Andrews (1995, forthcoming).

Hamwic has yielded large numbers of the secondary series sceattas, the introduction of which may have been c 710 (Metcalf 1993A, 64); there are also several continental sceattas, which seem to have been increasingly excluded from English kingdoms as the eighth century progressed. This suggests that Hamwic initially rode a wave of relative prosperity, and again the other non-ferrous metalwork is consistent with this view, not because it is rich in quality, but because those few categories which clearly span the seventh- to eighth-century transition are distributed throughout the town, without any obvious sign of skewing to the waterfront, as was perceived in the pottery (Timby 1988, 117–20). The two disc-headed pins, 169/568 and 169/634 (fig 12), seem unlikely to have had currency for very long after c 700, and are from Six Dials at the north end. Spiral-headed pins (fig 11), which are probably eighth-century or earlier rather than later, also occur at Six Dials, one of that area's six being from an early eighth-century context. There are also three spiral-headed pins from Cook Street in the far south – a site which incidentally produced only a single sceat, a Series X, of c 710–c 750 (Metcalf 1993C). Cook Street was the site of an early cemetery; one grave included a linked pin suite, 254/1370 (fig 13), another type unlikely to have extended long into the eighth century.

There are several cemeteries in Saxon Southampton, although few have graves which definitely contained objects deliberately deposited in them. Exceptions include the two buckles, 20/9 and 20/28 (fig 2), found in graves with weapons, one at least a foreign, eighth-century seax (Morton 1992, 51–2). There are other objects which are quite likely to have been grave goods, even though not positively with burials when found, such as the curious 'pendant', 13/1 (fig 6). The nineteenth-century discovery of two glass palm-cups, both reported to have been in graves (Morton 1992, 51), may indicate a nucleus of important burials in the central, eastern part of the town. The palm-cups have seventh-century burial parallels in Wiltshire at Swallowcliffe Down, and in Cow Lowe, Derbyshire, a grave which also included gold linked pins (Speake 1989, 81–3), of the sort which Hamwic's disc-headed but perhaps originally conjoined 169/568 and 169/634 (fig 12) seem to have aped in base metal. A recently discovered grave in Ipswich with weapons and palm-cups is attributed to the earlier seventh century (Gaimster *et al* 1989, 209), but nothing at Hamwic would justify a comparably early date – nor, of course, does Hamwic have other cemeteries close by, suggesting substantial pre-existing settlement units, as in the Ipswich area (Newman 1993).

The discussion of object 13/1's exact find-spot indicates the difficulty of being certain of contexts when features have been disturbed subsequently. It is clear, however, that at least a few people were buried with objects, and since this was a practice likely to have become increasingly uncommon as the eighth century progressed, there is a slight bias towards recovery of objects from the early part of Hamwic's chronology. There could also be a bias caused by costume change. The practice of suspending a number of objects from the belt may not have lasted much beyond the end of the seventh century:

Kentish ladies, and probably at least some of their 'Jutish cousins' on the Isle of Wight also, might have carried a rock-crystal ball and a silver spoon (Welch 1992, 63; Frankish ladies may have gone to even further extremes: it is worth noting here that a cowrie shell from Hamwic is drilled at one end, probably for suspension as shown in Wamers 1986, Abb 5). Some men were carrying amulets at the end of the eighth century, but these are more likely to have been fragments of Christian texts or saints' bones than anything associated with older ideologies (Meaney 1992, 116).

Apart from these two factors, there seems no obvious reason why loss-rates should have varied throughout Hamwic's period of occupation. The probability that Hamwic's fortunes ebbed and flowed, and the difficulty of recognising such fluctuations in the archaeological record, has been much discussed. There may have been an interlude between the end of the production of sceattas (c 760 Metcalf 1993A, 64), and the use of silver pennies later in the eighth century; unfortunately the town does not have the succession of occupation layers that Ribe boasts, enabling it to be said confidently that the Danish Series X sceattas 'dwindle progressively' there after c 740/50, until none are found after c 770/80 (Metcalf 1993B, 173). Ribe was clearly trading with Frisians and the Rhine mouths: despite the Series X finds, Hamwic must have had more links with north France, presumably through Quentovic and Rouen, areas where the nuances of the currency are less well understood (Metcalf 1993B, 263–5). Consequently, continental chronologies are less helpful to Hamwic's than they are likely to be to Kent's, London's or East Anglia's. This is no less true for other types of metalwork: it is not at present possible to identify artefacts specifically of the second half of the eighth century, and thus to discuss further Hamwic's prosperity at that time, except to say that that inability might possibly be symptomatic of an unadventurous period of stagnation or decline. Certainly there are no sites of any size which have not yielded spiral-headed pins or other objects probably early in the town's chronology, so there is no evidence of significant expansion beyond its first boundaries. Equally, there is no sign of contraction. An attempt to address this problem by seriation analysis (Cherry and Hodges 1978) was rightly criticised for failing to take account of different strata within features (Holdsworth 1984, 337). Nevertheless, it is a form of analysis potentially worth pursuing when all the Hamwic material has been processed, using only closed contexts. This might also refine some of the dating of the non-ferrous metalwork, but it is felt that to attempt it at present would be premature.

The history of Hamwic in the ninth century depends greatly upon interpretation of the numbers of coins found; put crudely, upon the reasons why silver pennies are less frequently recovered than the earlier sceattas, to the extent that any losses at all are significant. The recent Cook Street excavation, Site 254, produced no pennies (Metcalf 1993C) to add to the short list of excavated ninth-century coins (Metcalf 1988, 22–3), but did yield a convex-sided strap-end of the type conventionally dated to the ninth century. It is one of eight from the town, not a large number but enough to be useful, perhaps hinting at continuing activity despite the relative paucity of pennies, but much more strongly hinting by their distribution that the whole of the town was still in use. It would seem that its population remained quite large, even if its coinage suggests a less buoyant economy than was once enjoyed, and even if there was some contraction, as the evidence of property amalgamations at Six Dials suggests (Andrews 1995, forthcoming).

The end of Hamwic is more controversial in its dating than is its beginning. The shorter the period of Hamwic's ninth-century use, the more constricted becomes the dating of the strap-ends. Unfortunately they are base metal, so that such decoration as they have is too simple to compare very convincingly to decorated silver in coin-dated hoards. The Trewhiddle style on some was still used in the later part of the century, but none of the Hamwic strap-ends has clear evidence of its later versions. The penny sequence from twentieth-century excavations extends to the late ninth century, with a single coin of Alfred (Metcalf 1988, 54), but earlier records are of coins well into the tenth (Pagan 1988A, 70). Nothing in the metalwork has to be later than the ninth century, and there are some notable absences if occupation really went beyond c 900 – cast openwork strap-ends and other objects similarly influenced by Carolingian acanthus ornament, for instance (eg the Wareham mount, Webster 1991, no 256). Bayley notes that brass alloys would be expected in a tenth-century assemblage, and that Wilthew's analyses have not revealed much (Bayley 1992A, 809). This is consistent with the Hamwic pottery, which includes only a 'very sparse scatter of possible late Saxon types' (Timby 1988, 116).

The non-ferrous metalwork is not securely enough dated to make a major contribution to an understanding of Hamwic's chronological history. Nevertheless, an early impetus from c 700 seems to be visible, and it is difficult not to associate this with the expansionism of Kings Caedwalla and Ine, building on the successes of their predecessors – even if it was perhaps not a king who actually created the town. Pressure from Mercia no doubt limited Wessex during much of the eighth century (Yorke 1990, 140–1), and defence would have yielded no booty, or captives to sell as slaves (see below). The up-turn in Wessex's fortunes in the early ninth century under Egbert reversed this trend, and the metalwork suggests that Hamwic benefited to a limited extent; certainly it does not seem to suggest decline immediately after c 825, with the capture of Essex and Kent diverting attention eastwards (discussed by Morton 1992, 77). This theory anyway perhaps suggests too much direct interest in those territories by King Egbert himself; it was his son, Aethelwulf, who led the victorious army, and who was given the new territories to rule (*ASC sa* 825, 839). Both kings had sufficient resources to resist the worst of the generally prevailing trend to currency debasement (Metcalf and Northover 1989), which may indicate relatively buoyant trading in Wessex up to c 850, despite the Viking raids of the 830s and early 840s, let alone any problems created for European traders by internecine wars between Carolingian claimants in the 820s and 830s. Nevertheless, the Hamwic metalwork sequence does not seem to extend beyond the end of the ninth century. Whatever direct impact on Hamwic the 840s raid(s) had, Viking disruption made trading a dangerous occupation (Morton 1992, 70–7); presumably King Alfred's successes and his consolidation of his kingdom could not restore Hamwic's fortunes after 878, with the Vikings' continuing activities elsewhere allowing Hamwic's former trading partners no opportunity to recover.

PRODUCTION

There is an impressive range of evidence, studied above by Bayley, Morton, Oddy and Wilthew, for non-ferrous metalworking in Hamwic, represented by crucibles used in melting alloys, by cupels for separating precious metals from base metals, by clay and stone moulds, by debris from wire production, and by the unique grinding mortar.

The grinding mortar, 169/752 (fig 31), represents direct evidence for the use of gold, applied with the use of mercury to other metals to gild them. There are not very many objects from Hamwic that can now be recognised as having been gilded, and another hint that the process was infrequently carried out may be supplied by the stone of which the mortar is made, a non-local sandstone from the Mendip/Bristol area. That stone may have been selected because it was considered especially suitable, and it is worth noting that gold-workers may have had particular contacts with the Bristol area, since the Coalfield is one of the more likely sources of the mid-Saxon touchstones found in Winchester (Oddy and Tylecote 1990, 77). Other Southampton evidence for gold processing is its presence in a cupel at sites SOU 31 and SOU 169, and in several crucibles. Bayley considers that gold was an impurity within silver in the crucibles, but that at site SOU 31 there is enough to indicate its refining, and at SOU 169 the cupel had been used to melt gold scrap.

There is more evidence of silver working, recognised by Bayley in a few cupels and in a larger number of crucibles, just as there are more silver objects. Litharge is reported from a site some 50 metres north of Six Dials at Brintons Road, SOU 349 (Gaimster *et al* 1989, 191). Indirect evidence includes the Type 49 sceattas, which are presumed from their quantity within Southampton and rarity outside it to have been minted in the town (Metcalf 1988, 28–9), and less certainly those of Type 39 (*ibid*, 27).

The majority of the evidence is of various alloys of copper. As well as many crucibles, there are the fragments from site SOU 8 identified by Oddy as debris from production of wire from the folding process. At least one of the clay piece-moulds found in Cook Street, site SOU 254, was used for copper alloy, but Bayley cannot be certain that all or even any of the others were. Scraps of wire, castings and so forth may also be production debris, but are usually impossible to distinguish from broken objects. There is not a significant number of half-finished objects, or failed castings, which might mark a production site, an occasional misshapen head not necessarily creating an unusable and rejected pin. Wilthew's analyses do not suggest that particular alloys could ever be identified as particular to Southampton; he suggests that the consistent use of leaded bronze for spiral-headed pins, and for most of the pins with decorated spherical heads, could be evidence of their production at a single site, but an alternative is that that alloy was consistently chosen for those types of pin. Bayley notes that the alloys which contain relatively little or no lead, the majority, would be more likely to have been used for wrought than cast objects.

Although lead was present in two clay moulds, in cupels and in crucibles, it was probably there either as an incidental inclusion or used as part of the separation process of gold and silver from other metals. Although there are many lead fragments and at least one piece that suggests a cast ingot, 32/179 (fig 27), there are few objects and those crude, like the disc, 169/2831 (fig 19), or the weights, eg 169/790 (fig 26). This suggests that pewter had little if any role in Hamwic, and lead was for practical not decorative purposes. Disc-brooch 31/1653 (fig 1) may be an exception, if it is indeed a lead alloy.

No structures or hearths found in the Hamwic excavations can be associated with non-ferrous metalworking, nor have tools specific to the task been recognised (very detailed X-radiographs would be required for such things as 'needle files' to be identified: cf Hinton 1993A, 155–6). Production debris is widely spread, and does not suggest that the craft was in any way zoned. Indeed, it must be borne in mind that the recorded evidence may substantially underrepresent actual survival. The nineteenth-century excavators would not have retained anything which they would have regarded as dross, and subsequent excavators may not have recognised, and therefore discarded, small pieces of stone which were actually mould fragments, or other grinding mortars. It is very likely that there are more scraps of folded wire than those from site SOU 8, and bits of wire and castings might be either production waste or fragments of broken objects. Bayley points out that many of the clay piece-mould fragments were only found in wet sieving, so that many others can be assumed to have been lost without trace. Slag has not been systematically retained, and has not been discussed here partly for that reason and partly because of the difficulty of distinguishing Saxon from later pieces.

The metalworking debris may therefore have a worse collection rate than have recognisable objects, which makes its recognised quantity rather more impressive than it might seem at first glance. It is not possible to say if metalworking was practised throughout Hamwic right from its start, though there are two indications that silverworking was one of the first crafts there, as a crucible for it was from one of the earliest contexts at Cook Street (Garner 1993, 123) and the Series H sceattas, which include Types 38 and 49, probably date from *c* 710 or soon after, if they conform with other secondary series (Metcalf 1993A, 64). It certainly cannot be said that enough debris is found in early Hamwic contexts to justify a claim that one reason for its foundation was to concentrate craft production within it, but equally that argument is not precluded, at any rate for silver working. It does seem, however, that debris from metalworking of different kinds is widely enough spread to show that it rapidly became one of the town's specialised craft activities. The quantity seems comparable to Anglian York (Bayley 1993A), but both seem to have less than at least some later urban sites such as Lincoln (Bayley 1991). The fixed property boundaries laid out at an early date at Six Dials (Andrews 1995, forthcoming) perhaps imply that household units were already the norm for craft production in eighth-century Southampton.

EXCHANGE SYSTEMS AND HAMWIC'S FUNCTION

If it is correct that there was relatively less metalworking in the *wic* sites than in later towns, it may reflect lower internal population levels and less 'market penetration' of hinterlands. Attempts to review

DISCUSSION

the latter are restrained by various factors. Unlike Helgö (Holmqvist 1972), Saxon Southampton has not produced any moulds for making cast objects that would be clearly distinguishable when found. Nor are any of the objects, wrought or cast, stylistically distinctive enough to be attributed to Hamwic if found outside it, although the relief-bird disc-brooches would be claimants if discovered. Consequently, it cannot be certain that any of the buckles, pins, tweezers and such-like that were used and lost in Chalton and Abbots Worthy in Hampshire (Champion 1977, 369; Davies 1991) were made in Hamwic, even though similar things have been found in it. Non-ferrous metalworking is likely to have taken place at such sites, at least on an occasional basis, even though only Meonstoke, Hampshire, in Wessex has produced any evidence from rural excavations, in the ambivalent guise of unused crucibles (Hughes 1986, 9–10; the lug on the side of a crucible from a Saxon pit at Portchester (Cunliffe 1976, 108 and 221) suggests that it is Roman, residual in its context: cf Bayley 1993A, 1233). Mould fragments from Mucking, Essex (Webster 1993), and failed brooch castings from Cassington, Oxfordshire (Dickinson 1993, 35 and figs 57–9) indicate that copper-alloy working was practised in the fifth and sixth centuries at rural sites, as it was, further afield but contemporaneously with Hamwic, at Wharram Percy, Yorkshire (Bayley 1992B), either by resident or more probably by itinerant smiths. The recent report of a copper-alloy punch for making ring-and-dot stamps, found with a spherical-headed pin decorated with ring-and-dot, at Aldbourne, Wiltshire, strongly suggests a mid-Saxon craftsman in a rural environment (Robinson 1994).

Hamwic's smiths would not have been able to draw on their local area for raw materials, except for what came in for recycling. There is therefore no demonstrable trade into the town of the sort that is inferred from the bone evidence about animals and their produce (as Bourdillon and Coy 1980), and from some of the pottery (Timby 1988, 110), nor can inland contacts be discussed in the same way with metalwork as with the stones (Addyman and Hill 1969, 79–81) and the coins (Metcalf 1990, fig 3.3, Series H distribution map; the relative paucity of these sceattas in Wessex may imply little monetary trading, but does not preclude other regular exchange mechanisms such as barter).

Because it is not possible to recognise any particular object as having been made in Hamwic and lost in its hinterland, it is difficult to assess the argument that the 'immense amounts of commodities' that might have been produced 'should have transformed the material culture of Wessex' (Hodges 1989, 89). The seventy-eight type A–C pins that might possibly have been lost in an average year may represent only a fraction of those that were not, but do not really suggest numbers to justify adjectives like 'immense', or presumptions that production must have been seasonal because otherwise too many objects would have been made. Intermittent production is perfectly possible, but it need not have been linked directly to a seasonal fair.

It is not yet possible to make a detailed comparison of the Hamwic metalwork with the objects found in the 1980s and early 1990s in eastern England at such sites as Flixborough and Brandon (Leahy 1991, Webster 1991, 82–7). A qualitative judgement is that whereas most of the Hamwic objects would not look out of place in those settlements, the reverse is not always the case. At both, for instance, there are some much more elaborate pin-heads than almost all that have been found in Hamwic. It is also notable that Hamwic's metalwork has nothing to indicate an ecclesiastical presence; there is nothing with the Latin literacy of inscribed pieces such as an alphabet ring (Leahy 1991, no 69b) or a cross mount (Webster 1991, no 66a), nor are there any styli. This could merely be a reflection of the level of material prosperity at the churches of Wessex. Even Winchester has produced no eighth-century metal artefacts of quality, only window glass suggesting anything distinctive (Biddle 1990E). Indeed, this is broadly true of Wessex as a whole, which has little gold, few sculptures and no illuminated manuscripts attributable to the eighth century. The ninth saw some increase in secular gold and silver, and more sculpture. In the intellectual sphere, the death of Aldhelm and the departure of Boniface seem to have left Wessex increasingly isolated after the early part of the eighth century. It is possible, therefore, that Wessex's churches would not reveal themselves in their metalwork. On the other hand, the Hamwic collection is consistent with the view that the settlement was almost entirely secular, despite the presence in it of churches, including one that was referred to as a *mynster* in the eleventh century (Morton 1992, 50–1).

These are not unimportant considerations, since they impinge on interpretations of Hamwic's functions. By the time of the town's foundation, gold had become very difficult to obtain in western Europe. Direct supply by subsidy payment had ceased, and the African caravan routes and the Near Eastern mines were under Arab control. Sales of slaves probably still brought small amounts of gold (and silk and spices) into the west, with the consequent instability that the means of acquisition of such slaves might bring. If a gloss on a letter of AD 743 is correct, gold was then valued at a ratio of 12:1 against silver on the Continent (Grierson 1991, 20), so was probably even more highly valued in England. By the same time, garnets also seem to have become either unobtainable, as Avar and other conquests disrupted Bohemia, or unsought, if they were perceived as lacking interest when set against anything but a gold background. That the former is more likely is suggested by the almost desperate chipping down of old garnets evidenced in, for instance, the Boss Hall, Ipswich, brooch (Evans 1991, 52–3) and the efforts made to repair the Caistor St Edmund brooch (Ashwin, 175–6 in Nenk *et al* 1991). In effect, many of the more showy items that gave lustre to seventh-century aristocrats were simply not available in the eighth century. Consequently, if kings were expected to be the suppliers of these things to keep their people gift-dependent, there was insufficient gold for the purpose. Either there had to be substitutes available from various parts of northern Europe – wine and sword-blades, fine textiles, furs and glass vessels – or a different sort of dependency had to be created, one based on land. This would not have been an immediate change, but a process of transition.

A consequence of this process of transition for Hamwic is that it calls into question the extent to which the port served either to 'direct' trade and goods to the kings of Wessex, for their own consumption or for redistribution to their subjects, or whether royal interest in it would mainly have been to extract a revenue from traders' tolls. That documentary evidence for London suggests the latter may be no more than an example of the way that texts have particular concerns (Kelly 1992, 16, cites two examples of pre-emption, one of which is a Domesday entry of doubtful application to mid-Saxon conditions; the second was to apply only to one of two – or three – ships. This may, therefore, be an indication that the practice was exceptional). Nevertheless the calibre of the Hamwic metalwork that was lost in the town suggests nothing that would much have interested kings, except insofar as they could make use of the sceatta coins to ensure that tolls were paid to them in a measurable medium. The glass may, of course, be different, and may be associated with wine drinking amongst the elite in Wessex – what is recovered in Hamwic being the breakage element in what was passing through. If the sceattas were of interest to kings because they could be used for toll payments, the range of their weights and the variety of their alloys seem to indicate that they had face value as units (cf Metcalf 1988, 33: 'if the coins had royal backing and were in any case not required to compete in other kingdoms or overseas, their intrinsic value may not have been of vital importance.'). This may help to explain the virtual absence of weighing equipment, if it was not considered necessary to check the coins' actual unitary value at each transaction.

Apart from sceattas, it is glass that might be most recognisable in the countryside as evidence of Hamwic's trading connections with its hinterland; again it is Winchester that is the first place where fragments might be sought, but none has yet been positively identified there (Biddle 1990E), and only Portchester has any to show (Harden 1976). The Hamwic pottery imports are similar, with little being found in the rest of Wessex at such sites as Chalton (Timby 1988, 110), Abbots Worthy (although a little of the pottery there could be continental, it is not identified as one of the Hamwic import types: Fasham and Whinney 1991, 56), or Ramsbury, Wiltshire (Haslam 1980, 30–2). Portchester had a slightly larger amount (Cunliffe 1976, 187), but coastal Portchester is at least as likely to have received such things directly as through Hamwic. Indeed, it is the prosaic lava quernstones which seem at present to be the best indicator of occasional arrivals of imported goods at inland sites, as at Ramsbury (Williams 1980). In reverse, two of the things in this catalogue which originated outside Hamwic, at least as raw materials, are stone objects – sandstone for the grinding mortar from the Bristol area, chalk for the mould from somewhere more local, but at least five miles away.

As Hodges has recently shown, however, imported pottery indicates that Hamwic was much more closely involved with northern France than with the Rhineland, the source of the lava quernstones (Hodges 1991; see also Morton 1992, 65–6). This is not demonstrable from the non-ferrous metalwork, since the few objects like the double-ended hooks (fig 20) and equal-arm bow-brooches (fig 1) which are either imports or most visibly affected by continental influences, are not specific to a particular region; although the former are now best recorded from northern France, an example at Dorestad has been noted. There were already some pre-700 links between England and the Normandy area, as an increasing number of cemeteries is showing (Pilet et Auduc-le Bagousse 1990, 34–5; Pilet *et al* 1992, 40), and Wessex coin finds include a Rouen gold *triens* from near Swindon (Metcalf 1990A, 206). Hamwic may have been able to exploit some existing connections. On the other hand, there is no E-ware pottery to suggest that it was able to take advantage of whatever links once existed with south-western France, attested by 'Jutish' objects in cemeteries like Herpes (James 1988, 113–14). The only hint of trade with that area comes at the end of the eighth or in the ninth century, with two coins (Brown 1988; Metcalf 1988, 25; a third coin, from Carthage, is sixth century and might have come via south-west France, at any time: *ibid*; an alternative is to see it as having originally been brought into south-west Britain with sixth-century ARSW pottery, later finding its way into Hamwic with a cargo of tin).

It is notoriously difficult to recognise, let alone to quantify, English exports in exchange for wine and other imports (eg Kelly 1992, 14). Hunting dogs are recorded at earlier and later dates; wool is always possible; since Irish leather was distributed in the seventh century in the Loire (James 1982), unrecorded English trade in hides is possible, and Andrews has found evidence of their production in Hamwic (1995, forthcoming); Charlemagne's letter to King Offa is evidence that English cloth reached the Continent, but this may have been work of the highest quality, fit for kings – evidence of diplomatic gift exchange, not of regular trade. Yet if St Willibald could expect to catch a cross-channel ship passing down the Solent in 721 (Morton 1992, 60), and St Aldhelm a little earlier could wait for one in the Wareham area (Hinton and Hodges 1977, 81), fairly frequent voyages from Wessex can be inferred. Lead, despite its weight, may have been worth shipping, via Hamwic from the Mendips presumably. Whether Wessex could have obtained tin when Hamwic was founded is uncertain, but the expansion of the kingdom as far west as Exeter by 680 (Yorke 1990, 137) would certainly suggest control at least of Dartmoor's supplies. Perhaps most important of all were slaves. Although Astill has pointed out that these are usually donated as part of gift-exchange systems in early societies, not traded as a means of making good labour deficiencies (1985, 221–2), documentary references make it clear that slave-trading was actually on a relatively large scale, with the Islamic world as the main destination (Pelteret 1981; Loyn 1962, 86–9). Whether or not *wealh* had yet acquired its synonymity of 'slave' and 'Briton' is uncertain, as is the extent to which Wessex's westwards expansion brought Britons into enslavement, but Ine's law-code is quite explicit in showing that his Wessex subjects were involved in slaving at the end of the seventh century, since he forbad anyone to sell 'his own countryman, bond or free', which implies that the practice was sufficiently frequent to require legislation – and makes no proscription against selling people from other kingdoms (Whitelock 1955, 365 cl 11). The ring-headed pin, 31/882 (fig 13), could be the loss of an Irish slave or slaver, and gives a hint about Hamwic's trading connections so far unrecognised in other data.

THE RANGE OF OBJECTS

The ring-headed pin is one of the most distinctive objects in the Hamwic collection. Despite the relative lack of gold and silver, others also have considerable individual interest. The two disc-brooches, 31/1653 and 258/331 (fig 1), have designs remarkable for being without recognised parallel elsewhere. The two finger-rings, 31/653 and 36/103 (fig 3), also seem to be unique to Hamwic. With these categories of object, however, it needs to be borne in mind that base-metal items are less likely to be casually observed and reported than those of gold and silver, so that any parallels that can be drawn are more likely to have come from excavated assemblages. Furthermore, copper alloys do not lend themselves to fine workmanship such as the best filigree, so that direct imitation of some types of gold finger-ring would have been difficult for the makers of the two Hamwic rings to achieve in the materials that they were using. Other base-metal rings, found without a context, might well be difficult to recognise as they would not be in modes familiar from the better-known precious-metal rings.

Perhaps the most intriguing individual Hamwic object is the fitting with three pendants, 13/1 (fig 6), for which no satisfactory analogue has been cited. It may suggest that a range of amuletic objects continued to be carried at least in the early part of the eighth century. Very different except for the absence of good parallels are the single-riveted, spherical-ended strap-ends (fig 14), which seem quite common in Hamwic, but not elsewhere, and might suggest some fashion particular to the port; if so, this is a marked contrast to the other strap-ends, to the hooked tags (fig 4) and to the pins (figs 7–13). Not particular to Hamwic, but unexplained, are the 'forks' and 'spoons' (fig 24).

Attention should not be focused only upon the relatively few exotic objects found at Hamwic. The preponderance is of things quite carefully made, but produced in quantity and with very sparing use of valuable metals – a pattern that is reminiscent of the town's meat supply, which was plentiful but basic (eg Bourdillon 1979, 183–5). It is as though the townsfolk were mostly well able to obtain small objects of limited value, but that the most precious things would seem to have been beyond them – there is no equivalent in the non-ferrous metalwork to the hints at York or Dorestad of a distinctively richer element, discussed above. This equates with the documentary record which does not suggest that the trading area at Hamwic had a royal residence or rich church immediately adjacent to it, as York had. Nevertheless, that two of Hamwic's graveyards contained burials within penannular ditches (Morton 1992, 175, 177; Garner 1993, 90–1) suggests that there was some internal social hierarchy. Furthermore, of course, the number of silver coins that were buried or lost, and the gold *solidus*, indicate no small amount of disposable wealth amongst the townspeople; the broken glass may represent vessels that they used, but may have come from vessels intended for other destinations. If, as has been suggested, Wessex's thegns and aristocrats deigned to visit Hamwic to attend a seasonal fair (Hodges 1989, 89), they were careful not to leave too many tokens of their presence behind.

There is one hint of a much wealthier element in Hamwic, in the nineteenth-century record of glass vessels, apparently palm cups, found in Hamwic at sites SOU 47 and 48 with burials (Morton 1992, 51). As such vessels usually accompany people otherwise recognisable as wealthy, such as the lady buried at Swallowcliffe in the late seventh century with two palm cups and other fineries (Speake 1989, 81–2), Hamwic may have had richer denizens, at least in its early years. The *wic* at London also had at least one burial with glass vessels, and may have had other rich graves (Vince 1991, 415), but the grave with the vessels is attributed to the late sixth/early seventh century, and the 'warrior-grave' within Ipswich with palm cups is also thought earlier in date than anything yet proven for Hamwic (Gaimster *et al* 1989, 209). The very rich female burial of the late seventh or early eighth century at Boss Hall (Evans 1991, 51–3) was inserted into a cemetery some distance from Ipswich and her wealth may not have derived from the port: she may, for instance, have been a member of a land-owning family in the area. In the same way, the prosperous lady buried in the Brooks at Winchester at the end of the seventh century is unlikely to have depended on the town for her support, as there seems to have been little activity within it at the time (Hawkes 1990). Such graves may not, therefore, necessarily reflect a town's self-generated wealth. The 'glass-vessel' burials at London and Hamwic, together with Ipswich's 'warrior', all early in the occupation of these *wic* sites, could indicate deliberate planting of a power-wielding group at the inception of such places.

'MARGINALITY', GENDER AND ETHNICITY

Another possibility to be considered in relation to the paucity of expensive metalwork in Hamwic is that its townspeople did not lack the resources necessary to acquire such things, but did not seek them. If a display of wealth still involved prestige, and its acquisition was a sign of competitive aggression, the absence from the town of such things may be an indication that its inhabitants were slightly outside the norms of the society that surrounded them. They might, indeed, be seen as 'socially marginal', a concept applied to those living in the new emporia by Randsborg (1991, 156).

A few objects might at first glance reinforce this view; the two disc-brooches, 31/1653 and 258/331 (fig 1), which lack analogues, carry a design comparable to that on one of the Southampton sceatta types, as though some sense of a Southampton idiom was being expressed. Single-riveted, spherical-ended strap-ends may have been particular to the place. A few things which are unusual in an English context may have been brought from overseas. The presence of foreign visitors in Hamwic is strongly hinted at by the two site 20 burials with buckles (fig 2) and weapons, one of the latter apparently a continental seax (Morton 1992, 51–2; Holdsworth 1980, 39). The ring-headed pin, 31/882 (fig 13), probably came from Ireland, perhaps brought by a slave or a slaver. These are indications of outsiders at Hamwic who would have contributed to the place's sense of difference.

Not long ago, an equal-arm bow-brooch would have been claimed as an import, but recent work suggests that many brooches of this type were in fact made in England: it is always difficult to be sure that a particular artefact type which seems a rarity is not actually a common-place that has gone unrecognised. The recovery of three equal-arm bow-brooches (fig 1) in Hamwic may not, therefore, be any particular mark of distinctiveness. Similarly, the double-ended hooks, 30/178 and 34/8 (fig 20), are not necessarily imports, even though all but one of the cited parallels is from overseas; at present, however, it seems that they were things not normally seen in England, and may have been a little exotic in an English context. Again, the two gilt finger-rings, 31/653 and 36/103 (fig 3), also suggest something slightly exotic: not necessarily imported, but perhaps made for people who had seen such things worn by strangers, and wished them for themselves.

Saxon Southampton seems, therefore, to have had at least a small number of visitors whose customs had an effect upon the townsfolk, just as it is likely that some of those townsfolk voyaged overseas and subsequently displayed an element of the unusual in their tastes as a result of their experiences. For the most part, however, the metalwork suggests that Hamwic conformed not only with the rest of Wessex, but also with a wider zone that included north France as well as the rest of England; ethnic differences were no longer being clearly expressed through costume fittings. Most of the objects would not have looked out of place in other contexts, as the cited parallels show: the exceptions are really marginal to the majority of the other objects, rather than evidence of the 'marginality' of Hamwic as a whole, and their importance is easily exaggerated. The likeness to some birds on Type 49 sceattas of birds on the two disc-brooches (fig 1) may not have been as recognisable to a Southamptonian of the eighth century as it is to one (perhaps only one?) of the twentieth.

A Wessex *ceorl* who had occasion to visit Hamwic might, therefore, have felt that the people whom he saw in its streets were not very different in their costume from himself and his wife. It is often asserted that the place must have been peopled initially from the area around it, and the metalwork in general supports such a view. The recent excavation of the cemetery at site SOU 254 also has a bearing on this question, for it adds further examples of types of grave already known in Hamwic, such as those surrounded by penannular ditches, which are in traditions well-established in southern England (Garner 1993, 91; Morton 1992, 179), and now recognised also in Ireland (O'Brien 1993, 98–9) – suggesting contacts that perhaps make the ring-headed pin seem less out of place. Also well-established was the custom of burying little groups of objects in bags. It is therefore worth stressing that the linked pin suite, 254/1374 (fig 13), one of the very few indubitable Hamwic grave finds, was apparently not being worn when deposited. Instead, it was placed, perhaps in a bag, by the skeleton's shoulder. This rite has also been observed outside Winchester, at Winnall, providing an interesting example of shared local customs.

Cemeteries, of course, provide the evidence for one of the key aspects in consideration of the 'marginality' of the new emporia. Randsborg has noted a heavy bias towards males in their populations, (1991, 156) to which the Hamwic evidence may be compared. Unfortunately, the numbers of sexable skeletons from its graveyards are small, but the largest, at site SOU 31, has a reported ratio of exactly 2:1 (trenches A and B contained thirty-four identified adult male, seventeen female burials, and five of children: Morton 1992, 135 and MF1, C1 and C7). This may not be consistent throughout Hamwic; the much smaller site SOU 254 assemblage had one certain and three possible males, against two certain and one possible females (McKinley and Garner 1993, 86–8), but the later group from Six Dials has six identified males to three identified females (Andrews 1995, forthcoming). Andrews (*ibid*) points to an inherent bias against the representation of young females, however, because of differential bone survival, a substantial factor in Hamwic's acid soils. Despite this problem, some gender imbalance towards a male population seems possible. To what extent can the non-ferrous metalwork be considered in relation to these sex ratios?

When they occur in graves, a few categories of object are solely found with one or other sex, and slightly more are very much more likely to be with one than the other. Of course, it is not always possible to be certain that objects chosen for deposition directly reflected the users of those objects in daily life. Furthermore, there are not very many categories that are found both in sixth- and seventh-century graves, and in Hamwic. It is therefore difficult to be sure that any are actually sex-specific, finger-rings being an example. Twisted wire and plain band types are normally found in female graves, but the inscriptions on more elaborate rings of the eighth and ninth centuries at least as often carry men's as women's names. The two finger-rings from Hamwic cannot therefore be assumed to have been worn by women. In the same way, pins, Hamwic's most common items, are usually assumed to have been worn with women's costume – but largely because of linked pins in cemeteries. Evidence as to who used the eighth- and ninth-century pins, and how they were used, is sparse, and equal use by males and females is not precluded.

Possibly more revealing are paucities and absences, the infrequency of disc-brooches being an example. Although it has been argued in the discussion of that category that few such brooches were worn in the eighth century, it is just possible that their scarcity in Hamwic is because they were normally female attire, and that there would have been relatively fewer of them worn in a town than in a settlement with a normal population balance. Perhaps a better indicator is the apparent absence of toilet implements other than the relatively common tweezers (fig 18); in southern English graves, tweezers may be with males or females, although elsewhere they are actually male-associated. Ear-scoops and their like are much more often with females, and Hamwic has none of these implements at all, even though those from Barking Abbey show that at least one section of the female population continued to use them (Webster 1991, nos 67i–l).

Overall, the non-ferrous metalwork does not provide convincing evidence of a male predominance in Hamwic's population, but there is at any rate nothing to contradict the hint provided by the skeleton evidence that is currently available that there was indeed some, perhaps slight, imbalance of the sexes. But the overwhelming similarity of most of the objects to those in the rest of England suggests that although the emporium was markedly different in its function, and that some aspects of its population and culture reflected those differences, it was not 'marginal' in the sense of standing apart and being kept at a distance. The place was as much an integral part of the society that produced it as were the recently arrived Christian churches, and like them is a reflection of the changes that that society was undergoing.

CONCORDANCE

(Excludes pin shafts, table 1; Roman coins, table 2; crucibles and cupels, tables 6–16. For locations see Frontispiece and Catalogue Preface: 'Eastern side' = sites close to the River Itchen; 'Clifford Street area' = north central zone; 'Six Dials' = north; 'St Mary's' = southern area around the church; 'Central area' = north of St Mary's.)

Site 4 (Eastern side)
2	Pin, Type Bb 1ii	4	Pin, Type Ba 2iii	5	Tweezers
6	Buckle pin	7	Mount	37	(Fork/) spoon
84	Pin, Type Fa 1ii				

Site 5 (Eastern side)
1	Pin, Type Ab 1ii	2	Mount	3	Pin, Type Aa 2ii
5	Mount	6	Pin, Type Ab 1ii	61	Chain
67	Hook	70	Unidentified object	71	Strap-end, Type B
72	Strap-end, Type B	73	(Hook/) handle		

Site 7 (Eastern side)
1	Brooch, Type C

Site 8 (Eastern side)
19	Pin, Type Aa 1i	26	Chain	33	Pin, Type Ba 1i
38	Pin, Type Aa 1i	89	Tile mould	91	Tile mould
92	Tile mould	94	Stone mould	95	Stone mould

Site 11 (Eastern side)
1	Pin, Type Ca 1iii	3	Strap-end, Type D	91	Unidentified object

Site 13 (Eastern side)
1	Pendant	2	Buckle		

Site 15 (Clifford Street area)
1	Brooch, Type A	2	Mount	3	Mount
4	Strap-end, Type C	5	Strap-end, Type A	6	Pin, Type Bb 1i
7	Pin, Type Ca 2ii	218	Pin, Type Bb 2ii	281	Buckle
287	Pin, Type Aa 1ii	289	Buckle		

Site 18 (Eastern side)
16	Unidentified object

Site 20 (Eastern side)
1	Pin, Type Ab 2iii	2	Strap-end, Type B	3	Pin, Type Ca 1i
6	Unidentified object	8	Pin, Type Aa 2ii	9	Buckle
28	Buckle				

Site 23 (Six Dials)
1	Pin, Type Bb 1i	2	Pin, Type Ca 2ii	4	Pin, Type Bb 2ii
5	Pendant	6	Pin, Type K	10	Buckle plate

Site 24 (Six Dials)
1	Unidentified object	2	Pin, Type Bb 2i	3	Pin, Type Aa 2i

4	Strap-end, Type B	5	Strap-end, Type B	7	(Fork/) spoon
9	Mount	10	Pin, Type K	12	Tweezers
13	Pin, Type Bb 2ii	14	Pin, Type Ab 2ii	17	Strap-end, Type A
18	Pin, Type Ca 2i	21	Strap-end, Type E	23	Pin, Type Ba 2iii
24	Pin, Type Ac 1ii	25	Strap-end, Type A	26	Unidentified Object
27	(Fork/) spoon	144	Pin, Type Ab 1ii	398	Pin, Type Ab 1ii
648	Identified object	809	Strap-end, Type E	819	Pin, Type Bb 2i
821	Pendant	822	Pin, Type Aa 1i	824	Strap-end, Type A
826	Pin, Type Ca 1i	830	Pin, Type Ca 1ii	832	Mount
834	Strap-end, Type C				

Site 26 (Six Dials)

144	Pin, Type Ab 1ii	145	Mount	177	Pin, Type Fa 1i
181	Strap-end, Type C	193	Mount	300	Pin, Type Ca 2i
304	Mount	393	Pin, Type Ca 2iii	398	Pin, Type Ab 1ii
585	Identified object	593	Fork	624	Pin, Type Aa 2ii
666	Pin, Type Aa 1ii	679	Pin, Type Bb 2ii	765	Pin, Type Ca 2i

Site 30 (Six Dials)

1	Mount	66	Pin, Type Bb 1iii	68	Pin, Type Ca 2i
72	Pin, Type Ac 2ii	73	Pin, Type Fb 1ii	99	Pin, Type Ca 2i
161	Pin, Type Bb 2ii	177	Strap-end, Type B	178	Hook
183	Unidentified object	266	Pin, Type Ia 2i	328	Pin, Type Ga 1ii
330	Pin, Type Ab 1iii	356	Mount	442	Pin, Type Aa 1ii
493	Hook				

Site 31 (Six Dials)

11	Pin, Type Ab 1ii	13	Buckle pin	31	Pin, Type Ad 2ii
101	Tweezers	157	Pin, Type Bb 2ii	254	Loop
520	Pin, Type Da 1i	547	Mount	574	Pin, Type Ca 2ii
600	Pin, Type Ca 2i	622	Strap-end, Type B	653	Finger-ring
668	Hooked tag	672	Pin, Type Ac 2ii	677	Pin, Type Bb 2i
869	Fork	882	Pin, Type Ga 2i	910	Strap-end, Type A
919	Hook	982	Pin, Type Aa 1ii	1025	Pin, Type Ab 2iii
1058	Pin, Type Bb 2ii	1247	Pin, Type Ac 1i	1258	Pin, Type Bb 1i
1266	Ring	1324	Hook	1391	Loop
1428	Pin, Type Bb 2ii	1434	Pin, Type Bb 2i	1460	Pin, Type Bb 2i
1464	Pin, Type Ad 2ii	1466	Pin, Type Aa 2iii	1482	Hooked tag
1487	Pin, Type Bb 2ii	1562	Pin, Type Bb 2i	1563	Pin, Type Ba 2ii
1567	Pin, Type Bd 1i	1644	Pin, Type Da 1ii	1645	Pin, Type Bb 2ii
1647	Loop	1648	Pin, Type Da 1i	1653	Brooch, Type B
1849	Mount	1869	Loop	2102	Pin, Type Ca 2i
2474	Unidentified object	2630	Loop	2642	Buckle pin
2644	Pin, Type Aa 1i				

Site 32 (Clifford Street area)

4	Mount	5	Unidentified object	6	Mount
87	Buckle plate	134	Brooch, Type A	156	Mount
157	Pin, Type Aa 1i	159	Pin, Type Fb 1ii	160	Pin, Type Ca 2iii
161	Pin, Type Ca 2i	162	Pin, Type Ac 2ii	163	Pin, Type Aa 2i
164	Pin, Type Bb 2ii	165	Pin, Type Bb 2ii	166	Strap-end, Type D
167	Pin, Type Ab 1ii	168	Pin, Type Ca 1iii	169	Pin, Type K
170	Hooked tag	171	Pin, Type Da 1ii	172	Strap-end, Type C
173	Loop	177	Identified object	179	Unidentified object
194	Stone mould	196	Pin, Type K	197	Mount
316	Strap-end, Type A	317	Strap-end, Type A	420	Pin, Type Ac 2ii
455	Strap-end, Type C	456	Pin, Type Ba 2iii	457	Pin, Type Bb 2ii
458	Pin, Type Ab 2ii	459	Pin, Type Aa 1ii	526	Weight

CONCORDANCE

Site 33 (St Mary's)
83	Hook	84	Hook	86	Ring
89	Strap-end, Type A				

Site 34 (Central area)
6	Brooch, Type D	8	Hook	84	Mount

Site 35 (Central area)
5	Pin, Type Ab 2ii	11	Pin, Type Ab 1i	34	Pin, Type Ba 2i

Site 36 (Clifford Street area)
94	Strap-end, Type E	95	Pin, Type Ca 2i	96	Key
97	Pin, Type Ba 2iii	98	Unidentified object	99	Strap-end, Type A
100	Mount	101	Ring	103	Finger-ring
104	Unidentified object	112	Hooked tag	117	Identified object, bell
190	Hooked tag	347	Pin, Type Ad 2iii		

Site 38 (Eastern side)
38	Ring	39	Hooked tag	40	Tweezers
42	Pin Type Ab 1ii	44	Disc		

Site 39 (Clifford Street area)
40	Tweezers	41	Pin, Type K	42	Loop
43	Hook	44	Pin, Type Ca 2ii	45	Pin, Type Aa 2ii

Site 44 (St Mary's)
1	Strap-end, Type A	2	Pin, Type Aa 2iii		

Site 85 (Central area)
14	Pin, Type Ad 2iii				

Site 99 (Central area)
25	Pin, Type Aa 2iii	75	Tweezers	91	Mount
108	Mount				

Site 169 (Six Dials)
1	Pin, Type Ab 2ii	6	Pin, Type Ab 1i	21	Pin, Type Ca 2i
145	Mount	180	Pin, Type Bb 2i	189	Strap-end, Type B
213	Pin, Type Ab 2iii	238	Loop	245	Pin, Type Bb 2ii
318	Buckle	327	Pin, Type Bb 1ii	341	Pin, Type Aa 1i
397	Strap-end, Type B	442	Pin, type Ba 2i	457	Unidentified object
488	Hooked tag	549	Disc	555	Pin, Type Ca 1ii
568	Pin, Type Ed 1i	616	Pin, Type Ca 1ii	634	Pin, Type Ed 1i
669	Mount	748	Pin, Type Aa 2ii	749	Mount
752	Mortar	790	Identified object	817	Pin, Type Bb 1ii
818	Pin, Type Ha 1ii	914	Pin, Type Da 1i	915	Pin, Type Ba 1i
1163	Pin, Type Bb 1ii	1270	Strap-end, Type C	1286	Pin, Type Bb 1i
1297	Unidentified object	1408	Pin, Type Da 1i	1409	Pin, Type Aa 2iii
1447	Hook	1461	Stone mould	1465	Strap-end, Type B
1503	Pin, Type Aa 1ii	1515	Loop	1564	Ring
1585	Hook	1600	Hooked tag	1605	Pin, Type Ca 1i
1611	Hook	1698	Pin, Type Aa 1ii	1747	Pin, Type Bb 2i
1821	Unidentified object	1867	Pin, Type Ca 1ii	1905	Pin, Type Bb 2ii
1973	Pin, Type Aa 2iii	1879	Mount	2037	Strap-end, Type D
2041	Unidentified object	2169	Strap-end, Type C	2244	Pin, Type Aa 2iii
2323	Buckle pin	2376	Pin, Type Ca 2ii	2390	Pin, Type Ca 2i
2418	Pin, Type Da 1i	2469	Pin, Type Bb 2i	2499	Pin, Type Aa 2ii
2548	Tweezers	2568	Pin, Type Aa 2i	2622	Hooked tag

2700	Ring	2831	Disc	2930	Pin, Type Ca 2i
2955	Pin, Type Bb 2ii	2959	Pin, Type Ed 1i	2960	Mount
2998	Pin, Type Ab 1ii				

Site 177 (Central area)

4	Pin, Type Bb 1ii	53	Strap-end, Type A	234	Pin, Type Aa 2iii
251	Buckle	313	(Hook/) handle	562	Pin, Type Ab 2ii
567	Pin, Type Aa 2ii	595	Pin, Type Aa 1i	629	Pin, Type Ab 2iii
652	Pin, Type Da 1i	821	(Hook/) handle		

Site 184 (St Mary's)

86	Pin, Type Bd 2ii	124	Pin, Type Aa 1ii	377	Disc

Site 254 (St Mary's)

107	Pin, Type Da 1i	114	Pin, Type Aa 2ii	115	Pin, Type Ad 2ii
144	Pin, Type Da 1i	811	Brooch, Type A	1149	Strap-end, Type C
1305	Identified object	1308	Pin, Type Ca 2i	1370	Pin, Type Ia 1ii
1494	Identified object	1523	Pin, Type Aa 2ii	1595	Hook
1613	Pin, Type Ad 2ii	1679	Pin, Type Da 1i	2293	Clay mould
2294	Clay mould	2315	Clay mould	2321	Clay mould
2322	Clay mould	2350	Clay mould		

Site 258 (Six Dials)

27	Pin, Type Aa 2iii	80	Strap-end, Type D	102	Tweezers
118	Pin, Type Bb 1i	138	Pin, Type Ca 1i	181	Pin, Type Aa 1ii
183	Unidentified object	260	Pin, Type Bb 1iii	270	Pin, Type Ba 2ii
310	Pin, Type Aa 2ii	331	Brooch, Type B	370	Scale-pan
400	Pin, Type Bb 1ii				

Site 349 (Six Dials)

35	Pin, Type Ab 2iii	38	Pin, Type Bb 1ii	42	Pin, Type Ab 1ii
80	(Tweezers/) toilet implement	148	Pin, Type Bb 2i	150	Tweezers
151	Pin, Type Ad 2iii				

SUMMARY

The large collection of non-ferrous metal objects from Hamwic (Saxon Southampton) is catalogued: the principal categories are Brooches, Finger-rings, Hooked tags, Loops, Pendants, Pins, Strap-ends, Tweezers, Handles, Keys, Mounts, 'Forks' and 'spoons', and Scales and weights. A miscellany of copper alloy was used, but there are no brasses. Although there are no gold objects, some are gilt, and there is a mortar used for grinding gold and mercury into an amalgam. There are a few silver objects.

Metalworking evidence of various sorts is represented by moulds, crucibles and cupels, the stone mortar, and fragments, including residues of a folded wire process. There are no concentrations of debris to suggest that any particular zone of Hamwic had a metalworking specialisation.

The collection shows many connections with other sites in England, and with trading emporia on the Continent. Places of manufacture cannot be determined, though two unusual disc-brooches seem likely to be Hamwic's own products. Although some objects might be seventh-century in date, all may be eighth-century or later; one sub-category of strap-end is likely to be ninth century, but Hamwic's decline and virtual abandonment cannot be exactly charted. The paucity of gold and silver objects suggests no great wealth variation within its population. Although different in many ways from any other settlement within Wessex, Hamwic was an integral part of that kingdom and its culture.

SOMMAIRE

L'importante collection d'objets en métal non-ferreux provenant de Hamwic (Southampton à l'époque Saxonne) est inscrite dans un catalogue. Les catégories principales comprennent des fibules, des bagues, des pattes à cochets, des boucles, des pendentifs, des épingles, des passants, des pinces, des poignées, des clés, des montures, des 'fourchettes' et 'cuillères' ainsi que des balances et poids.

Divers alliages de cuivre étaient utilisés, mais il n'y a pas d'objets en laiton. Bien qu'on ne trouve aucun objet en or, certains sont dorés, et il y a un mortier utilisé pour broyer l'or et le mercure de façon à en faire un amalgame. Il y a peu d'objets en argent.

Les moules, les creusets et les coupelles, le mortier en pierre, ainsi que les fragments, y compris les restes d'un procédé pour plier les fils métalliques sont la preuve que différents types de ferronerie existaient. Il n'y a aucune concentration de débris qui suggère qu'une zone particulière de Hamwic se soit spècialisée dans le travail des métaux.

La collection indique que de nombreux liens existaient avec d'autres sites d'Angleterre ainsi qu'avec les centres de commerce du Continent. Il n'est pas possible de déterminer quels étaient les endroits chargés de la fabrication bien que deux fibules discoïdes semblent appartenir aux produits de Hamwic. Bien qu'il se peut que certains objets datent du VIIe siècle, il est possible qu'ils soient tous du VIIIe siècle ou plus récents.

Certains genres de passants datent probablement du IXe siècle, mais il n'est pas facile d'indiquer avec exactitude le déclin et en fait l'abandon de Hamwic. Le manque d'objets en or et en argent laisse supposer qu'il n'existait pas de grande différence de richesse parmi la population. Bien que différente à bien des égards de quelque autre colonie du Wessex, Hamwic faisait partie intégrante de ce royaume et de sa culture.

ZUSAMMENFASSUNG

Die umfassende Sammlung von Nichteisenmetallgegenständen aus Hamwic (sächsisches Southampton) ist katalogisiert: Die Hauptkategorien sind Fibeln, Fingerringe, Anhänger mit Haken, Schlaufen, Anhänger, Anstecknadeln, Riemenzungen, Pinzetten, Griffe, Schlüssel, Beschlagen, 'Gabeln' und 'Löffel', und Waagen und Gewichte. Verschiedene Arten von Kupferlegierungen wurden benutzt, aber kein Messing. Goldgegenstände sind nich vorhanden, jedoch aber vergoldete und ein Mörser, der dazu benutzt wurde, Gold und Quecksilber zu einem Amalgam zu zermahlen. Außerdem sind einige Silbergegenstände vorhanden.

Das Vorhanden sein von Gußformen, Schmelztiegel und Kupolöfen, der Steinmörser und Bruchstücke, einschließlich der Uberberreste von einem Drahtfaltungsprozess, ist ein Beweis dafür, daß es Metallarbeiten gab. Es gibt jedoch keine Ansummlung von Trümmern, die darauf schließen lassen würde, daß sich eine spezielle Zone in Hamwic auf Metallarbeit spezialisiert haätte.

Die Sammlung zeigt viele Verbindungen mit anderen Grabungsstätten in England und mit Handelsemporien auf dem Kontinent. Herstellungsorte können nicht festgestellt werden, jedoch sind zwei ungewöhnliche scheibenfibeln wahrscheinlich aus Hamwic's eigener Herstellung. Obwohl einige Gegenstände aus dem 7. Jahrhundert stammen könnten, kommen wahrscheinlich alle aus dem 8. Jahrhundert; eine Subkategorie von Riemenzungen stammt eventuelle aus dem 9. Jahrhundert, jedoch können Hamwic's Zerfall und geradezu Aufgabe zeitlich nicht genau festgelegt werden. Der Mangel an Gold-und Silbergegenständen läßt darauf schließen, daß es keinen großen Reichtumsunterschied in Hamwic's Bevölkerung gab. Obwohl Hamwic sich in Vielem von anderen Niederlassungen in Wessex unterscheidet, war es ein integraler Bestandteil dieses Königreiches und seiner Kultur.

BIBLIOGRAPHY

Unless otherwise stated, books and pamphlets were published in London.

Addyman, PV, 1964, 'A dark-age settlement at Maxey, Northants', *Medieval Archaeol*, 8, 20–73
Addyman, PV, and Hill, DH, 1969, 'Saxon Southampton: a review of the evidence', *Proc Hampshire Fld Club Archaeol Soc*, 36, 61–96
Aldsworth, FR, 1978, 'The Droxford Anglo-Saxon cemetery, Soberton, Hampshire', *Proc Hampshire Fld Club Archaeol Soc*, 35, 93–182
Andrews, P (ed), 1988, *The Coins and Pottery from Hamwic*, Southampton Finds Volume One, Southampton City Museums
Andrews, P, 1993, 'Iron objects', 94–5 in Garner 1993
Andrews, P, 1995, *Excavations at Hamwic, Volume 2: Excavations at Six Dials*, Counc Brit Archaeol Res Rep, forthcoming
Armstrong, P, Tomlinson, D, and Evans, DH, 1991, *Excavations at Lurk Lane, Beverley, 1979–82*, Sheffield Excavation Rep 1
Arnold, CJ, 1982, *The Anglo-Saxon Cemeteries of the Isle of Wight*, British Museum
Arnold, CJ, 1988, *An Archaeology of the Early Anglo-Saxon Kingdoms*, Routledge
ASC, The Anglo-Saxon Chronicle, trans and ed D Whitelock, Eyre and Spottiswoode, 1961
Astill, G, 1985, 'Archaeology, economics and early medieval Europe', *Oxford J Archaeol*, 4, 215–31
Audin, A, 1955, 'Destination des agrafes Mérovingiennes à double crochet', *Rev Archaeol de l'Est et du Centre-Est*, 6 (1955), 158–9
Ayers, BS, 1988, *Excavations at St Martin-at-Palace Plain, Norwich 1981*, E Anglian Archaeol Rep 37
Ayers, BS, 1994, *Excavations at Fishergate, Norwich, 1985*, E Anglian Archaeol Rep 68
BM 1923, British Museum, *A Guide to the Anglo-Saxon Antiquities in the Department of British and Later Medieval Antiquities*, British Museum
Bailey, RN, 1971, 'An Anglo-Saxon pin-head from Pontefract', *Yorkshire Archaeol J*, 42, 405–6
Baldwin Brown, G, 1915, *Arts in Early England*, Vols 3 and 4, Edinburgh, Murray
Bayley, J, 1982, 'Non-ferrous metal and glass working in Anglo-Scandinavian England: an interim statement', PACT, 7ii, 487–96
Bayley, J, 1984, 'Some technological finds from Lion Walk and Balkerne Lane', 214–5 in Crummy, P, *Excavations at Lion Walk, Balkerne Lane and Middleborough, Colchester, Essex*, Colchester Archaeol Rep 3
Bayley, J, 1988A, 'Non-ferrous metalworking: continuity and change', 193–208 in Slater, EA, and Tate, JO (eds), *Science and Archaeology, Glasgow 1987*, Oxford, Brit Archaeol Rep Brit Ser 196
Bayley, J, 1988B, 'Crucibles and moulds', 184–8 in Daniels 1988
Bayley, J, 1991, 'Anglo-Saxon non-ferrous metalworking: a survey', *World Archaeol*, 23i, 115–30
Bayley, J, 1992A, *Anglo-Scandinavian Non-Ferrous Metalworking from 16–22 Coppergate*, Counc Brit Archaeol, Archaeology of York, The Small Finds, 17/7
Bayley, J, 1992B, 'The metalworking evidence (with a note on the stylistic evidence of the moulds by JT Lang)', 59–66 in Milne, G, and Richards, JD, *Two Anglo-Saxon Buildings and Associated Finds, Wharram, A Study of Settlement on the Yorkshire Wolds, 7*, York Univ Archaeol Pub 9
Bayley, J, 1992C, 'Non-ferrous metalworking in England: Late Iron Age to early medieval', Univ London, unpublished Ph D thesis
Bayley, J, 1993A, 'Crucibles', 1232–5 in Rogers 1993
Bayley, J, 1993B, 'Non-ferrous metalworking: crucibles and moulds', 95–6 in Garner 1993
Bergman, K, and Billberg, I, 1976, 'Metallhantverk', 199–212 in Mårtensson, A (ed), *Uppgrävt förflutet för PK-banken i Lund en investering i arkeologi, Archaologica Lundensia*, 7
Biddle, M, 1990A, *Object and Economy in Medieval Winchester* Oxford, University Press
Biddle, M, 1990B, 'Dress and hair pins', 552–60 in Biddle 1990A
Biddle, M, 1990C, 'Weights and measures', 908–28 in Biddle 1990A
Biddle, M, 1990D, 'Tweezers', 690–2 in Biddle 1990A
Biddle, M, 1990E, 'Early medieval vessel glass', 933 in Biddle 1990A
Bourdillon, J, 1979, 'Town life and animal husbandry in the Southampton area, as suggested by the excavated bones', *Proc Hampshire Fld Club Archaeol Soc*, 36, 181–91
Bourdillon, J, and Coy, J, 1980, 'The animal bones', 79–120 in Holdsworth 1980

Brodribb, AC, Hands, AR, and Walker, DR, 1972, *Excavations at Shakenoak Farm, near Wilcote, Oxfordshire,* Vol 3, Oxford, Brit Archaeol Rep

Brown, H, 1988, 'An Islamic dirham', 25–6 in Andrews (ed) 1988

Bruce-Mitford, RLS, 1956, 'Late Saxon disk-brooches', 171–201 in Harden, DB (ed), *Dark-Age Britain,* Methuen

Bruce-Mitford, RLS, 1983, *The Sutton Hoo Ship-Burial,* Volume 3ii, Care Evans, A (ed), British Museum Pubs

Bruce-Mitford, RLS, 1993, 'Late Celtic hanging-bowls', 45–70 in Vince, A (ed), *Pre-Viking Lindsey,* Lincoln Archaeol Studies 1

Buckton, D, 1986, 'Late 10th- and 11th-century cloisonné enamel brooches', *Medieval Archaeol,* 30, 8–18

Bu'lock, JD, 1960, 'The Celtic, Saxon and Scandinavian settlement at Meols in Wirrall', *Trans Hist Soc Lancashire Cheshire,* 112, 1–28

Burnam, JM, 1920, *A Classical Technology Edited from Codex Lucensis 490,* Boston

Capelle, T, 1970, 'Metallschmuck und Gussformen aus Haithabu (Ausgrabungen 1963–1964)', 9–23 in Schietzel, K (ed), *Berichte über die Ausgrabungen in Haithabu,* Bericht 4, Neumünster

Capelle, T, 1976, *Die frühgeschichtlichen Metallfunde von Domburg auf Walcheren,* Rijksdienst voor het Oudheidkundig Bodemonderzoek, 5

Capelle, T, 1978, *Die karolingischen Funde van Schouwen,* Nederlandse Oudheden, ROB 7, Amersfoort

Caple, C, 1986, 'An analytical appraisal of copper-alloy pin production: 400–1600 AD', University of Bradford, Ph D thesis

Caple, C, 1991, 'The detection and definition of an industry: the English medieval and post-medieval pin industry', *Archaeol J,* 148, 241–55

Carr, J, 1985, 'Excavations on the Mound, Glastonbury, Somerset, 1971', *Proc Somerset Natur Hist Archaeol Soc,* 129, 37–62

Carter, A, 1982, Review of Holdsworth 1980, *Medieval Archaeol,* 36, 231–2

Champion, TC, 1977, 'Chalton', *Current Archaeol,* 59, 364–9

Cherry, JF, and Hodges, R, 1979, 'The dating of Hamwih: Saxon Southampton reconsidered', *Antiq J* 58, 299–309

Clark, J, 1979, 'Saxon – early medieval and undated finds', 118–21 in Canham, R, 'Excavations at Shepperton Green 1967 and 1973', *Trans London Middlesex Archaeol Soc,* 30, 97–121

Collis, J, and Kjølbye-Biddle, B, 1979, 'Early medieval bone spoons from Winchester', *Antiq J,* 59, 375–91

Cook, AM, and Dacre, MW, 1985, *Excavations at Portway, Andover 1973–1975,* Oxford Univ Committee Archaeol Mono 4

Costa, D, 1964, *Nantes: Art Mérovingien – Musée Th Dobrée,* Paris

Couchman, CR, 1979, 'Work of Essex County Council Archaeological Section, 1978', *Essex Archaeol Hist,* 1, 32–77

Crowther, DR, 1983, 'The small finds', 250–4 in Millett, M, 'Excavations at Cowdery's Down, Basingstoke, Hampshire', *Archaeol J,* 140, 151–279

Cunliffe, B, 1976, *Excavations at Portchester Castle Vol II: Saxon,* Soc Antiq

Daniels, R, 1988, 'The Anglo-Saxon monastery at Church Close, Hartlepool, Cleveland', *Archaeol J,* 145, 158–210

Davies, SM, 1991, 'The finds', 40–6 in Fasham, PJ, and Whinney, RJB, *Archaeology and the M3,* Hampshire Fld Club Archaeol Soc Mono 7

Decaens, J, et al, 1971, 'Un nouveau cimetière du haut moyen âge en Normandie, Hérouvillette (Calvados)', *Archéologie Médiévale,* 1, 1–87

Denford, GT, 1986, 'A keystone garnet disc brooch from Ampfield' *Proc Hampshire Fld Club Archaeol Soc,* 42, 160–1

Detsicas, AP, and Hawkes, S, 1973, 'Finds from the Anglo-Saxon cemetery at Eccles, Kent', *Antiq J,* 53, 281–6

Dickinson, TM, 1973, 'Bronze lace-tags from Site F', 116–17 in Brodribb, AC, Hands, AR, and Walker, DR, *Excavations at Shakenoak,* Vol 4, Oxford, Brit Archaeol Rep

Dickinson, TM, 1990, 'The metal objects', 181 in McCarthy, MR, *A Roman, Anglian and Medieval Site at Blackfriars, Carlisle, Excavations 1977–79,* Carlisle

Dickinson, TM, 1993, 'Early Saxon saucer brooches: a preliminary overview', *Anglo-Saxon Studies Archaeol Hist,* 6, 11–44

Dolley, M, 1971, 'The nummular brooch from Sulgrave', 333–49 in Clemoes, P, and Hughes, K (eds), *England before the Conquest,* Cambridge, Univ Press

Dornier, A, 1977, 'The Anglo-Saxon monastery at Breedon-on-the-Hill, Leicestershire', 155–68 in Dornier, A (ed), *Mercian Studies,* Leicester, Univ Press

Drescher, H, 1984, 'Glockenfunde aus Haithabu', 9–62 in Schietzel, K (ed), *Bericht über die Ausgrabungen in Haithabu,* Bericht 19

Dunstable Library and Museum, 1925–26, *Museum: First Annual Rep (1925–26) of the Committee,* Dunstable

Edwards, N, 1990, *The Archaeology of Early Medieval Ireland,* Batsford

Evans, AC, 1991, 'Grave group', 51–3 in Webster and Backhouse (eds)

Evison, VI, 1966, 'A caterpillar-brooch from Old Erringham Farm, Shoreham-by-Sea, Sussex', *Medieval Archaeol,* 10, 149–51

Evison, VI, 1976, 'Comment on a tag-end', 247–8 in Farley, M, 'Saxon and medieval Walton, Aylesbury: excavations 1973–4', *Rec Buckinghamshire,* 20 ii, 153–290

Evison, VI, 1988, *An Anglo-Saxon Cemetery at Alton, Hampshire,* Hampshire Fld Club Mono 4

Fairbrother, J, 1990, *Faccombe Netherton. Excavations of a Saxon and Medieval Manorial Complex,* British Museum Occ Paper 74

Fanning, T, 1990, 'Die bronzenen Ringkopfnadeln aus der Ausgrabung in Hafen von Haithabu', 127–70 in Schietzel (ed), 1990

Fasham, PJ, and Whinney, RJB, 1991, *Archaeology and the M3*, Hampshire Fld Club Archaeol Soc Mono 7

Fisher, GC, 1979, 'Finger-rings of the early Anglo-Saxon period', unpublished M Phil thesis, Univ of Oxford

Frere, SS, and Stow, S, 1983, *Excavations in the St George's Street and Burgate Street Areas*, Archaeology of Canterbury 7, Kent Archaeol Soc

Gaimster, DRM, Margeson, S, and Barry, T, 1989, 'Medieval Britain and Ireland in 1988', *Medieval Archaeol*, 33, 161–241

Gaimster, DRM, Margeson, S, and Hurley, M, 1990, 'Medieval Britain and Ireland in 1989', *Medieval Archaeol*, 34, 162–252

Garner, MF, 1993, 'Middle Saxon evidence at Cook Street, Southampton (SOU 254)', *Proc Hampshire Fld Club Archaeol Soc*, 49, 77–128

Gingell, CJ, 1975/6, 'Excavation of an early Anglo-Saxon cemetery at Collingbourne Ducis', *Wiltshire Archaeol Mag*, 70/1, 61–98

Goodall, AR, 1984, 'III: non-ferrous metal objects', 68–75 in Rogerson, A, and Dallas, C, *Excavations in Thetford 1948–59 and 1973–80*, East Anglian Archaeol Rep 22

Goodall, AR, 1991, 'The copper alloy and gold', 148–54 in Armstrong *et al* 1991

Goodall, IH, 1990, 'Heckle or woolcomb teeth', 214–16 in Biddle 1990A

Goodall, IH, and Keene, D, 1990, 'Harbicks (shear-board hooks)', 239–40 in Biddle 1990A

Graham, AH, and Davies, SM, 1993, *Excavations in the Town Centre of Trowbridge, Wiltshire, 1977 and 1986–1988*, Salisbury, Wessex Archaeol Rep 2

Graham-Campbell, J, 1982A, 'A Middle Saxon gold finger-ring from the Cathedral Close, Exeter', *Antiq J*, 62, 366–7

Graham-Campbell, J, 1982B, 'Some new and neglected finds of 9th-century Anglo-Saxon ornamented metalwork', *Medieval Archaeol*, 26, 144–51

Graham-Campbell, J, 1995, *The Viking Age Gold and Silver of Scotland (AD 850–1100)*, Edinburgh, National Museums of Scotland

Graham-Campbell, J, and Okasha, E, 1991, 'A pair of inscribed Anglo-Saxon tags from the Rome (Forum) 1883 hoard', *Anglo-Saxon England*, 20, 221–9

Gray Hill, N, 1937, 'Excavations on Stockbridge Down', *Papers Proc Hampshire Fld Club Archaeol Soc*, 13iii, 247–59

Grierson, P, 1991, *Coins of Medieval Europe*, Seaby

Haith, C, 1991, Entries in Webster and Backhouse (eds), *passim*

Haldenby, D, 1990, 'An Anglian site on the Yorkshire Wolds', *Yorkshire Archaeol J*, 62, 51–63

Haldenby, D, 1992, 'An Anglian site on the Wolds – continued', *Yorkshire Archaeol J*, 64, 25–39

Hall, RA, 1984, *The Viking Dig*, Bodley Head

Hall, RA, 1986, 'Archaeological aspects', 15–25 in Pirie, EJE, *Post-Roman Coins from York Excavations 1971–81*, Counc Brit Archaeol, Archaeology of York, 18/1

Halleux, R, 1981, *Les Alchimistes Grecs: Tome 1: Papyrus de Leyde, Papyrus de Stockholm, Fragments de Recettes*, Paris

Harden, DB, 1976, 'The glass', 232–4 in Cunliffe 1976

Harper, PO, and Meyers, P, 1981, *Silver vessels of the Sasanian Period: Volume 1: Royal Imagery*, New York, Metropolitan Museum of Art

Haslam, J, 1980, 'A middle Saxon iron smelting site at Ramsbury, Wiltshire', *Medieval Archaeol*, 24, 1–68

Haslam, J (ed), 1984, *Anglo-Saxon Towns in Southern England*, Chichester, Phillimore

Hattat, HJ, 1987, *Brooches of Antiquity. A Third Selection of Brooches from the Author's Collection*, Oxford, Oxbow Books

Hawkes, SC, 1990, 'The Anglo-Saxon necklace from Lower Brook Street', 621–7 in Biddle 1990A

Hawthorne, JG, and Smith, CS, 1963, *Theophilus: On Divers Arts*, Chicago Univ Press (reprinted New York, 1979)

Henig, M, 1981, 'The bronze', 44–5 in Rowley, T, and Brown, L, 'Excavations at the Beech House Hotel, Dorchester-on-Thames, 1972', *Oxoniensia*, 46, 1–55

Hill, D, Barrett, D, Maude, K, Warburton, J, and Worthington, M, 1990, 'Quentovic defined', *Antiquity*, 64, 51–8

Hinchliffe, J, 1986, 'An early medieval settlement at Cowage Farm, Foxley, near Malmesbury', *Archaeol J*, 143, 240–59

Hinton, DA, 1977, 'A late Saxon strap-end from Andover, Hants', *Proc Hampshire Fld Club Archaeol Soc*, 34, 80

Hinton, DA, 1978, 'Late Saxon treasure and bullion', 135–58 in Hill, D (ed), *Ethelred the Unready*, Oxford, Brit Archaeol Rep Brit Ser 59

Hinton, DA, 1980, 'The bronze, iron, lead and wood', 73–5 in Holdsworth 1980

Hinton, DA, 1990A, 'Buckles and buckle-plates', 506–26 in Biddle 1990A

Hinton, DA, 1990B, 'Hooked tags', 548–52 in Biddle 1990A

Hinton, DA, 1990C, 'Split-end strap-ends', 500–2 in Biddle 1990A

Hinton, DA, 1993A, 'A smith's hoard from Tattershall Thorpe, Lincolnshire: a synopsis', *Anglo-Saxon England*, 22, 147–66

Hinton, DA, 1993B, Note in Graham and Davies 1993, 83

Hinton, DA, 1993C, 'Non-ferrous metal objects', 92–4 in Garner 1993

Hinton, DA, and Hodges, R, 1977, 'Excavations in Wareham, 1974–5', *Proc Dorset Natur Hist Soc*, 99, 42–83

Hinton, DA, and Welch, M, 1976, 'Iron and bronze', 195–219 in Cunliffe 1976

Hodges, R, 1981, *The Hamwih pottery: the local and imported wares from 30 years' excavations at Middle Saxon Southampton and their European context*, Counc Brit Archaeol Res Rep 37

Hodges, R, 1989, *The Anglo-Saxon Achievement*, Duckworth

Hodges, R, 1991, 'The 8th-century pottery industry at La Londe, near Rouen, and its implications for cross-channel trade with Hamwic, Saxon Southampton', *Antiquity*, 65, 882–7

Holdsworth, P, 1976, 'Saxon Southampton: a new review', *Medieval Archaeol*, 20, 26–61

Holdsworth, P, 1980, *Excavations at Melbourne Street, Southampton, 1971–76*, Counc Brit Archaeol Res Rep 33

Holdsworth, P, 1984, 'Saxon Southampton', 331–43 in Haslam (ed) 1984

Holmqvist, W, 1972, *Excavations at Helgö IV. Workshop*, Kungl Vitterhets Historie och Antikvitets Akademien, Stockholm

Holmqvist, W, 1979, *Vikingar p & Helgö och Birka*, Stockholm

Hübener, W, 1972, 'Gleicharmige Bügelfibeln der Merowingerzeit in Westeuropa', *Madrider Mitteilungen*, 13, 211–69

Hughes, M, 1986, *Excavations at Meonstoke 1985/6*, Hampshire County Council

Hull, MR, 1967, 'The Nor'nour brooches', 28–64 in Dudley, D, 'Excavations on Nor'nour in the Isles of Scilly, 1962–6', *Archaeol J*, 124, 1–64

Hunter, JR, and Heyworth, M, Volume on Hamwic glass (forthcoming)

Jackson, S, 1988, 'Copper alloy objects', 182–3 in Daniels 1988

Keen, L, 1975, '*Illa mercimonia que dicitur Hamwih*: a study in early medieval urban development', *Archaeologia Atlantica*, 1 (1975), 165–90

James, E, 1982, 'Ireland and western Gaul in the Merovingian period', 362–86 in Whitelock, D, McKitterick, R, and Dumville, D (eds), *Ireland in Early Medieval Europe*, Cambridge, Univ Press

James, E, 1988, *The Franks*, Oxford, Blackwell

Keen, L, 1975, '*Illa mercimonia que dicitur Hamwih:* a study in early medieval urban development', *Archaeologia Atlantica*, 1 (1975), 165–90

Keen, L, 1986, 'Late Anglo-Saxon strap-ends from Dorset', *Proc Dorset Natur Hist Archaeol Soc*, 108, 195–6

Kelly, S, 1992, 'Trading privileges from eighth-century England', *Early Medieval Europe*, 1, 3–28

Kemp, RL, 1993, 'The archaeology of 46–54 Fishergate', 1205–16 in Rogers 1993

Knocker, GM, 1956, 'Early burials and an Anglo-Saxon cemetery at Snell's Corner near Horndean, Hampshire', *Proc Hampshire Fld Club Archaeol Soc*, 19, 117–70

Kruse, SE, 1992, 'Late Saxon balances and weights from England', *Medieval Archaeol*, 36, 67–95

Leahy, K, 1991, 'Selected finds from a high-status site at Flixborough, South Humberside', 94–101 in Webster and Backhouse (eds) 1991

Leeds, ET, 1945, 'The distribution of the Angles and Saxons archaeologically considered', *Archaeologia*, 91, 1–106

Leman, P, 1981, 'Contribution à la localisation de Quentovic, ou la relance d'un vieux débat', *Revue du Nord*, 53 no 251, 935–45

Leman, P, 1990, 'Quentovic: état des recherches', *Revue du Nord*, 72, 175–8

Liddell, DM, 1933, 'Excavations at Meon Hill', *Papers Proc Hampshire Fld Club Archaeol Soc*, 12 ii, 127–60

Lins, PA, and Oddy, WA, 1975, 'The origins of mercury gilding', *J Archaeol Sci*, 2, 365–73

Liversage, D, 1983 'An unpublished Irish grave group from Norway', *Acta Archaeologica*, 54, 147–51

Loyn, HR, 1962, *Anglo-Saxon England and the Norman Conquest*, Longmans

Maaskant-Kleibrink, M, 1980, 'A gold ring set with a Roman ringstone from Dorestad, Hoogstraat I', 207–11 in van Es and Verwers 1980

MacGregor, A, and Bolick, E, 1993, *Ashmolean Museum, Oxford: A Summary Catalogue of the Anglo-Saxon Collections (Non-Ferrous Metals)*, Oxford, Brit Archaeol Rep Brit Ser 230

Margeson, S, 1993, *Norwich Households: Medieval and Post-Medieval Finds from Norwich Survey Excavations 1971–78*, East Anglian Archaeol Rep 58

McKinley, JI, and Garner, MF, 1993, 'The cemetery', 84–9 in Garner 1993

Meaney, AL, 1981, *Anglo-Saxon Amulets and Curing Stones*, Oxford, Brit Archaeol Rep Brit Ser 96

Meaney, AL, 1992, 'Anglo-Saxon idolators and ecclesiasts from Theodore to Alcuin: a source study', *Anglo-Saxon Stud Archaeol Hist*, 5, 103–25

Meaney, AL, and Hawkes, SC, 1970, *Two Anglo-Saxon Cemeteries at Winnall, Winchester, Hampshire*, Soc Medieval Archaeol Mono 4

Metcalf, DM, 1988, 'The Coins', 17–59 in Andrews (ed) 1988

Metcalf, DM, 1990A, 'A "Porcupine" sceat from Market Lavington, with a list of other sceattas from Wiltshire', *Wiltshire Archaeol Natur Hist Mag*, 83, 205–8

Metcalf, DM, 1990B, Distribution map, 53 in Hinton, DA, *Archaeology, Economy and Society*, Seaby

Metcalf, DM, 1993A, *Thrymsas and Sceattas in the Ashmolean Museum Oxford, Volume 1*, London, Royal Numismatic Soc and Ashmolean Museum, Oxford

Metcalf, DM, 1993B, *Thrymsas and Sceattas in the Ashmolean Museum Oxford, Volume 2*, London, Royal Numismatic Soc and

Ashmolean Museum, Oxford

Metcalf, DM, 1993C, 'Coin', 91–2 in Garner 1993

Metcalf, DM, and Northover, JP, 1985, 'Debasement of the coinage in southern England in the age of King Alfred', *Numismatic Chron*, 145, 150–76

Metcalf, DM, and Northover, JP, 1989, 'Coinage alloys from the time of Offa and Charlemagne to *c* 864', *Numismatic Chron*, 149, 101–20

Mortimer, C, 1988, 'Anglo-Saxon copper alloys from Lechlade, Gloucestershire', *Oxford J Archaeol*, 7ii, 227–33

Morton, AD (ed), 1992, *Excavations at Hamwic: Volume 1*, Counc Brit Archaeol Res Rep 84

Munby, J, 1984, 'Saxon Chichester and its predecessors', 315–30 in Haslam (ed) 1984

Musée national 1988, *Un Village au temps de Charlemagne*, Musée national des arts et traditions populaires, 29 Nov 1988 – April 30 1989, Editions de la Réunion des Musées nationaux, Paris

Nenk, BS, Margeson, S, and Hurley, M, 1991, 'Medieval Britain and Ireland in 1990' *Medieval Archaeol*, 35, 126–238

Newman, J, 1993, 'The Anglo-Saxon cemetery at Boss Hall, Ipswich', *Bull Sutton Hoo Res Committee*, 8, 32–5

O'Brien, E, 1993, 'Contacts between Ireland and Anglo-Saxon England in the seventh century', *Anglo-Saxon Stud Archaeol Hist*, 6, 93–102

Oddy, WA, 1985, 'Vergoldungen auf prähistorichen und klassischen Bronzen', 64–71 in Born, H (ed), *Archäologische Bronzen: Antike Kunst Moderne Technik*, Berlin, Museum für Vor-und Frühgeschichte

Oddy, WA, 1988, 'The gilding of Roman silver plate', 9–25 in Baratte, F (ed), *Argenterie Romaine et Byzantine, Actes de la Table Ronde, Paris, 11–13 octobre 1983*, Paris

Oddy, WA, Bimson, M, and La Niece, S, 1981, 'Gilding Himalayan images: history, tradition and modern techniques', 87–101 in Oddy, WA, and Zwalf, W (eds), *Aspects of Tibetan Metallurgy*, British Museum Occ Paper 15

Oddy, WA, and Meeks, ND, 1978, 'A Parthian bowl: study of the gilding technique', *MASCA*, 1, 5–6

Oddy, WA, La Niece, S, and Stratford, N, 1986, *Romanesque Metalwork: Copper Alloys and their Decoration*, British Museum Pubs

Oddy, WA, and Tylecote, RF, 1990, 'Objects associated with gold working', 76–84 in Biddle 1990A

Owen-Crocker, GR, 1986, *Dress in Anglo-Saxon England*, Manchester, Univ Press

Pagan, HE, 1988A, 'The older coin finds from Southampton', 60–70 in Andrews (ed) 1988

Pagan, HE, 1988B, 'The imitative Louis the Pious solidus from Southampton and finds of other related coins in the British Isles', 71–2 in Andrews (ed) 1988

Peers, C, and Radford, CAR, 1943, 'The Saxon monastery of Whitby', *Archaeologia*, 89, 27–88

Pelteret, D, 1981, 'Slave raiding and slave trading in early England', *Anglo-Saxon England*, 9, 99–114

Pilet, C, et Alduc-le Bagousse, A, 1990, 'Les Nécropoles de Giberville (Calvados). Fin du Vème siècle-fin du VIIème après J–C', *Archéologie Médiévale*, 20, 3–140

Pilet, Ch, Alduc-le Bagousse, A, Blondiaux, J, Buchet, L, et Pilet-Fermière, J, 1992, 'Le village de Saunerville, "Lirose", fin de la période gauloise au VIIe siècle après J–C', *Archéologie Médièvale*, 22, 1–190

Pretty, K, 1972, 'Two bronze spiral-headed pins', 84–6 in Brodribb, ACC, Hands, AR, and Walker, DR, *Excavations at Shakenoak Farm, near Wilcote, Oxfordshire: Part III, Site F*, Oxford, privately printed

Pritchard, F, 1991, 'Small finds', 120–278 in Vince (ed) 1991

Rahtz, P, 1979, *The Saxon and Medieval Palaces at Cheddar: Excavations 1960–62*, Oxford, Brit Archaeol Rep Brit Ser 65

Randsborg, K, 1991, *The First Millennium AD in Europe and the Mediterranean*, Cambridge, Univ Press

Robinson, PH, 1994, 'Devizes Museum', *Counc Brit Archaeol Wessex Newsletter* (April 1994), 24–5

Roes, A, 1954, 'Agrafes du haut Moyen Age à double crochet', *Revue Archaeol de l'Est et du Centre-Est*, 5, 330–4

Roes, A, 1965, *Vondsten van Dorestad*, Groningen, Wolters

Roesdahl, E, 1977, *Fyrkat: En jysk vikingeborg.II: Oldsagerne og Gravpladsen*, Copenhagen, I Komm hos Herm HJ Lynge og søn

Roesdahl, E, *et al*, 1981, *The Vikings in England*, British Museum

Roesdahl, E, and Wilson, DM (eds), 1992, *From Viking to Crusader: Scandinavia and Europe 800–1200*, Nordic Council of Ministers, Paris/Berlin/Copenhagen

Rogers, NSH, 1993, *Anglian and Other Finds from Fishergate*, Counc Brit Archaeol, Archaeology of York, The Small Finds, 17/9

Ross, S, 1992, 'Dress pins from Anglo-Saxon England: their production and typo-chronological development', Univ of Oxford, D Phil thesis

Schietzel, K (ed), 1990, *Berichte über die Ausgrabungen in Haithabu, Bericht 27: Das archäologische Fundmateriel V Neumünster*, Karl Wachholz Verlag

Scull, C, 1986, 'A sixth-century grave containing a balance and weights from Watchfield, Oxfordshire', *Germania*, 65, 105–38

Scull, C, 1990, 'Scales and weights in early Anglo-Saxon England', *Archaeol J*, 147, 183–215

Scull, C, 1992, 'Excavations and survey at Watchfield, Oxfordshire', *Archaeol J*, 149, 124–281

Sherlock, D, and Woods, H, 1988, *St Augustine's Abbey: Report on excavations, 1960–78*, Maidstone, Kent Archaeol Soc

Smallridge, A, 1969, 'A late eighth-century disc from Mavourne Farm, Bolnhurst, Beds', *Bedfordshire Archaeol J*, 4, 13–5

Smith, C Roach, 1857, *Collectanea Antiqua IV* (printed for subscribers)

Smith, CS, and Hawthorne, JG, 1974, 'Mappae Clavicula: a little key to the world of medieval techniques', *Trans American Philosoph Soc* (new ser), 64iv

Smith, RA, 1923, 'Early Anglo-Saxon weights', *Antiq J*, 3, 122–9

Speake, G, 1989, *A Saxon Bed Burial on Swallowcliffe Down: Excavations by F de M Vatcher*, Hist Buildings Monuments Comm England

Spufford, P, 1988, *Money and its Uses in Medieval Europe*, Cambridge, Univ Press

Stamper, PA, 1977, 'Anglo-Saxon buckets: a discussion and gazetteer', Univ of Southampton, BA dissertation

Stead, IM, and Rigby, V, 1989, *Verulamium: The King Harry Lane Site*, English Heritage

Taylor, J, and Webster, L, 1984, 'A late Saxon strap-end mould from Carlisle', *Medieval Archaeol*, 28, 178–80

Timby, J, 1988, 'The middle Saxon pottery', 73–122 in Andrews (ed) 1988

Tweddle, D, 1992, *The Anglian Helmet from Coppergate*, Counc Brit Archaeol for York Archaeol Trust, The Archaeology of York, The Small Finds, 17/8

van Es, WA, 1976, 'La grande fibule de Dorestad', *Rijksdienst voor het Oudheidkundig Bodemonderzoek*, Overdrukken 80

van Es, WA, and Verwers, WJH, 1980, *Excavations at Dorestad 1. The Harbour: Hoogstraat I*, Nederlandse Oudheden 9, Amersfoort

Vince, A, 1990, *Saxon London: An Archaeological Investigation*, Seaby

Vince, A, 1991, 'The development of Saxon London', 409–35 in Vince (ed) 1991

Vince, A (ed), 1991, *Aspects of Saxo-Norman London: II Finds and Environmental Evidence*, London Middlesex Archaeol Soc Special Paper 12

Wade, K, 1988, 'Ipswich', 93–100 in Hodges, R, and Hobley, B (eds), *The Rebirth of Towns in the West*, Counc Brit Archaeol Res Rep 68

Waller, J, 1972, 'Dress pins', 27–45 in Holmqvist 1972

Wamers, E, 1986, *Archäologische Reihe Schmuck des frühen Mittelalters*, Frankfurter Museum für Vor-und Frühgeschichte

Waterman, DM, 1959, 'Late Saxon, Viking and early medieval finds from York', *Archaeologia*, 97, 59–105

Webster, L, 1991, Entries in Webster and Backhouse (eds) 1991, *passim*

Webster, L, 1993, 'The brooch mould', 62–3 in Hamerow, H, *Excavations at Mucking. Volume 2: The Anglo-Saxon Settlement, Excavations by MU Jones and WT Jones*, English Heritage Archaeol Rep 21

Webster, L, 1995, 'The Iona Abbey ring bezel', 49–50 in Graham-Campbell 1995

Webster, L, and Backhouse, J (eds), 1991, *The Making of England. Anglo-Saxon Art and Culture AD 600–900*, British Museum Press

Welch, MG, 1976, 'Iron and bronze', 205–14 in Hinton and Welch 1976

Welch, MG, 1983, *Early Anglo-Saxon Sussex*, Oxford, Brit Archaeol Rep Brit Ser 112

Welch, M, 1992, *Anglo-Saxon England*, English Heritage/Batsford

Werner, J, 1992, 'A review of *The Sutton Hoo Ship Burial Volume 3*: some remarks, thoughts and proposals', *Anglo-Saxon Stud Archaeol Hist*, 5, 1–24

West, S, 1985, *West Stow: The Anglo-Saxon Village*, East Anglian Archaeol 24, Suffolk Co Planning Dept

White, R, 1990, 'Scrap or substitute: Roman material in Anglo-Saxon graves', 125–52 in Southworth, E (ed), *Anglo-Saxon Cemeteries: A Reappraisal*, Alan Sutton, Stroud

Whitelock, D (ed), 1955, *English Historical Documents c 500–1042*, Eyre and Spottiswoode

Whitfield, N, 1990, 'Round wire in the early Middle Ages', *Jewellery Stud*, 4, 13–28

Whitwell, B, 1991, 'Flixborough', *Current Archaeol*, 126, 244–7

Williams, DF, 1980, 'Lava querns', 33 in Haslam 1980

Williams, V, 1988, 'Non-ferrous metal objects', 63–7 in Ayers 1988

Williams, V, 1994, 'Non-ferrous metal objects', 14–15 in Ayers 1994

Wilson, DM, 1964, *Anglo-Saxon Ornamental Metalwork 700–1100 in the British Museum*, British Museum

Wilson, DM, 1984, *Anglo-Saxon Art from the Seventh Century to the Norman Conquest*, Thames and Hudson

Wormald, CP, 1982, 'Viking studies: whence and whither', 128–53 in Farrell, RT (ed), *The Vikings*, Phillimore, Chichester

Yorke, B, 1990, *Kings and Kingdoms of Early Anglo-Saxon England*, Seaby

Youngs, SM (ed), 1989, *'The Work of Angels': Masterpieces of Celtic Metalwork, 6th–9th Centuries AD*, British Museum Press

Youngs, SM, Clark, J, and Barry, TB 1983, 'Medieval Britain and Ireland in 1982', *Medieval Archaeol*, 27, 161–229

INDEX

Page numbers of illustrations are given in italics

Abbots Worthy 35, 46, 99, 100
Aethelwulf, K 97
Aldbourne 20, 99
Aldhelm, St 99, 101
Alfred, K 96, 97
Alfriston 3, 5
Alton 5, 25, 35, 46
Ampfield 5
amulets, 'amulet-capsules' 13, 96, 102
Andover, *see* Portway
animal ornament 41, 42, 50, 54
animals 99, 102
arm-rings 65
assaying 88
attachments, *see* mounts
awls 35

bags 10, 12, 35, 103
balances, beam- 56, 58, 60
balls, rock-crystal 96
Barking Abbey 36, 104
bars 50, 63, *64*, 65
   see also mounts
Barton-on-Humber 60
base metals, *see* metals
Bawsey 42
beads, glass 9, 54
bells 50, 62, *63*
belts 8, 12, 13, 44, 54, 95–6
Beverley 56
binding-strips, *see* mounts
Birka 10
Bitterne, *see* Southampton
Bolney 31
Bologna 9
bone 35, 54, 56, 93
Boniface, St 99
books 54
Bourton-on-the-Water 29
boxes 50, 55
Boxmoor 5
Brandon 1, 29, 30, 31, 36, 50, 56, 99
brass, *see* metals
Breedon-on-the-Hill 54
Brintons Road, *see* Southampton
bronze, *see* metals
brooches *4*, 35, 47, 54, 68; 'ansate' 3; button 35; disc- 3, *4*, 5, 54, 98, 99, 100, 101, 103, 104; equal-arm bow- 3, *4*, 101, 103; gold 93, 94; pseudo-cameo 94; Roman bow- *4*, 6, 93;

saucer- 34; small-long *4*, 5, 95;
buckets 12, 50, 54
   see also vessels
buckles and buckle-fittings 6, *7*, 8, 35, 68, 95, 99, 103
burials, *see* cemeteries
Burton-on-Trent 3

Caedwalla, K 97
Caistor St Edmund, brooch 100
Canterbury 30, 59
Carlisle 30, 42
Carthage 101
caskets 50, 54
Cassington 99
cemeteries 1, 3, 5, 6, 7, 8, 9, 10, 12, 13–14, 25, 29, 30, 32, 34, 35, 37, 38, 41, 46, 47–8, 54, 56, 58, 59, 60, 62, 82, 94, 95, 101, 102, 103, 104
   see also shroud-hooks
chain 8, 12, 34, 47
chalk 84, 100
Chalton 20, 25, 28, 46, 99, 100
Charlemagne 101
châtelaines 13, 56
Cheddar 82
Chessell Down 7
Chichester 5
churches 56, 99, 102, 104
   see also Southampton, St Mary's
Clifford Street, *see* Southampton
clips 62
cloth 47, 60, 101
   see also textiles
coins 1, 10, 42, 56, 65, 93, 96, 97, 99, 101, 102
   see also gold, hoards, pennies, Roman, sceattas, *solidi, trientes*
Collingbourne Ducis 5, 34
Compton Verney 5
Cook Street, *see* Southampton
copper alloy, *see* metals
costume 8, 30, 35, 36, 95–6, 103, 104
Cottam and Cowlam 11, 94
counters 58
Cow Lowe 95
Cowdery's Down 12
craft specialisation 81, 98
crosses 54, 99
crucibles 68, 76, 77, 78, 79, 82, 84, 86, *87*, 88–92, 97, 98, 99
cupels 78, 79, 84, 86–92, 97, 98

daub 77
discs 32, 46, *47*, 56, 84, 98
distributors, *see* loops
dogs 101
Domburg 11, 20, 25, 28, 29, 94
Dorestad 11, 20, 25, 28, 30, *47*, 62, 94, 101, 102
double-ended hooks, *see* hooks, double-ended
draw plates 37
dress, *see* costume
dress-fasteners 8, 35, 47
   see also brooches, buckles, pins
drinking horns 54
Droxford 5, 6, 25, 35, 46

ear-rings 9
ear-scoops, *see* tweezers and other toilet items
Eccles 29
Egbert, K 97
embroidery 50
emission spectroscopy 81, 82
emporia 94, 97, 103–4
   see also wic sites
enamel 43
exchange *see also* gifts, trade
Exeter 9, 101

Faccombe-Netherton 82
fasteners, garment-, *see* dress-fasteners
Faversham 35
feasts 56
females, *see* women
ferrules 62, *63*
files 98,
finger-rings *8*, 9, 42, 54, 55, 80, 94, 101, 102, 103, 104
Flixborough 1, 30, 36, 56, 94, 99
'forks' and 'spoons' 55–6, *57*, 102
furs 100

garment-fasteners, *see* dress-fasteners
garment hooks, *see* hooked tags
garnets 30, 34, 94, 100
gartering 38
gems 9
gender 104
   see also men, women
Germany 89, 93
Giberville 47, 48

gifts 100, 101
gilding, *see* metals, mercury
Girton 30
glass 33, 34, 37, 54, 93
   see also beads, fittings, pin-heads, vessels, window
Glastonbury 38
gold, *see* metals
graves, *see* cemeteries
Gravesend 54
gunmetal, *see* metals

hair-pins 35, 36
Haithabu 11, 82, 85
Halstock 42
Hampshire 3, 5
Hamwic (Saxon Southampton), comparison with other sites 5, 94; distributions in 37, 68; end of 96–7; foundation of 96–7; functions of 97–101, 104; hinterland of 98–101, 103; prosperity of 96, 102; size of 95, 96, 98
   see also Southampton
handles, *see* hooks and handles
hanging-bowls 12
harbicks 47
Hartlepool 30, 40, 87
hearths 78, 80, 81, 86, 98
'heating trays', *see* cupels
heckles 35
Hedeby, *see* Haithabu
heirlooms 96
Helgo 36, 99
helmets 12
Hérouvillette 82
Herpes 47, 48, 101
Highdown 3, 5
Hitchin, ring from 9
hoards 7, 42, 56, 59, 96
hooked tags 9, *10*, 11, 41, 43, 50, 102
hooks and handles 48, *49*, 50, 55
hooks, double-ended 47–8, *49*, 101, 103
Horndean 7, 9, 12, 38

Ine, K 95, 97, 101
ingots 58, 63, *64*, 65, 85, 93, 98
inscriptions 99
Iona, ring from 9
Ipswich 1, 60, 94, 95, 100, 102
Ireland 32, 101, 103
ironwork 93
Isle of Wight 3, 5
Itchen, River 1

'Jutish' culture 5, 96, 101

Kentish culture 5, 54, 58, 59, 96
keys and locks 50, *51*, 62
Kingston-by-Lewes 40
Kingston Down 62
Kingsworthy 29, 46
knives 7, 12, 34

lace-tags 38, 44
lava 100, 101
lead, *see* metals
leaded bronze, *see* metals
leather 12, 37, 44, 54, 81, 101
Lincoln 12, 98
limestone 78, 84
linen, *see* textiles
litharge 97
locks, *see* keys
London 1, 3, 32, 60, 85, 94, 96, 100, 102
loops and distributors 11, *12*, 13, 32, 38, 62
   see also rings
Lund 82

males, *see* men
Malmesbury 7
manufacturing, *see* metalworking
manuscripts 99
'marginality' 103–4
Marinus, Pope 10
Maxey 38
Mediterranean influence 8
Melbourne Street, *see* Southampton
men 36, 46, 103–4
Meols 56
Meon Hill 10
Meonstoke 99
merchants, *see* traders
metallurgy 66–73
metal plating 62, 93
metals 8, 12, 56, 85, 87, 97–8: brass 66–73, 81, 88, 89, 93, 96–7; bronze 29, 66–73, 81, 82, 88; copper 66, 75, 81, 82, 93, 97; copper alloy 2, 7, 12, 28, 31, 35, 36, 37, 82, 84, 85, 86, 88, 98, 101, 102; gold 5, 30, 31, 34, 58, 80–2, 88, 89, 93, 94, 95, 97, 98, 99, 100, 101; gunmetal 66–73, 88, iron 7, 12, 35, 37, 50, 56, 62, 81; lead 2, 37, 58, 60, 62, 65, 66–73, 80, 81, 82, 84, 88, 93, 98, 101; leaded bronze 21, 29, 67, 98; mercury 9, 21, 25, 30, 54, 80–2, 89, 93, 94, 97; niello 2, 42–3; scrap 5, 46, 58, 68, 79, 93, 97, 98, 99; silver 2, 20, 34, 36, 42, 54, 56, 60, 66–73, 81, 85, 88, 93, 94, 96, 97, 98, 100, 101; tin 56, 66–73, 82, 84, 88, 93, 101; zinc 66–73, 82, 84, 88
metalworking 12, 14, 25, 35, 36–7, 42, 46, 50, 65, 68, 79, 82, 86, 88, 93, 97–9
   see also moulds, wire-folding
Minster Lovell jewel 54
minting 5, 88, 97
mortar, grinding *80*, 81–2, 89, 93, 97, 98, 100
moulds 36–7, 42, 78, 79, 82, *83*, 84, *85*, *86*, 87, 97, 98, 99, 100
mounts 9, 32, 44, 47, 50–1, *52*, 53–4, 58, 62
Mucking 99

nails, *see* mounts
nail-cleaners, *see* tweezers
necklaces 5, 8
neck-rings 65
needles 4, 50
net-sinkers 55, 62
niello, *see* metals
Norwich 1, 3, 48

Offa, K 101
Old Erringham 3

padlocks, *see* keys
pails, *see* buckets
palm-cups 95, 102
   see also vessels, glass
pastry-cutter 54,
pendants 5, *13*, 14, 46, 47, 95, 102
pennies 93, 96
   see also coins
pewter 98
pins 14–37, 66–71, 76, 79, 80, 93, 94, 95, 99, 102, 104; bi-conical 14, 25–8, 35, 67, 95; classification of 14–15; cuboid 14; disc 14, 30, *31*, 32, 35, 37, 47, 54, 67; discussion of 35–7; headless 14, 34–6; linked 8, 14, 32, *33*, 34, 35, 36, 95, 103, 104; miscellaneous 14, 34; oval 14, *33*; polyhedral 14, 21, *22*, 23–5, 35, 67; rhomboid 14, *31*, 32; ring 14, 32, *33*, 101, 103; spherical 14–15, *16*, *17*–19, *20*, 21, 25, 35, 36, 37, 67, 98, 99; spiral 14, 28, *29*, 30, 35, 36, 37, 67, 95, 96, 98
   see also buckles and buckle-fittings, chain, hair-pins
pits with metalworking residues 75, *76*, 77–9, 84, 85
pit with grinding mortar 80
plant ornament 54
playing-pieces 58
plugs 62
plumb bobs 62
Poitiers 93
Pontefract 31
Portchester 25, 29, 54, 99, 100
Portway 5, 35, 46
Poslingford 42
pottery 93, 95, 97, 99, 100–1
Poundbury 43
production, *see* metalworking
punches 99
purses 10

Quentovic 47, 94, 96
quernstones 100, 101

Ramsbury 100
Reculver 46
Rhine, River 96
Ribe 96
rings 12, 46, 54, *55*, *63*, 93, 94, 99

see also arm-, ear-, finger-, neck-rings
rods 12, 50, 62, 63, *64*, 68
Roman, bow-brooch *6*, 93; brick 78; coins 6, 47, 58–61, 93; crucibles 86, 99; keys 50; pins 37; reused objects 6; rings 9; sites 1; tile 84–5; tweezers 46
Rome 10
Rouen 94, 96, 101
Roundway Down 30, 34

St Albans 13
sandstone 80, 97, 100
scale-pans 47, 56, *59*, 60
sceattas 3, 4–5, 60, 93, 95, 96, 97, 98, 99, 100, 103
  see also coins
Schouwen 94
scramasax 7, 95, 103
  see also knives
scrap 93, 95
  see also metals
sculpture 99
seax, *see* scramasax, knives
Sevington 42, 56
shells, cowrie 96
ships and shipping 101
shrines 62
shroud-hooks 47
Shudy Camps 12
silk, *see* textiles
silver, *see* metals
Six Dials, *see* Southampton
slag 75, 88, 89, 98
slaves 60, 97, 100, 101, 103
smiths 99
  see also metalworking
soil conditions 11
solidi 5, 59–61, 93, 94, 102
  see also coins
Southampton 32, 41, Bitterne 6; Brintons Road 97; churches 14; Clifford Street 2; Cook Street 29, 37, 83–4, 95, 96, 98; Melbourne Street 2; mint 5, 88, 97; St Mary's area 2; St Mary's *mynster* 1, 99; Six Dials 2, 29, 80, 82, 95, 96, 97, 98; Standford Street 75; Westgate 3

spices 100
spoons 56, 96
  see 'forks'
spurs 8
stone 79, 80, 93, 99, 100
  see also chalk, lava, mortar, moulds, limestone, sandstone
strap-ends 8, 37, 50, 54, 68, 94; cast openwork 96; folded *43*, 44; single-riveted, spherical terminals 37–8, *39*, 40, 41, 102, 103; single-riveted, various terminals 39, *40*, 41; two-riveted, flat shafts 11, 40–1, *42*, *43*, 96; two-riveted, various *43*
strap-slide 7
strips 63
studs, *see* mounts
styli 54, 99
Sutton Hoo 56
Swallowcliffe 56, 95, 102
Swindon 101
swords 100

tacks, *see* mounts
tags, *see* hooked tags, lace-tags
Tattershall Thorpe 58, 62
Test, River 1
textiles 12, 34, 36, 37, 100
Theophilus 81
Thetford 1, 5, 56
tile 76, 77, 78, 79, 84
tin, tinning *see* metals
toilet items, *see* tweezers and other toilet items
tolls 100
tools 82, 98
tooth-picks, *see* tweezers and other toilet items
Totternhoe 3
touchstones 97
traders, trading 32, 58, 60, 97, 100–1
tremisses, *see trientes*
Trewhiddle 7, 42, 96
trientes 5, 58–61, 101
  see also coins
Trowbridge 43
tuyère 86
tweezers and other toilet items 14, 38, 44, *45*, 46, 68, 99, 104

urbanism 94

vessels 12
vessels, glass 60, 100, 102
  see also palm-cups
Vikings 60, 97

Wareham 96, 101
washers 55
Watchfield 12
weapons 95, 103
weight systems 58–61, 100
weights 56–61, 62, *63*, 98
  see also scale-pans
wergild payments 5
Westgate, *see* Southampton
West Stow 12, 56
Wharram Percy 99
Whitby Abbey 20, 25, 28, 56, 94
wic sites 94, 98, 102
  see also emporia
Willibald, St 94, 101
Winchester 1, 7, 11, 20, 25, 28, 32, 56, 59, 97, 99, 100, 102
window glass 99
wine 60, 100
Winnall 5, 7, 9, 30, 32, 34, 35, 38, 103
wire 14, 30, 35, 37, 42, 50, *64*, 65, 79, 82, 97
wire-folding 36–7, *79*, 97–8
Witham, hanging-bowl 54
Witham, River, pins 31
women 30, 35, 36, 46, 47, 56, 62, 102, 104
wood 12, 35, 44, 54
wool 101
wool-combs 35, 37
woollens, *see* textiles
'work-boxes' 13

X-radiographs 98
X-ray fluorescence 2, 66–73, 81, 82, 84, 86, 88, 89–92, 94

York 1, 3, 5, 6, 9, 12, 20, 25, 28, 30, 32, 35, 36, 50, 54, 58, 59, 60, 82, 85, 87, 94, 98, 102

zinc, *see* metals